D1554000

Jewcentricity

Jewcentricity

Why the Jews Are Praised, Blamed, and Used to Explain Just About Everything

Adam Garfinkle

WILEY

John Wiley & Sons, Inc.

Published by John Wiley & Sons, Inc., Hoboken, New Jersey
Published simultaneously in Canada

For general information about our other products and services, please contact our Customer Care Department within the United States at (800) 762–2974, outside the United States at (317) 572–3993 or fax (317) 572–4002.

Wiley also publishes its books in a variety of electronic formats. Some content that appears in print may not be available in electronic books. For more information about Wiley products, visit our web site at www.wiley.com.

Library of Congress Cataloging-in-Publication Data:

Garfinkle, Adam M., date.
    Jewcentricity : why the Jews are praised, blamed, and used to explain just about everything/Adam Garfinkle.
      p.   cm.
    Includes index.
    ISBN 978-0-470-19856-8 (cloth)
      1. Jews—Identity. 2. Antisemitism. 3. Jews—United States—Identity. 4. Jews in popular culture—United States. 5. Arab-Israeli conflict—Influence. I. Title.
DS143.G35 2009
305.892'4—dc22

                                            2009006811

Printed in the United States of America
10 9 8 7 6 5 4 3 2 1

To Rachel Reinitz (1907–2007), my teacher

Contents

Preface

As *The American Interest* magazine prepared a few years back to move from a quarterly to a bimonthly publication, a question arose as to what to call our six issues. As founding editor of *TAI*, I rejected the standard January/February, March/April system as too bland for a magazine whose intention was to be anything but. The problem, of course, is that we have only four names for the seasons, leaving two issues to be dubbed something else. We decided to call July/August the "Vacation" issue and November/December the "Holidays" issue.

The latter term, of course, intended to evoke images of Thanksgiving and the ecumenical celebratory fecundity of December. It frankly didn't occur to me that, schedules and lead times in the magazine business being what they are, the preparation of the "Holidays" issue would always occur close to the Jewish High Holy Days. As it happened, the first one went to press in September 2006 smack-dab between Rosh Hashanah and Yom Kippur in what was then the Jewish New Year of 5767.

I confess, too (it was the season, after all), to having been awe-struck during those Days of Awe by an intense concentration of Jewcentricity: the assumption, idea, intimation, or subconscious presumption that Jews are to be found at the very center of many, if not most—in extreme cases all—important historical events. Examples of Jewcentricity from the silly to the sublime were everywhere I looked. It was for this reason, aided by the fact that some expected material never showed up, that I wrote the first "Holidays" seasonal note on "The Madness of Jewcentricity."

It seemed to strike a nerve: the essay vaulted to the top of the "Arts & Letters" Web site and was mentioned in *New York Times* columnist David Brooks's annual "Sydney Awards" column. As one result, literary agents started calling me from New York City, asking if they could represent me in selling the Jewcentricity book to commercial publishers.

"What book?" I answered.

"The book you *have* to write," they replied.

"Oh, *that* book. . . . I see."

I did see, you see, for I had written books before. I knew well how the excitement of an ambitious moment can morph into months of headaches, procrastination, and guilt. Nonetheless, suffering in the purse from the travails of financing three private college tuitions, I listened to these heralds of cash against my better judgment. In the end, I accepted their reasoning but not their help, turning instead to a friend who was also, in theory at least, my literary agent: Sharon Friedman.

I say "in theory" because our supposed business relationship, years old though it was, had never produced a nickel of income for either of us. The reason was that between writing federal commission reports and then speeches for two secretaries of state, among other things, I had not had the time to produce anything she could sell. I felt I owed her a first right of refusal on trying to market *Jewcentricity*, and she accepted the challenge.

Our business relationship thus renewed, Sharon and I headed off to see the wizards of the American publishing world in New York City, hoping to find the sort of yellow brick road one can follow all the way to the bank. I, for one, learned a lot there. One publisher asked me whether I realized the irony inherent in writing a book on the excessive, even obsessive, interest in Jews.

"What do you mean?" I asked, not apparently realizing.

"Well," he answered, "don't you think it's odd to write a book whose purpose is to call attention to a phenomenon in order to persuade people not to call attention to it?"

After only a slight pause I responded, lying, "Not at all. After I get through with this subject, no one will want to discuss it for years."

In any event, we did place the book (though not with him), and the rest, as they say (but only in America), "is history."

This book intends to be elucidating and perhaps entertaining, but it makes no pretense to be of much use to scholars. It is for reasonably well-educated readers curious about the subject, not those whose day jobs consist of teaching about the various aspects of it. I have special sympathy for younger readers, defined as anyone who has yet to reach, say, thirty-five years of age. Over the years my students have sometimes stopped me in mid-lecture upon hearing about some event or piece of proper-noun vocabulary I took to be common knowledge—but wasn't. The most common excuse in defense of their ignorance was along the lines of, "Hey, we weren't born yet." Fair enough: so some books must be written more to compensate for the derelictions of parents than to engage the academy. This is one of them.

It is just as well, for an exhaustive scholarly book on Jewcentricity is probably impossible for any single mortal to write. Jews have been around for a long time and have inhabited more countries and climes for longer periods than any other more or less specifically defined group of people in recorded history. It follows that the material for a scholarly book on Jewcentricity is so vast that a conscientious author pursuing the subject would end up not with a book but a multivolume encyclopedia.

As it is, there is a fair bit of history in this book, although it is not a book of history as such. I do not apologize for this. Most Americans, who I assume will make up the majority of my readership, have little patience for history in what is perhaps the most forward-looking, pragmatic, and future-friendly civilization ever. But nothing about Jewcentricity today can be understood properly, or in some cases understood at all, without some grounding in history.

Some of this material, too, may seem esoteric to many readers, despite my effort to disappoint true scholars. This presents a problem for a writer as for a classroom teacher: simplify too much, as I may have done by retelling familiar Bible stories, and some readers will scold the dumbing-down of a captivating topic; simplify too little and many will find words and concepts lapping up and over their cognitive nostrils. So I've tried to find a fair middle ground that does justice to the subject, but without bringing in excessive detail or using unnecessary jargon. I have thus avoided excessive references in the text and in the notes that follow, but that presents a problem, too. To many readers such accoutrements come across as off-putting clutter. On the other hand, references and notes enable a motivated mind to trace back a paper trail of intellectual influence, and they enable an author to properly acknowledge debts to the original thinking of others. I have leaned toward sins of omission rather than commission here, liberally taking insights from others sometimes without so much as a pretense of acknowledgment. If there are still too many notes to suit your taste, dear reader, you may simply ignore them.

Some wit once said that the only difference between scholarship and plagiarism is that the scholar has forgotten where he found his materials. Since I have been thinking about these subjects for at least forty years, I honestly do not know for certain what is original and what is derivative here. If those living souls whose work I have ransacked without acknowledgment are irritated, sorry.

I know I won't please everyone with these various compromises, but I've tried. Where I've not succeeded, my editors at John Wiley & Sons, Eric Nelson, Marcia Samuels, and Alexa Selph, have exerted themselves to limit the damage I've done. I owe them a debt of gratitude for that, and so do you. I also am indebted, as all who read this book should be, to my friend Harvey Sicherman, who is the only peer colleague I asked to read my manuscript. He has helped in many ways, and I have taken all his suggestions to heart, even those whose direction I did not follow.

Finally, as for my wife, Scilla, and my children, Gabriel, Hannah, and Nate, they resisted repeated entreaties for help that I directed at them over the course of many months. None of them ever made it past the introduction, or provided a single written comment as requested. They have suffered for their delinquency by having to put up with numerous conversations—to which they sardonically refer as lectures—on the various subjects discussed below. They helped a lot.

INTRODUCTION

Jewcentricity Defined

Exaggeration misleads the credulous and offends the perceptive.
                                                    —ELIZA COOK

Jewcentricity is about exaggeration. More specifically, it is about the various roles Jews are imagined to play on the world stage that they do not, in fact, actually play. Some of this imagining is done by Jews, but most of it is done by non-Jews. Some of these roles are imagined to be benign, even transcendently wonderful. Some are imagined to be malign, even cosmically evil. But as unusual as the actual history of the Jews is, Jewcentricity by definition involves distortion that insists on its being even more unusual still.

As will be readily apparent to anyone even remotely familiar with history, this is a phenomenon that has been going on for a very long time. But why? Why the Jews?

Why, for example, do so many Arabs today believe that "the Jews" manipulate the greatest power in the world, the United States of America, turning tens of millions of Muslim brothers and cousins against one another? That the Jews have caused the current global economic dislocations? Why not the Gypsies, or the Swedes?

Why do millions of evangelical Christians think Jews hold the key to the Second Coming of Christ? Why not devout Christians themselves?

Why did multitudes of European anti-Semites of the nineteenth and early twentieth centuries believe Jews were trying to destroy the Church and take over the world? Why not Bosnian Muslims or renegade Knights Templar? When Asia suffered a sharp economic crisis in 1997–1998, why did Mohathir Mohammed, the leader of Malaysia—a country where there are virtually no Jews—blame the crisis on "the Jews"? Why not the Chinese, or Rotary International?

Why has Hugo Chávez, the firebrand leader of Venezuela, accused the Jews of plotting his downfall, even as he goes to the rostrum of the United Nations General Assembly waving and praising a book written by Noam Chomsky, who is, of course, a Jew? And why would the United Nations host antiracism conferences in Durban, South Africa, that in fact propagate one and only one particular form of racism—anti-Semitism in the garb of anti-Zionism? Why *that* one form of racism?

How does it come to be that a tiny minority of intellectuals in Japan manage to produce anti-Semitic rants despite the historical absence of Jews in those lands? Why not rant about Gujaratis, who also have had no communal presence in Japan? And why are there popular books in Korean that teach about the Talmud so readers can become wealthy like the Jews? Why not popular versions of the Vedas so that readers can become rich like maharajas?

Let *us* be careful not to exaggerate; that's the last thing we should do in a book about other people's exaggerations. Jewcentricity is not a fully universal phenomenon, at least not yet. It is still mostly confined to the Abrahamic world (the part of human civilization that includes what we commonly call the West and the Muslim world), and certainly not everyone in that world is Jewcentric. Most people these days are not obsessed with any particular group (except perhaps Northside Chicagoans about the Cubs in the spring of any given year). Still, examples of Jewcentricity abound, ranging from the silly to the sublime, in basically four types.

First there are non-Jews who obsess over Jews in a negative way, irrationally blaming Jews for everything they dislike and fear. These are the anti-Semites.

Second, there are non-Jews who obsess over Jews in a positive way. These philo-Semites today populate the ranks of millenarian and evangelical Christians in the United States and abroad, for example, but they are found in other forms, as well, in a range of expressions.

Third are Jews who obsess positively over themselves. Some Jews distort the idea of the Chosen People into a form of religious chauvinism offensive to non-Jews and to a lot of their fellow Jews, too.

Some Jews exaggerate their chosenness in secular terms, claiming Jewish origins for everything from Byzantine art styles to the U.S. Constitution to sliced bread.

Finally there are "self-hating" or "self-loathing" Jews, Jews who obsess over the fact that they are Jews who would rather not be. Some go to considerable lengths to distance themselves from being identified as Jews. Others identify themselves as Jews but exert themselves to defame everything commonly associated with Jews, Jewishness, and Judaism. (As I will explain, however, the label "self-hating" is itself usually an exaggeration.)

All four manifestations of Jewcentricity not only exaggerate the significance of Jews, in often curious and sometimes counterintuitive ways, they often goad one another, pushing the tendency to misperceive and to exaggerate to greater heights. Some of this feeding and goading is fairly harmless. Indeed, some of it is so silly that it qualifies as a form of entertainment. But just as a little knowledge can be a dangerous thing, a little exaggeration can be, too—and a lot of exaggeration even more so. Not that Jews aren't interesting (although that is merely a matter of taste), and not that Jews aren't statistically unusual in some ways—winning Nobel Prizes, for example, greatly out of proportion to their percentage in the population. Still, enough is enough, and too much is much too common.

Jews are not entirely alone, of course, in being an object of exaggerated importance. In the United States the Lyndon LaRouche cult exaggerates wildly the power of the queen of England and the pope. There are backwoods conspiracy nuts who think the United Nations is coming any day now with its black helicopters to take over the U.S. government. Some black cultists are sure, on the other hand, that an omnipotent U.S. government deliberately spread HIV/AIDS and crack among black urban communities. There are those who believe humankind never traveled to the moon, that fluoridated drinking water is a Communist plot, and that aliens regularly take afternoon tea in Roswell, New Mexico. What various cults outside the general confines of the Western world believe (and do) is, if possible, even weirder.

But conspiracy cultists have for the most part been localized, few in number, and not in a position to influence mainstream politics and culture. Jewcentricity, on the other hand, in both its negative and its positive manifestations, has been widespread, long-lived, and occasionally very influential indeed. Nazi Jewcentricity, for example, may not by itself have started World War II, but it played a major role in defining its character and course. Evangelical Jewcentricity today has a significant influence on American attitudes and policies toward the Middle East. Indeed, as the focus of conspiracy theories and heavenly fantasies alike, no other group comes close to the Jews. Even as a focus of general interest, bordering sometimes on fascination, no other group of people matches the Jews.

This fascination is so commonly accepted that it has become an object of humor, at least in most Western countries and certainly in the United States. Examples range from the punch-line lyric in Tom Lehrer's classic song "National Brotherhood Week"—"And everybody hates the Jews"—to the widely known, wry definition of anti-Semitism attributed to the Jewish comedian Jackie Mason as "disliking Jews more than is absolutely necessary." But what *explains* this fascination? Where did it come from, and where is it going? That is the quest of this book.

It only remains for an introduction to lay out the plan of argument presented below. Most broadly, part one, "Jewcentricity in History," sets out the seminal historical predicates of the subject. It shows Jewish Jewcentricity, in the form of the concept of the Chosen People, to be the original source of Jewcentricity from which both positive and negative forms of gentile Jewcentricity arose. From this history we get a sense of where Jewcentricity may be headed in a world where images and perceptions are becoming increasingly global and virtual. Jewcentricity used to require the actual presence of Jews to flourish in given places. This may no longer be the case.

Part two, "Jewcentricity in America," looks more specifically at various manifestations of Jewcentricity, again from the silly to the sublime, in history and on the contemporary scene. All four types of Jewcentricity pour themselves into the broader American social context in which they exist. This is why Jewcentricity in America has been and remains both like and unlike Jewcentricity elsewhere.

Part three, "Jewcentricity in the Middle East," carries the analysis from America to the Middle East—back to where it all began—and tries to bring together the book's three parts into a whole. Jewcentricity in history and Jewcentricity in America come together in the fact that today the American Jewish community is the largest and most influential Jewish community in the world outside of Israel, and that America is for historical reasons the most Jewcentric gentile nation that has ever existed. These two parts in turn join with the third, with the Middle East, through the major role the United States plays in the region. What we witness today, therefore, is a joining of the three streams of Jewcentricity—the historical, the American, and the Middle Eastern—in a mélange of images, arguments, and confusions that veritably invite misunderstanding and exaggeration. We will return to the truth uttered in song by Bob Dylan, that we are "living in a political world"; we should not doubt that, unfortunately, we are also living in a Jewcentric one.

PART ONE

Jewcentricity
in
History

I

Chosen

To exaggerate is to weaken.

          —JEAN FRANÇOIS DE LA HARPE

The origins of Jewcentricity lie in the historical odyssey of an idea, a Jewish idea about the purpose of Jewish people. But it is the collision of that idea with the long and eccentric history of the Jews that has given particular shape to Jewish self-image and behavior alike over the centuries. More specifically, the strategies that Jews devised to survive as a people—a nation lacking a common land, a common spoken language, and political independence for more than two thousand years—have often proved perplexing to the non-Jews in whose midst the vast majority of Jews have lived.

Those survival strategies, motivated and shaped by the moral tenets of a religious faith that has claimed the Jews to be God's chosen people, set Jews apart and led most host societies to encourage Jews to remain apart.[1] Separated from, but still within, their host communities, nearly everything the Jews did to enable themselves to continue their mission as the Chosen People *made* them chosen, and everything that made them chosen more often than not made them pariahs in the eyes of others. This chosen/pariah dialectic is the motor, the innermost source, of Jewcentricity.

Some of this Jewish desire for communal separation amid the larger society, and the willingness of non-Jews to enable or to tolerate

9

it, is clearly tied to the simple fact of difference. But some of it has its origins in the discomfort caused by ambiguity. Just as people often fear difference, they often go to great lengths to dispel, explain, or ignore (as the case may be) ambiguity. Human beings live by the categories they devise to organize experience, and when things, events, or other people violate their principles of categorization, they strive to restore the explanatory power of their cognitive frameworks. Just as dirt is "matter out of place"—as the British anthropologist Mary Douglas, quoting Lord Chesterfield, took pains to explain—the Jews in their global sojourn have often seemed to others "people out of place," hence a kind of social dirt.[2] As the Israeli writer A. B. Yehoshua once put it:

> We have a tendency to drive the non-Jews crazy. There is something in our existence which leads whole civilizations to be obsessed with us. Earlier we drove the Europeans crazy and now we drive crazy also the Arabs. Something in *our undefined existence* causes this madness. . . . To live without borders, without taking responsibility. To be here and also there, yet not here and not there, and to maintain such an elusive existence, such an unclear identity. . . . It is about time we should understand that our ambiguous identity is causing individuals and groups who suffer a chaos of identity to cast on us awesome implications.[3]

Is Jewcentricity, then, mainly the result of a prolonged interciv-ilizational misunderstanding? The kind where one episode tends to generate further episodes, gradually but ineluctably encrusting relations between civilizations to the point that no one can figure out how it all got started? Well, yes. However, the gentile misunderstanding of the Jews has become more protracted, ornate, interwoven, shifting, and ironic than any other roughly similar misunderstanding ever known. A central reason for this, at least for those societies that have been formed by Christian and Islamic religion, is that Jewish ideas have influenced them at one level even as flesh-and-blood Jewish communities have engaged them at another. The idea of chosenness itself radiated outward, became transformed as other "chosen" Abrahamic faiths sought to separate and distinguish themselves from their Jewish origins, and was then hurled back at the Jewish communities within. This is what led the redoubtable Israel Zangwill to say that the Jew is "the great misunderstood of history."[4]

But that is not quite all there is to it: there is a circularity to the misunderstanding at the heart of Jewcentricity, because Jews have often misunderstood in turn the source of gentile misunderstanding. They understood traditionally that chosen meant different, not necessarily better, and they assumed that this distinction would also be clear to others. It was often, however, not so clear; difference, when associated with superior achievement of various kinds, easily blends into presumptions of snobbery. When who God in fact chose became a matter of theological dispute, and vulnerable Jews in Diaspora grew defensive about their own claims, "different" sometimes elided into "better," and the whole cycle began again. This would almost be amusing—a kind of reverse version of O. Henry's famous story "The Gift of the Magi"—if it were not so serious. But there it is—a misunderstanding that has shifted its bases and gears throughout the centuries and is doing so still.

To understand contemporary manifestations of Jewcentricity, we have to reckon with the fact that it is a phenomenon that has been many centuries in the making. Where did it all start? How did Jews become known worldwide as the people that considers itself chosen? Why the Jews?

The annals of history and anthropology are full of creation stories centered on the ancestors of the very writers of those stories. The idea that humankind itself is, as the Hebrew Bible suggests, the "crown of creation," is of course widespread, and the idea that a particular group with its own language and culture is the diadem at the center of that crown is not much less so. Indeed, the presumed cosmic union of land, people, and god is a formula so typical of ancient cultures that merely to summarize the principal examples would consume the better part of any given afternoon.[5]

Ancient Israel is certainly one of those examples, though a minor one by conventional measures. The people of Israel were small in number, built no great monuments, constructed no great cities, conquered no then-known-world-spanning empires. Yet the people of Israel turned out to have anything but a minor impact on history, and that is because its version of its own origin was and remains an example of ancient ethnocentrism with a twist.

Ancient Israelites (also called Hebrews, and later and until today called Jews for reasons we will come to in a moment) came to believe that their ancestor Abraham was called by God Himself to propagate the revolutionary idea of monotheism. Monotheism was revolutionary not only because it proclaimed a single God, but also because the biblical creation story made clear that humanity was a parallel unity to a single God, having descended from one divinely created couple, Adam and Eve. And even more important than the idea that there is only one God was the astounding idea, for the time, that God is one, that God and his creation form a unity. (This is what the verse "Hear O Israel, the Lord our God, the Lord is One" actually means.) In other words, creation makes sense as a whole: there is a first cause, and all other causes are consistent with it.

That there is only one God, one brotherhood of man, and that God is the author of a creation that is itself a unity, were ideas that changed the world. They posited the first universal moral vision, and they arguably established the earliest foundations for modern science. But there is even more to the twist than that: Abraham's relation to a land, within the ancient conceptual trinity of land, people, and god, was *not* to the land of his birth, Ur Kasdim in Mesopotamia, in what is today Iraq, or the land of his sojourn, the region of Haran, in what is today southern Turkey. Rather, as all those who know the biblical story are aware, God told Abraham to leave his native land and go to a new land God would show him. That turned out to be Canaan, later called the Land of Israel, part of which is Judea, and which has been generally known since Roman times as Palestine.

That land, and more besides, was to belong to Abraham's posterity, but not by a right fixed by might. Rather, Canaan was to belong to Abraham's seed through his son Isaac by dint of a covenant, a reciprocal and conditional relationship between the Creator of the universe and what became the people of Israel. (The rest of "the land between the two rivers" was to belong to the descendants of Abraham's other sons, notably Ishmael, but also the six sons he had with Keturah after the death of Sarah, as related in Genesis 25:1–6.) This, too, the idea of a conditional, covenantal relationship between a single God and a single people whose purpose was to minister to a universal brotherhood of mankind, was a new idea. The Israelites were the only "chosen people" of the ancient world who defined themselves more by a creed than by a bloodline and whose moral mission trumped the importance of their ties to a land.

It is on account of the singular purpose of Israel that the biblical narrative tells a story that was revolutionary in another way, as well. In every other ancient religious narrative, God is an ally of the existing temporal powers and the hierarchy that sustains them. Not in the Hebrew Bible, whose main protagonists are not rulers or warriors but ordinary people with extraordinary concern for living a morally informed life. In the story, if not in actual fact, Abraham leaves the most sophisticated urban culture of his day, crosses the river (hence the origin of the name Hebrews, from *avar*, to cross over), and sets off through the wilderness. The anti-hierarchical theme of the story is then replicated and greatly magnified with the story of Moses. Other ancient epics tell stories of noble-born children who somehow become the wards of slaves or the poor and are then restored to their rightful noble places. But Moses is born to slaves and ends up being raised as a prince of Egypt, only to reject privilege and associate his life with the underlings of society. As Jonathan Sacks puts it, the Moses story is an antimyth, arguably the world's first and certainly the most powerfully long-lasting antimyth in literature.[6]

A people who believe in a God who disdains earthly power isn't likely to endear itself to those in power, even when those in power happen to be Jews. This notion, that political rule deserves respect only when it is just, is an indelible feature of the Jewish worldview. It is how within the biblical narrative the prophets of Israel, armed with the antimyth of the Exodus, show their mettle. Indeed, from the time of Moses' audiences with Pharaoh onward, one sees the manifestations of this dynamic playing out in Jewish history, sending forth sparks of opposition to tyranny that lit the tinder of Jewcentricity hither and yon.

Ideas have real social and ultimately political consequences, and the ideas embedded in the stories of credit and blame that human communities tell about God and creation especially so.[7] What the Israelites believed about God set them apart from their neighbors, and over time the distinctions grew. For example, since there was only one God, gods fighting each other could not explain the forces of nature or disputes among peoples. Since the "Jewish" God did not die and get reborn with the seasons as gods typically did in pagan, or pantheistic, religions, the Israelites did not copy the resurrection rites of their neighbors, which often involved child sacrifice. Since God was beyond sexuality, the Israelites had no fertility rites either—no group copulations as with the Sumerians or institutionalized temple prostitution as with the Greeks—rites often associated with sexual excess and perversion.

Perhaps most important, God was an ally of both liberation and historical change; He was not merely a God in and of nature, but a God in and of history. This had two major implications that lay at the root of defining what was and has long remained different about the Jews.

First, since God was first cause in a world that made internal logical sense, it fell to people to figure out their own way in that world. Only after God, or the gods, were expelled from the immanent here and now, exported to heaven, so to speak, could human reason begin to take hold as a means to understand reality.

Second and closely related, in the Jewish view history mattered as something more than just a series of events. It meant something. It progressed toward a goal, rather than cycling back around itself like the seasons. It was free to become what its actors wished it to become. An omnipotent God is a god who can control the world in such a way as to turn events toward those who recognize Him.

The rabbis understood this from the Torah text, specifically from how God describes himself to Moses at the burning bush. When Moses asks God to tell him who is sending him to Pharaoh, God answers with just three Hebrew words: "*Eheyeh asher eheyeh.*" Cryptic as this sentence seems, and despite the many translations it has attracted, it is actually quite simple grammatically. As the first and last words are the future tense, first person of the verb *to be*, it means, "I will be that which I will be." In other words, I am free, and you humans I have created in my spiritual image, you are free, too. What you do matters to your future, which is yours to shape.

That is why the Hebrew Bible, unlike other ancient stories, amounts to an effort to write history, however arguable the result in terms of accuracy. As many observers have pointed out, it never mattered in other ancient narratives if what happened in the stories was literally true, for what was true did not happen in real human time but in heaven, among the gods. Abraham and the early Israelites essentially realized, which is to say brought into collective consciousness, the idea of a concrete now. History started to matter because it was understood to cumulatively create the present, just as action in the present created the future. One's behavior and decisions mattered, too, not just because they affected how the crops would grow or how to make one's family safe from the elements and hostile neighbors, but because they shaped the character of life, the quality of consciousness itself. That realization, so taken for granted now and thus so easy to underestimate as a revolutionary force, defines the inner logic of the Hebrew Bible.

And that—all that—is why, in turn, roughly a millennium after Abraham and the other patriarchs of Israel, what Jews believed and how Jews acted contrasted so vividly with what, say, Greeks believed and how Greeks acted. Whatever their material and philosophical achievements, the ancient Greeks practiced infanticide and slavery, and exalted pedophilia and homosexuality as the preferred natural order of things. Why not? Their pantheon of gods did the same. Above all, when Jews and Greeks encountered one another in the fourth and third centuries BCE, the Greeks still aligned their temporal power with those of their whimsical gods; the Hebrews decided that their chosen status did not align with conventional political and military power, and they often stood athwart it—and would outlast it.

To review here the whole skein of Jewish history as related by the biblical narrative we cannot afford. The more familiar one is with that narrative, the clearer its historical impact on Jewish thinking and behavior becomes, but what matters, in any event, is that the biblical text has an underlying theme; it is not just a chronicle of sometimes touching, sometimes obtuse stories. The theme inheres in the unfolding of the Jews' chosenness in history; it is the extended tale of the divine mission given to Abraham. The Hebrew Bible amounts to a continuous reinforcement of the idea of the Chosen People: the Jews believe in God's having chosen them; the Jews then act a certain way as a result; something happens that is necessarily interpreted in the light of chosenness; that interpretation impels further understanding and behavior, which is interpreted again in the light of the chosen mission; and so on and on. Out of all this comes not only a historical narrative studded with a presumed meaning but a theology pointing forward to redemption.

We have already limned how it all starts: Abraham accepts God's call, as do his son Isaac and his grandson Jacob. We know about Jacob's eleventh son, Joseph, the descent into Egypt and the Exodus from it, the revelation at Mount Sinai, the forty years in the wilderness, the death of Moses, and the slow conquest of the land under Joshua and the Judges. We know, too, about Saul as king, about David, who supplanted him, and about David's son Solomon, who built the first Temple in Jerusalem. We "know" all of this from the Hebrew Bible, not from corroborative historical and archeological sources, for they range from scarce to nonexistent. Biblical and historical accounts start to merge after the time of Solomon, as the odyssey of Jewish history merges with that of the wider world. It is from this point that the Jewish theology of chosenness collides with the broader flow of history, and it is this collision that has shaped the Jewish theology-in-history that endures to this day.

King David conquered Jerusalem from the Jebusites and made it his capital sometime around 1000 BCE. The Jewish people, now about four and half centuries after the Exodus, enjoyed something very close to ordinary stability. Having ignored Samuel's advice and taken for themselves a king like the other nations (Samuel I, chapter 8), they had fairly well de-Jewcentrized themselves. They had a government, a territory, a place in the regional order, and a religious culture that, if the prophets can be believed, bore little resemblance much of the time to the code Moses delivered to the people from God. After David's death Solomon consummated the highest form of Jewish ritual obligation by building the Temple in which the Levites, the priestly caste, could fulfill their divinely mandated tasks. All seemed well, more or less, as these things go.

When Solomon died, something indeed utterly normal happened: his children fought over the kingdom, with the result that it split in two, in 933 BCE. The northern part was called Israel, with its capital Samaria and its own rival temple and priesthood; the southern part was called Judah (capital Jerusalem). Then in 722 BCE, the Northern Kingdom was destroyed by the Assyrian Empire; ten of the twelve tribes were carried off into captivity, vanishing from history as descendants of the Patriarchs.[8] This meant that the majority of Israelites who remained in their own land under their own government were of the Kingdom of Judah and were descended from Jacob's son Judah. Hence, ultimately, the word "Jew" to describe them.[9]

The Kingdom of Judah experienced its ups and downs over the decades, as all kingdoms do. But the idea of the Chosen People with its chosen mission was never entirely extirpated. Sometime around the year 621 BCE, under the reign of King Josiah, the Torah (the first five books of the Hebrew Bible) was more or less canonized as it exists today as part of a religious revitalization movement generated by the king. Alas, the good times of what has become known as the First Commonwealth did not last long, for the power of the Babylonian Empire bore down on the eastern Mediterranean. The Kingdom of Judah remained more or less independent until 586 BCE, when it was conquered by Babylonian armies under King Nebuchadnezzar. Solomon's Temple was razed, and many, but not all, of the people were carried off as captives to Babylon.

The Babylonian Empire, however, was itself soon conquered by the Persian Empire—upon which Cyrus the Great gave the Jews permission to return to their land and rebuild the Temple. Led by

Ezra, this they did. The rebuilding took a while to complete, not least because most of the Jews, having gotten used to Babylon and thriving there, declined to return to Judea. Nonetheless, the Second Temple was dedicated in 516 BCE, just seventy years after the Babylonians had destroyed the first one.

The Persian Empire fell in turn to the Greeks, and the Greeks in time gave way to the Romans, who conquered Judea and Samaria in the year 63 BCE. It was during this extended period between the end of the First Commonwealth and the start of the Roman era that the rest of the Hebrew Bible beyond the Torah was written and compiled, along with several other books that did not ultimately make it into the canon. The Hebrew Bible as a whole was canonized sometime in the first century CE. It was then that the books were given their names and put in the order they retain today.

The Second Temple stood until the Romans destroyed it in the year 70 CE in punishment for Jewish rebellion. The Jews soon rebelled again against Roman rule, most significantly in a revolt led by Shimon Bar Kochba starting in 133 CE. They were defeated and the people subsequently massacred in large numbers. Most of those who survived were sold as slaves or otherwise deported.[10] The Arch of Titus, which can still be viewed today in Rome, depicts some of these events—from the Roman point of view, of course.

From about the year 135 onward, Jews inhabited no territory on which their majority lived, lacked political independence, and, within a few generations after their dispersion, possessed no common spoken language—neither Hebrew, Aramaic, nor Syriac Greek. (They did have in common the written Hebrew language and a version of Aramaic as languages of prayer and study, which turned out to be critically important.) Yet the Jews as a people, as a corporate entity, managed to survive anyway. Moreover, starting in the mid-nineteenth century and consummated in May 1948, the Jews managed to reconstitute themselves on part of their ancient land as an independent nation, speaking a language similar to that of the Hebrew Bible—after a hiatus of about 1,878 years, give or take a few months. That, in a nutshell, is Jewish history.

No other people has ever pulled off a feat like this, and it is *how* the Jews managed to do it—managed not to become the historical fossils that Arnold Toynbee, Oswald Spengler, and other theorists of history claimed they must be—that provides the protracted context for the various and sundry manifestations of Jewcentricity that have dotted the history of the Common Era.

• • •

So how did the Jews do it? The basic answer is at once simple and profound: the continuous compounding of the concept of chosenness has been accomplished through the cultivation of memory. Enjoined by the Torah to remember the past, the Jews created not only books but disciplines for the interpretation and study of those books. Because these books and their interpretations stretch over many centuries, when Jews study their religious literature they are in effect having an intergenerational conversation in which the contents and concepts of the Jewish historical memory are transmitted forward in time.

There have been three key source books for creating the common collective Jewish memory: the Hebrew Bible, particularly the Torah; the siddur, the prayer book; and the Haggadah, the story of the Exodus from Egypt. (The Talmud is also a very important book, but for other reasons we will come to later.) One can see how these books function as a vehicle for the collective memory of chosenness only by actually reading them, so let me take you on a highly selective and abbreviated tour of the Hebrew Bible, and describe the siddur and the Haggadah as we proceed below.

When God promised Abraham that He would make of him a great nation, here is what the Torah says He said:

> Go for yourself from your land, from your birthplace and the house of your father, to a land that I will show you. And I will make of you a great nation; I will bless you and make your name great, and you shall be a blessing. And I will bless those who bless you, and he who curses you I will curse, and all the families of the earth will bless themselves through you. (Genesis 12:1–3)

When God calls upon Moses to lead the children of Israel out of slavery in Egypt, again the Jews are called special, for the Bible says that never before had one people been taken out of the midst of another. It is a bit later on, however, at the time of the revelation on Sinai, that the biblical language of chosenness is most vivid. In Exodus, chapter 19, just before the revelation of the Ten Commandments, God instructs Moses to tell the children of Israel as follows: "You have seen what I did to Egypt, and that I have borne you on the wings of eagles and brought you to Me. And now, if you hearken well to Me and observe My covenant, you shall be to Me the most beloved treasure of people, for Mine is the entire world. You shall be to Me a kingdom of priests and a holy nation." In Deuteronomy, chapter 7, the language is similar but perhaps even more vivid. Moses tells the people, "For you are a holy people to the Lord, your God; the Lord, your God has chosen you to be for Him a treasured people above all the peoples that are on the face of the earth. Not because you are more numerous than all the peoples did God desire you and choose you, for you are the fewest of the people."

Not only is the language of chosenness dispersed throughout the Torah, it continues on into the Prophets, for the concept of chosenness, at the very heart of all forms of Jewcentricity, did not remain inert as the history of Israel proceeded. As it was compounded in the cycle of experience and interpretation, it became a kind of prism through which the experiences of the Jews were refracted back to them. When Israel was planted upon the land during the First Commonwealth (and the Second), it is evident from Samuel I and II, Kings I and II, and other books that the people often strayed and were then punished in order to bring them back to their mission. Thus the prophet Amos (3:2): "You alone have I known from all the families of the earth, therefore I punish you for your iniquities."

Of course the Israelites and then the Jews experienced the usual sort of trouble any state endures in the world: the challenges of diplomacy and war, corruption and poor leadership. But the prophets interpreted everything in moral terms, translating the political into the religious as their moral imaginations developed over time. Thus Isaiah, who spoke of Israel as "a light unto the nations," elaborated Israel's mission anew by arguing after the traumatic destruction of the Northern Kingdom that the purpose of Israel's suffering was to cleanse not just its own collective soul but that of the entire world. (It was a relatively short step from that idea in prophetic Judaism to the Christian idea, transmitted via the Essene sect, that Jesus, taking the place of Israel, suffered for the sins of the world.)

Established as a central concept in Jewish theology from the beginning—Israel as the center of the moral universe, the handmaiden of God, the engine of cosmic history—the Jews applied the idea of chosenness to their circumstances in all cases. Of those circumstances, two stand out as most formative: the destruction of the First and Second Commonwealths, with them the First and Second Temples, and with those disasters exile from the land.

How did the Jews adapt? For the sacrificial service in a temple they invented and substituted communal prayer in a synagogue. For this they relied on books: on the Torah, on the rest of the Hebrew Bible, and on an evolving and increasingly standardized liturgy—the siddur, the second of the three key books of memory in the Jewish

literary pantheon. In order for this adaptation to work, not just widespread literacy but study and interpretation of texts were paramount:
and so a community of the intellect came into being, starting in
Babylon and continuing thereafter.

Those interpretations, in turn, eventually formed the core of
other books, notably the Talmud, which served as a vehicle for the
interpretation of scripture in light of the needs of the day. Judaism
(although no one called it that at the time) stopped being what many
religions tend to be: static, conservative, and inclined against change.
Instead, Judaism became a system of belief that looked forward to
redemption from exile and restoration to its land. This followed from
the Abrahamic realization that human time was real and open-ended
rather than cyclical, and that human life could be shaped by human
agency. With the advent of rabbinic Judaism, that basic insight looked
forward to a messianic age that would repair a broken world. The
Jews accepted the authority of the clergy over that of scripture itself
in order to make the journey forward.

Once a basically optimistic attitude toward change became established within Jewish thinking, that attitude doubled back and affected
the interpretation of texts and of Jewish history itself. Texts became
open in the sense that their meanings looked forward, and their interpretation was linked to the realities of Jewish life as time progressed.
Had this not occurred, had the religious ideas of the Jews not become
both portable *and* future-looking, the Jews could not have survived as
a self-aware, self-defined people over nearly two thousand years after
the Roman Exile.

As things turned out, the Jews got two cracks at this form of adaptation, and without the experience of the first, the second might have
failed. As already suggested, the portability of Judaism was first pioneered during the Babylonian Exile, when the Jews figured out how
to maintain a separate existence in a larger society without putting
themselves in untenable opposition to it. It was also in Babylon that
the Jews began to understand what their prophets had warned them
about, what Abraham and Jacob and Moses and Samuel and Amos
and Hosea and Isaiah had been trying to tell them: religious duty was
not just for kings and priests but for ordinary people; not about external grandeur but about internal grace; not about sacrificing children
or even animals, but about setting aside one's own needs out of love
for and generosity to others.

The Jews also gained practical experience in Babylon that would
prove critical in later centuries, for here they first experimented with

how to create and maintain far-flung personal networks, as the Jews followed Babylonian trade routes to every corner of the then-known world. More than that, Babylon's culture was more highly developed than Israelite culture, and from Babylon the Jews took a lot—a script, a calendar, a language (a form of Aramaic), the Babylonians' knowledge of astronomy, and much else. But they grafted these elements onto their own sense of corporate identity, historical mission, and moral sensibilities.

Not only that, but after their restoration to the land of Israel under the Persians, Jews reinvigorated their national life with the lessons learned in Babylon. Here, too, the Jews had help. The two-century period of Persian overlordship was a creative and culturally interactive one, and one in which Jewish political and cultural autonomy was extensive. Thus, when the Jews encountered Alexander the Great in the third century BCE and endured the dominant influence of Hellenism over the next several centuries, they already knew how to live a parallel existence in temples of time and spirit. They had already devised a way to maintain their religious and spiritual life apart from the vicissitudes of politics.

Hellenism represented a challenge to Judaism and Jews at least as great as the Babylonian Exile and the Roman one. Jewish civilization probably would not have survived Hellenism had it not been for the prior experience in exile in Babylon, and it would not have survived exile after 135 CE had it not been for the centuries of simultaneous synergy with and separation from Hellenism. Looking back, the sequence was both necessary and uncanny in the way it presaged the next two millennia of Jewish survival.

With the Roman destruction of the Second Temple as a result of the failure of the Jewish uprising against Rome, and the subsequent massive destruction and exile, Jews suffered such a calamity that not even their prior experience might have sufficed to ensure continuity. But there are times when the force of personality, of genius (perhaps through divine help, who knows?) makes the difference. Yohanan ben-Zakkai was that force, for in the first century CE, at a place called Yavneh, he and his associates elaborated a system of portable identity that has lasted till today: rabbinic Judaism.

Several of the main elements of rabbinic Judaism were already in place in embryo: belief in the chosen mission of the Jewish people, which provided the will to survive; and a mobile structure of law and the educational institutions required to develop and propagate it, thanks to the experience of the Babylonian Exile. Ben-Zakkai and his associates, however, refined and extended what they had inherited. Ben-Zakkai himself, as best we can tell from the literature, focused on preserving the court system, fixing the religious calendar, and assuring the continuity of the House of David; his associates and their students did the rest.

To understand what the pioneers of rabbinic Judaism actually did is to understand the key elements of Jewcentricity itself. That is because the innovations of rabbinic Judaism not only defined the chosen behavior of Jews, they also prefigured the gentile reaction to it. We can describe the essence of the rabbinic system by enumerating ten interrelated innovations. Taken together, these innovations constituted, as we might describe it today, a transterritorial netcentric governance system. The system worked because it stressed human capital, social trust, and institutional coherence—the three qualities that enable all such systems to work.

First, rabbinic Judaism's pioneer generation faced the very real concern that the existence of slavery in the ancient world could destroy Jewish families in exile and literally put an end to Jewish continuity. So they ordained that Jews were responsible for the freedom and basic well-being of other Jews. "All Israel is responsible, one to the other," it says in the Talmud, and the first duty of free Jews was to ransom any Jew who had been enslaved.

Second, in order to keep Jewish numbers up to a minimum level for survival—this in the shadow of the mass murder perpetrated by the Romans after the failed Bar Kochba revolt—they reiterated and strengthened Ezra and Nehemiah's earlier, post–Babylonian Exile ban on intermarriage. They also ordered draconian penalties for infanticide, celibacy, and selling one's children into slavery. They fixed the principle of matrilineal descent, too. (In ancient Israel, the determinant of identity had been patrilineal for reasons related to tribal equities.) They did so in part for legal reasons: if a Jewish male who was not a Roman citizen married a woman who was a citizen, children of that union would not legally be the possession of the father and could not inherit his estate. The ruling also encouraged Jewish men to insist that non-Jewish women convert in order to marry, not a trivial matter given the parlous demographic condition of the Jews at the time.[11]

Third, having done what was required to maintain live Jewish bodies, the rabbis set about making sure that there would be Jewish hearts and minds within them. So they ordered universal education for all male children from the age of six and up and sanctioned education for females. It was more important, they said, for communities to build schools and pay teachers than to build synagogues and pay rabbis. Rabbis were to get paying jobs of their own. They ordered as well that Hebrew dictionaries and grammars be written so that the schools could teach the language of the Torah.

Fourth, they made sure that communities were properly functional. They ordered that anyplace where more than 120 Jewish males over the age of thirteen lived had to form a school and a synagogue, and have a charitable fund, a burial society, and, above all, a court so that they could take care of disputes among themselves without having to resort to the mediation of non-Jewish authorities.

Fifth, in order that these courts should apply a consistent set of laws, Jewish communities far and wide were knit together in a kind of legal confederacy. Senior sages discussed, debated, and handed down legal guidance based on the Torah. They did this over a long period, centered on certain academies where the next generation of rabbis were trained, but they also engaged in long-distance correspondence, establishing a network of communication that was later to have many uses. This is how the core commentary on the Torah, the Mishnah, grew ultimately into a written form from around the year 70 through about the year 200 CE, and it is how the commentary on the Mishnah, the Gemara, came into being between the third and the fifth centuries. (The two together formed the Talmud, which was eventually written down and thus in effect canonized by sometime around the end of the sixth century.[12])

Sixth, in order that Jewish belief and ritual standards remained unified, the early rabbis standardized the liturgy and defined the prayer rituals of the synagogue. They created the siddur, fixed the calendar, and extended the privilege of the public reading of the Torah during the prayer service to anyone who could master the skills.

They also extended the custom of having translators and interpreters on hand to make sure people understood what they heard, for Aramaic, not Hebrew, had long since become the everyday vernacular by the second century CE. This resulted in a continuous process of translation from Hebrew into Aramaic that turned ineluctably into a process of interpretation. The synagogue, which had been created during the Babylonian Exile, but which continued even when the Second Temple stood, now became as much a house of study and debate as of prayer. The Jewish concern not only with text but also with translation and interpretation became institutionalized and critically shaped the Jewish understanding of education. The Jews fused piety and learning, and democratized both. Indeed, over time, the critical role of learning distinguished the Jews in the Diaspora from the larger communities in which they lived: whereas most offices— political, ecclesiastic, and military—were either inherited directly or purchased through the privilege of exalted birth in most host societies, Jewish leadership, long since detribalized by two exiles, was far more meritocratic.

Seventh, the standardization of the liturgy went hand in hand with the standardization of Pharisaic beliefs. Of the three main groupings within early Judaism, the Pharisees had for some centuries during Hellenistic times taken a more liberal approach than the Sadducees and Essenes. They were more egalitarian, more oriented to the message of the prophets, and more conservative socially, disdaining Greek and later Roman mores. The Sadducees, associated with the government and the Temple service, were open to Hellenistic cultural ways but not to religious innovation or the democratization of personal religious obligation. With the collapse of the Second Commonwealth state, the Sadducees virtually disappeared, and the tiny Essene sect withdrew to monastic conditions outside the cities. So Pharisaic attitudes won out in part by default, and the way the prayer book reads illustrates this vividly, for example, in its affirmation of the idea of an afterlife, which was not part of the Sadducees' belief system.

The affirmation of chosenness naturally became a central part of the liturgy. When a person is called to the Torah, he recites a prayer whose translation is as follows: "Blessed art Thou, O Lord our God, who has chosen us from all other peoples, and given us His Torah. Blessed art Thou, O Lord, who giveth the Torah." Every single morning religious Jews—and the vast majority of Jews were observant and prayed according to the law before the last few centuries—recite this line: "Blessed art Thou, O Lord, who has not made me a gentile." Just before the central prayer of Judaism, the Shema, Jews recite:

> With abounding love Thou hast loved us, O Lord our God, and great and overflowing tenderness Thou hast shown us. . . . Thou hast chosen us from all other peoples and tongues, and hast brought us near unto Thy great Name forever in faithfulness, that we might in love give thanks unto Thee and proclaim thy unity. Blessed art Thou, O Lord, who hast chosen thy people Israel in love.

In the sanctification of the wine on the Sabbath and festivals, part of the prayer goes as follows: "For Thou hast chosen us and hallowed us above all nations, and in love and favor Thou hast given us the holy Sabbath as an inheritance."

In one of the closing prayers to every Jewish prayer service, the Aleynu prayer, taken from the heart of the ancient Yom Kippur service, Jews recite:

> It is our duty to praise the Lord of all things . . . since He hath not made us like the nations of other lands, and hath not placed us like the other families of the earth, since He hath not assigned unto us a portion as unto them, nor a lot as unto all their multitudes. For they prostrate themselves before vanity and emptiness and pray to a God that saveth not.[13]

Chosenness is not all the siddur expresses theologically. On pilgrim festivals (Passover, Weeks, and Tabernacles—Pesach, Shavuot, and Succot), the prayers clearly assign cause-and-effect explanations for Jewish history's ups and downs: "On account of our sins we were exiled from our land and removed far from our country, and we are unable to go up before Thee to fulfill our obligations in Thy chosen House, that great and holy Temple that was called by Thy Name, because of the hand of violence that hast been laid upon thy sanctuary." The prayer then asks for God to rebuild the Temple and "bring our scattered ones among the nations near unto Thee, and gather our dispersed from the ends of the earth." And not just on holidays did Jews for centuries pray for the Temple, for the ingathering of the exiles and for the rebuilding of Jerusalem, but every single day, in some prayers recited three times every day, they honed the obligations of memory.

The redemption of the land and the rebuilding of the Temple were associated in rabbinic Judaism with the coming of the messiah. The theology of rabbinic Judaism holds that there will be no third exile but instead the messianic age, when the Kingdom of Heaven is established on earth. Learning, they believed, from the disaster of the Bar Kochba revolt, a revolt aided by the fact that some famous rabbis hailed Bar Kochba as the messiah, the rabbis warned against trying to "force the end." God will decide when the Jews are worthy of redemption. What Jews need to do is remember always the mission, always the moral demands of being chosen, and try patiently to perfect their own conduct to "repair the world" until God decides to send the messiah and end the exile. So in the eighth of the ten elements of the rabbinic system, the early rabbis banned the idea of fighting to reconstitute Jewish sovereignty.

More than that, they inveighed against proselytizing and told Jews they had to be loyal citizens of the states in which they lived. They told them *"dina d'malchutah dina,"* the law of the kingdom in which you live is the law, except for when it might enjoin a Jew to contravene a few crucial, uncompromisable elements of faith (idol worship, incest, and the shedding of innocent blood). They said, be citizens of other countries, but keep your spiritual allegiance to Torah and to God; do not put Jews in danger, defenseless as we are, through acts of hopeless zealotry, but don't blend with the societies in which you live except to the extent you must. Dietary laws and strict Sabbath observance, as the rabbis, not the Hebrew Bible, defined them, helped reinforce the balance between integration and separation.

These eight strictures exhaust the literal and legal aspects of the ben-Zakkai revolution, but two additional elements of the post–Second Commonwealth system support and sustain the rest. The ninth element of the system, already noted in passing, is that religion has to be capable of progressive articulation. Built into the way one looks at texts must be the sense that study and thought will reveal new meanings for old words—and here we come upon the significance of the Talmud.

The logic of the Talmud, flowing from Mishnah into Gemara, depended on the need for and the possibility of progressive articulation during the roughly five centuries in which the Gemara was developed and then codified. This seed planted by ben-Zakkai continued to grow after the Talmud was closed and committed to writing. A system of rabbinic *responsa* arose thereafter, *responsa* being simply a continuation of the legal discussions that led to the Talmud by means of correspondence, debate, publication, and teaching. Indeed, the Jews never really "closed" any of their books except to open a new one. Had that not been so, Jews never would have survived in exile as a self-defined unitary people, and they never would have been able to defeat various schisms that developed along the way.

The tenth element of ben-Zakkai's system is the hardest of all to describe to contemporary Western readers. It is that in order for Judaism, or any law-based system of religious faith, to adapt, there has to be an underlying understanding of human nature that legitimates the logic inherent in the process. The early rabbis did have a concept of human nature, a simple and elegant one, but one so foreign to the intellectual vernacular of twenty-first-century America that it requires careful restatement.

Western intellectuals have been battling for centuries over the essence of human nature. To simplify only a little, there is Rousseau's view that people are basically good but society is corrupting, and the Hobbesian view of people as inherently selfish and corrupt, needing a strong social restraint to contain "the war of all against all." In its early modern European incarnation, this disagreement had a lot to do with the tension between religion and early science: Hobbes's view was consistent with Christianity, if not with the habits of Christendom, and in context conservative. Rousseau's view was anti- or post-Christian, and in context revolutionary. The rabbinic approach to the question of human nature rejects both Hobbes and Rousseau because they see human nature as fixed one way or the other.

Judaism does not have a fixed view so much as a characteristic approach to understanding human nature. Put simply, it is that people have a good and an evil inclination, and can choose, as individuals and communities, how to form their own moral characters. There is not only free will, there is an obligation to make choices and to take responsibility for them. The Talmud enjoins each Jew to imagine that the fate of the world rests on his or her next act, that a single decision can tip a cosmic scale. So there is no fixed human nature in the sense that we are inherently good or bad; it is God who is good, and we can be good only by becoming partners with God (and one another) in repairing the world. We are born morally neutral: whether we lean more toward our good inclinations, as we nestle into our inevitable social contexts, is ultimately up to us.

This is crucial to the evolution of Jewcentricity for the simple reason that for centuries Jews lived among people taught by premodern forms of Christianity to believe in fate and predestination, not in freedom and responsibility. Educated Jews tended to see Christianity as a throwback to pre-Abrahamic notions that denied the possibility of historical open-endedness and individual free will. This distinction made the Jews different in their own eyes, and in the eyes of others; it infused a moral intensity into their lives that was mostly missing from and strange to the societies in which they lived. Again: ideas, even abstract ones, matter.

These ten elements define the system of Jewish survival in exile. The keys, really, are memory and education on the one hand and freedom

and responsibility on the other. Hence the centrality of the Jewish ritual, done in the home rather than the synagogue, that fuses the two:
the Passover seder.

The Passover recitation of the Haggadah as the key lesson
for children has embedded the antimyth of the Hebrew Bible into
Jewish hearts and minds now for two thousand years. The recitation
of the "fact," generation after generation, that "you were a slave in
the land of Egypt" tells every Jew, in effect: remember that you were
once on the lowest rung of a strictly hierarchical society ruled by an
autocratic government, a society in which there was no social mobility, only stasis and hopelessness for the unfortunate. Remember, too,
that many still suffer under similar conditions. This is how the Jews
have nearly always seemed to end up on "the other side of the river,"
on the other side of the ideological railroad tracks, why Jews beseech
God on the High Holy Days to "sweep away the rule of tyranny
from the earth."

The Haggadah's emphasis on children has been particularly
important. The seder is all about imparting the chosen mission to
the next generation. For the Jews, as we have seen, maintaining the
Jewish people constituted an acute practical problem thanks to their
diasporic condition. Other ancient peoples built great structures to
intimidate others in the present and defy time itself. The Jews chose
a different method, learned so well because it is embedded in the
biblical narrative itself.

In Exodus, chapters 12 and 13, Israel is about to leave Egypt;
Moses is instructing everyone in the preparations God has ordered.
What does Moses say at the gateway to freedom? Does he talk of
freedom or redemption, or about the destination being a "land flowing with milk and honey"? Does he warn how dangerous the journey
might be? Not Moses. Not once but three times (Exodus 12:26–27;
13:8; 13:14) he says: "And when your children ask you, 'What do you
mean by this rite?', you shall say: 'It is because of what the Lord did
for me when I went free from Egypt.'" As Rabbi Sacks explains, as
the Jews have seen things, "you achieve immortality not by building
pyramids or statues—but by engraving your values on the hearts of
your children, and they on theirs, so that our ancestors live on in us
and we in our children, and so on until the end of time."[14]

In other words, freedom and the moral elevation it allows are not
achievements that, once attained, simply endure. They are fragile and
so must be earned in each generation. "Civilization hangs suspended,"
Rabbi Jacob Neusner has written,

by the gossamer strand of memory. If only one cohort of mothers and fathers fails to convey to its children what it learned from its parents, then the great chain of learning and wisdom snaps. . . . And the generation that will go down through time bearing the burden of disgrace is not the one that has said nothing new—for not much new marks the mind of any age—but the one that has not said what is true.[15]

Because Jews have believed this for many centuries, they have learned to see education as an ultimate beacon of hope. It is, after all, one of the few things over which a small and dispossessed people can maintain some control. But more important, education preserves memory, and memory is the gateway to the accumulated wisdom of the ages. That memory and that wisdom have enabled Jews to stand back from given social and political conditions in which they have found themselves and to see those conditions in a broader context.[16] Because they insisted they were chosen, and because they lived in ways that preserved the possibility of consummating their mission, they ended up choosing certain ways to see the world—like lenses in a pair of conceptual spectacles. And those ways of seeing, in turn, helped provide the means to navigate and survive in it.

Each element of the rabbinic system of exilic survival, and especially the system taken as a whole, created patterns of behavior that non-Jews could not readily understand, that seemed alien, often off-putting and occasionally even threatening. To take pre-modern European cultures as a point of comparison, other peoples did not make a point of banding together to redeem captives, did not prohibit intermarriage among different linguistic groups, did not stress education, did not organize themselves into a network of communities that transcended political borders and maintained a legal confederacy, did not practice unintelligible rituals in a liturgy written in an undecipherable alphabet, did not conduct key religious rituals in their homes without officiating clergy, did not maintain beliefs that they did not try to proselytize, did not abjure force to pursue social goals, did not keep adding to and changing the corpus of their religious literature, and did not entertain open-ended ideas of human nature that credited individual human freedom and moral self-reckoning.

It is on account of these differences that the interactions of Jews and non-Jews describe a unity in the manifold in the sense that regardless of the circumstances, the Jewish exilic system always managed to adapt. It persisted in good times and bad, for at the core of that system was its reason for being: that God loves the Jewish people, has given it a singular mission, and has therefore promised that Israel cannot be destroyed and will be redeemed from exile. Like Moses at the burning bush, the Jewish people have found it impossible to say no to that proposition—not that he, and they, didn't try. And so Israel, like the burning bush itself, has been constantly aglow, throwing off light while being continuously consumed.

This is a metaphorical way of saying that the concept of the Chosen People has a kind of indestructible circularity to it, as manifested by its own history and the witness of the rest of the world to it. Why do Jews insist on existing, and existing as Jews? Because they are chosen for a divine mission. How have Jews proved to themselves and others that they are chosen? By existing. Is this an inherently Jewcentric point of view, a highly self-regarding conceit? Not if it isn't an exaggeration. Alas, only God really knows, and He's not telling.

2

On Philo-Semitism

There is no disappointment in memory, and one's exaggerations
are always on the good side.

—GEORGE ELIOT

Having outlined the sources of Jewcentricity in the Jewish
idea of chosenness, it is time now to sketch how gentile Jewcentricity developed. Contrary to what may be
supposed, gentile exaggerations about Jews predate the rise of
Christianity and the Roman era in Jewish history. They go back
at least several centuries before that, when the Land of Israel was
a part of the Hellenistic world. Indeed, the epic collision between
Jews and Christians was fundamentally shaped by the preceding one
between Jewish and Hellenistic civilizations. That collision may be
likened to two atoms smashing into each other with immeasurable
force, producing two novel, fused molecules: Christianity—Greek
rationalism combined with the Jewish moral sensibility—and rabbinic Judaism—the Jewish sense of moral mission combined with
Hellenism's logical system.

Christianity's civilization is more Hellenistic than it is Jewish,
as its achievements in science and the arts suggest. But its church is
more Jewish than Hellenistic, or else Christians would have embraced
slavery, infanticide, pederasty, and homosexuality, as they were widely

31

practiced and praised in ancient Greek culture. At the same time, the Jewish "church" is Jewish in terms of basic moral sensibilities, but the forms of rabbinic Judaism, as we shall see, owe an enormous debt to Hellenism. To claim otherwise—to assert that the genius of the Talmud is purely Jewish, for example—is an example of Jewish Jewcentricity.

You could not ask for a better set-piece for a long-lasting love-hate relationship than that between Jews and Christians. The hate part of the relationship is not obscure. The love part, however, takes some explaining.

Of course Jews and Greeks disagreed with and opposed each other on several levels. But just as much about classical civilization appealed to Jews, much about Jewish civilization appealed to Greeks, and later to Romans and others. It is hard to imagine nowadays, but in classical times Judaism was widespread throughout the known world. In a Roman Empire of roughly forty-five to fifty-five million people (estimates vary, but this is the mean range), as many as seven million were Jews. Yet not all were born Jews, for as many as three of the seven million were converts. The Roman philosopher Seneca observed with alarm that Jewish customs were so prevalent in his time that average Romans might be taken over by them. (Seneca did not admire these customs; he referred to the Jews as "a criminal tribe.") Surely, as the historian Max Dimont put it, in the period between 100 BCE and 100 CE many "Sabbath candles flickered in Grecian and Roman homes."[1] The rabbis of that day encouraged conversion and accepted converts as full members of the Jewish people, ruling that they were not only permitted but obligated to say the prayer "Our God and God of our fathers" just like all other Jews.

Many gentiles who admired Jewish ideas and practiced some Jewish rituals did not convert, however, for they were daunted by the obligations of circumcision, kashrut (the Jewish dietary laws), and strict Sabbath observance. They were nonetheless attracted to Jewish civilization, and perhaps the main reason—which Christianity in due course capitalized on in spades—is simple enough: the Hebrew Bible's antimyth, its challenge to the powers that be, its refusal to accept the hopelessness of enforced hierarchy, appealed to those on the receiving end of Greek and Roman exploitation, violence, and indignity. But Judaism was able to appeal in full force to the non-Jews of the classical era only after they had access to the Hebrew Bible, and clearly the first translation of the Hebrew Bible into Greek—a work known as the Septuagint—made a major difference in this.

The project to translate the Hebrew Bible into Greek dates from around 270 BCE. Jewcentric legend, related in the Babylonian Talmud (Mo'ed; Megillah), has it that the pharaoh Ptolemy II Philadelphus asked seventy Jewish scholars to translate the Bible into Greek so that he could add it to the great library at Alexandria. The scholars were locked in separate rooms but all came up with identical translations, suggesting divine intervention in the process. The real reason for the creation of the Septuagint, however, is that Jewish leaders feared that Hellenized Jews would forget their faith if they lacked a Greek-language version of their own scriptures. Throughout the Near East and even in Jerusalem, Greek had become the lingua franca; not all Jews still read Aramaic, and many fewer spoke and understood written Hebrew.

It worked. So successful was the translation of the Torah into Greek, whatever its flaws, that most Hellenized Jews did not forget their heritage. More germane here, the creation of the Septuagint did indeed spread Judaism's popularity in the ancient world. Many a slave wished to be a slave to Jews, and even to convert to Judaism, once he learned that Jewish law prohibited mistreating slaves and that after seven years, Jewish owners were obligated to offer slaves their freedom. This is one reason that upper-class Greeks and later Romans disliked Jews and Jewish religion (and in due course early Christians and Christian religion, as well). This is why, no doubt, the Roman historian Tacitus referred to Jews as "the abhorrent ones." They were different, and their differences sowed doubt and disorder concerning the proper way of things—proper, that is, as defined by the Roman elite.

Thus both the positive and negative orientations of gentiles to Jews were established long before the advent of Christianity, and those predispositions tended to break down along class lines—elites were, for the most part, anti-Jewish, and those they subjugated often enough were not. But with the rise of Christianity, and particularly its growing dominance throughout the Roman Empire, everything changed. The appeal of early Christianity piggybacked on the popularity of Judaism, and Christians for a time were seen, and saw themselves, as a sect of Judaism. But once the Church became official and in possession, in effect, of a great empire—Constantine made Christianity the official religion of the Roman Empire in 312—the merger of Christian faith and imperial Roman politics forced the redefinition of Judaism as something alien and anti-thetical. And the Jews accommodated, wanting Christians to stop identifying themselves as a sect of Jews, for the heresy of thinking Jesus, a physical being, divine was more than any interpretation of Judaism, however plastic, could accept.

This separation between Christianity and Judaism took time, however, nearly three centuries. And before Rome became formally Christian not only slaves and the lowly were attracted to Judaism, but at least some exalted members of elite society were, too. The emperor Caracalla was so impressed with the ways and skills of the Jews that in 212 CE he granted them not only civic equality in the empire but also citizenship. Even Constantine did not revoke Jewish citizenship, allowing the Jews to mix and live, work and thrive in the empire. Partly as a result, the emperor Julian, who came to power in 361 hoping to restore the popularity of Roman religion and rituals, returned many rights to Jews that Constantine had revoked and, before he died in battle in 363, had a mind to champion the rebuilding of the Temple. Roman Christian officialdom cracked down after that, but even by the sixth century the appeal of Judaism was still sufficiently great that the Church imposed the death penalty on Christian converts to Judaism to stem a wave of defections. In other words, positive gentile Jewcentricity, not just the Jews, provoked negative gentile Jewcentricity.

The anti-Jewish attitudes of the established Roman Church had roots not only in these oscillating social dynamics but also in a strong attendant logic. For the first two or three centuries of Christianity, Jews were the useful "other" against which Christians defined themselves, and Jews in some respects redefined themselves in turn. The relationship was one of mutual hostility as Christians tried to seize the mantle of chosenness for themselves through the theology of supersessionism—the idea that the Christian Church had replaced the Jews as God's agent on earth. Plenty of prejudicial words and deeds were hurled at the Jews, most notably in the eastern, Byzantine, part of the empire. As a rule, political elites sought order, within which Judaism was a licit religion, while the clergy sought more active anti-Jewish legislation. If anti-Semitism, as defined in the next chapter, as an aberration of mind replete with demonization and conspiracy theories, has an ur-source, it is with John Chrysostom's eight sermons, delivered in Antioch in and around the year 387. Over the years Jews were prohibited from arguing with Jewish converts to Christianity, from disinheriting children who had converted to Christianity, from converting their servants to Judaism even if they asked to be converted, from building houses of worship, and more. In 425 the

Byzantines even abolished the Jewish patriarchy in Israel—the institution of the Exilarch (after which that institution set up shop farther east). The Church on occasion prohibited Christians from going to Jewish doctors, and one ruler, Justinian, tried to tell Jews which commentaries and translations of the Bible they could and could not use.

On the other hand, what became the western, or Roman Catholic Church, more or less ignored actual living Jews, as opposed to the notion of "Israel" or "the Jews" as an abstract historical-theological construct. Jews had, after all, disappeared from the political map, and before the sixth century there were not that many Jews living in what had been the Western Roman Empire. It was only after the sixth century, when in the western and southern parts of Europe Christianity reigned supreme in post–Roman Empire times, that Christians rediscovered the Jews as the only significant non-Christian group in their realms. It was at that point that the Jews' belief in their own chosenness became further annealed in the cauldron of Christian hostility.

The more Jews were persecuted by the Church, the more Jews clung to the belief in their chosenness, and the more the Jews did so, the more Christians interpreted assertions of Jewish election as an affront to the Church. Simple logic demands that there cannot be two chosen peoples, only one—and "chosen" in religious terms translates into "leader" in temporal terms. If the Church insists that it is the chosen of God, then the Jews cannot be. It follows that they need to stop claiming they are, and if they do not stop, they must somehow be made to stop. This point of view has cascaded through Christian sensibilities well into modern times. Arnold Toynbee wrote in his 1961 masterwork *A Study of History*, for example, that "[t]he most notorious historical example of idolization of an ephemeral self is the error of Jews. . . . [T]hey persuaded themselves that Israel's discovery of the One True God had revealed Israel itself to be God's chosen people."[2] Essentially, he accused the Jews of Jewcentricity, of exaggerating their own role in cosmic history long after their early bit part had come to an end, a statement that would have fallen snugly into context in any of the preceding dozen or so centuries.

The fact that Jesus was, of course, a Jew just tended to drive everyone slightly crazy. To Christians, Jews were too stubborn to follow what seemed to them an obvious logic from Isaiah to Jesus, from Judaism to Christianity. To Jews, that logic was a perversion of text and its interpretation. As they saw it, Christians were using one of their own, a Jew, to distort and deny the Jewish mission in the world. It also occurred to them that Christians could not fully affirm belief in their own religion without casting aspersions on the original, foundational form from which it came: It is a common human foible, after all, to reinforce one's own beliefs by denigrating those of others, the more so the closer those beliefs are to one's own. This is the obvious logical and psychological root of supersessionist theology, not only in Christianity but also in Islam.

It is the reason, too, that the rabbis during the early Christian era, the time when Jews and Christians first became mortal enemies and acknowledged that circumstance, concluded that anti-Semitism was for all practical purposes permanent. As Rabbi Shimon bar-Yochai put it at the time, "The law holds that Esau hates Jacob"[3]—everyone at the time understanding that Esau (also called Edom, in accordance with Genesis 25:30) and Jacob, being biological twins, symbolized the insight that it is from such closeness that real hatred comes; the Jews coming to understand, too, that Esau was a metaphor for the officially Christianized Roman Empire, the Jews' worst nightmare come true in the merger of their conqueror with their most dangerous once-internal heresy: the assertion of Jesus's divinity.

Yet within the negative there still abided the positive. The fact that Christians affirmed monotheism and revered the Hebrew Bible as precursor to their own scripture represented a major achievement of the original Abrahamic mission. How could this Jewish success at having been a light unto the nations lead to such prejudice and pain, and from the very source of that success? How could Christians elevate one Jew so high and want to push all the rest down so low? How impious must we be, the exiled Jews asked, to deserve such a strange fate?

Under the circumstances, it is not hard to see how, in times when religion was paramount in society in a way it no longer is in Western countries, Jews and Christians developed their tangled love-hate relationship. The problem, much of the time, was that what each admired about the other was precisely what the other preferred not to emphasize. Jews should have been delighted that Christian morals and monotheism came from Judaism, but Christians rarely wanted to talk about that. Christians should have respected Jews for the fact that they had discovered both history and moral reasoning through the Jew named Jesus, but Jews definitely did not want to talk about that.

It was asymmetry, however, not irony or theology alone, that most definitively shaped the relationship. An obvious asymmetry concerned power: Christians in Europe and Byzantium had it; Jews did not. And the temptation to abuse power is rarely held in check by respect for those of different races or religions. More subtle, but in the long run perhaps more important, was a seemingly abstract, and rather esoteric, asymmetry in how Jews and Christians saw the relationship between culture and faith.

Christians, like Muslims later on, did not separate the message of monotheism from the theological and ritual package in which it came. For them there was only one correct religion, and it was the duty of Christians to proselytize that right religion until all the world accepted it. (Divisions within Christianity, almost from the start, mightily complicated that project, but that is another story.) The rabbis, on the other hand, held that a universal moral message could be expressed, indeed probably *had* to be expressed, in a great diversity of cultural forms. The Jewish vision of messianic times did not require that everyone become Jewish, only that everyone recognize the oneness of God and act accordingly. As the rabbis saw it, just as not every Jew could be or needed to be a priest, so not every moral person in the world could be or needed to be a Jew. To be true to the mission and to ensure its continuity, Jews took upon themselves obligations both moral and ritual that did not bind non-Jews. But that did not make non-Jews worse people; the rabbis even articulated a mystical notion that in every generation there are thirty-six righteous gentiles whose existence justifies God's not destroying the world.

Since many non-Jews in premodern times had difficulty, it seems, with the idea that universal moral truths could take more than one cultural and ritual form, they frequently misread the Jewish notion of chosenness not as respect for diversity but as clannish arrogance. They have read, as many still do, Jewish concern over the future of the Jewish people as a racial proclivity rather than a spiritual one, and, unfortunately, some less philosophically disposed but still observant Jews have contributed to that misperception by manifesting their fears and sense of vulnerability as general hostility, and compensatory arrogance, toward non-Jews.

Despite the hostility that often characterized Jewish-Christian relations, the seed of philo-Semitism never died. Over time, however, the social and cultural attraction of Jews and Jewish ideas acquired a character separate from religious attraction. Since philo-Semitism could not find practical expression in the Church, it migrated to domains outside the Church. Thus throughout the medieval and especially the early modern period, the Jewish quarter of many European cities ended up being

attractive cosmopolitan places in which the wealthier and more intellectually adept of the gentile population sometimes preferred to live.
In most cities and towns, the Jews were limited to certain areas by
official decree, although this was not the same as a ghetto—the first
of these being established in 1516 in Venice—where Jews were locked
in at night. In many cases, Jews simply chose to live near one another
so they could walk to synagogue and to the ritual bath, and have other
community facilities like butcheries and bakeries close to hand. Non-
Jews readily moved in nearby. Thus when a new pope, Paul IV, ordered
the establishment of a restricted ghetto on the banks of the Tiber in
1555, he did not create anything new: the neighborhood was already
there. As Dimont pointed out: "His problem was not getting the Jews
into the Jewish quarter, but getting the Christians out. They liked it
there, and only successive turns of the Inquisitional screw forced them
out. It took over a century before Rome's Jewish quarter became a
hundred percent Jewish."[4]

With the advent of the Renaissance and the Enlightenment,
attitudes toward Jews grew even more diverse. Those who affirmed
anti- or post-Christian views but disliked Jews could dislike them for
their parochialism—like Voltaire and Kant. Those who reaffirmed
Christian tenets in the face of modern challenges could dislike them
for their role in pioneering modernity. Others, however, could and
did take more historical and philosophical attitudes not in evidence
in earlier times. Thus could Michelet say in his 1864 book, *Bible of
Humanity*: "The Jews' vices are those which we have produced in them;
their virtues are their own." And thus could David Lloyd George say
to the Jews a half century later, in an odd, almost self-congratulatory
vein: "You may say you have been oppressed and persecuted—and that
has been your power! You have been hammered into very fine steel,
and that is why you have never been broken."[5] The Jews had their
share of gentile admirers, some religious but modern Christians, some
secularists. Indeed, with the Renaissance there arose, albeit in limited
form, the phenomenon of Christians converting to Judaism not merely
to wed a Jewish spouse, but out of conviction.

Philo-Semitism, however, has had a modern career more consequential than that manifested by the respect of the erudite and the
reflective, and a more ironic one as well. In modern times equality as
a norm in all things has overtaken assumptions of natural hierarchy,
and among some Jews the idea of the Chosen People fell on hard
times. Starting early in the nineteenth century, many Jews in western
Europe began to doubt and even to regret the very idea of their own

chosenness. Thus the Reform movement that began in Germany in around 1810 and, far more recently, the Reconstructionist movement in the United States, edited the idea of the Chosen People out of their theology and their prayer books. They became adept over the years at dismissing, ignoring, apologizing for, or abstracting into meaninglessness the idea of Jewish chosenness. Since a religion is in the end whatever its adepts say it is, one hesitates to label forms of Judaism that have jettisoned the idea of chosenness as inauthentic. But one has to wonder whether such Jews have really understood the role of chosenness in Jewish history, which is to say its pivotal role in Jewish survival. As the historian Salo Baron once aptly put it, the "Jewish religion without the 'Chosen People' is unthinkable, neither could it, like the other religions, be transplanted from Jews to other people."[6]

No doubt, liberal Jews of the nineteenth, twentieth, and, let us assume, the twenty-first centuries did not jettison the idea of chosenness for theological or philosophical reasons. Most thought instead that doing so would reduce the hostility of non-Jews. If that was really all there was to it—Christians and Jews coming to their senses and realizing that all the medieval fuss and hard feelings between them were simply misunderstandings arising from an unsophisticated interpretation of the scriptures—we would have been close to done with all the nastiness and tragedy of olden times. If that had been so, then the nineteenth and twentieth centuries would have been delightful, if a little less exciting, times for Jews in Europe. Clearly, however, that is not what happened, and what did happen requires some accounting. Gentile Jewcentricity grew in these centuries, in both its negative and its positive forms. It is the latter that most interests us now; the former we take up in the next chapter.

Oddly enough, whereas many Jews in recent centuries seem not to have understood how the idea of divine election has affected Jewish historical morale, certain non-Jews—Protestant Christians in the main—have insisted on Jewish chosenness for reasons of their own. Having reimported the idea into their theological system in fairly recent times, they have reshaped and reinterpreted it for use in ways that Jews never could have imagined, but that affect Jews nonetheless. By and large, this reinterpretation started out as an Anglo-American phenomenon, but it now reaches practically around the world from its current core in the United States.

American Protestantism, in all its sectarian diversity, is divided theologically between those who refer to themselves as supersessionists and those who refer to themselves as dispensationalists. Supersessionism, sometimes called replacement theology, is based on the classical view of Christianity, both Catholic and Protestant, which holds that Jews are no longer God's Chosen People because they refused to accept Jesus as Christ, as savior. The Church has instead superseded the Jews, and Judaism.

The failure of the Jews to accept Jesus as Christ, or messiah, brought upon them a curse—they are doomed to wander the earth, loathed and abused by all. The term "wandering Jew" therefore has a general theological basis; it is not just a description of a mostly European sociohistorical fact. The term has a specific textual basis as well, one with truly bizarre historical manifestations. In the Gospel of Matthew, 16:28, Jesus is quoted as saying that some who proved inhospitable to him in his ordeal would not taste death until the Second Coming. By legend, this was transmuted into a single person, *the* Wandering Jew. This individual was spotted all over Europe for centuries, and there were even several people, including some Jews, who claimed to *be* the Wandering Jew.[7] It is not too much to say that because of this belief, persecution of the Jews carried with it a kind of catchall justification: Christians persecuted a people whom, they believed, God Himself had already cursed.

The idea of the Church as having superseded the Jews was carried over into Protestantism. As those who know their church history are aware, there were many revolts against the Church of Rome before Martin Luther nailed his Ninety-five Theses to the church door in Wittenberg in 1517. But that man, on that date, marked the beginning of the Protestant Reformation for practical purposes. Luther believed he was returning to the true Christian faith, and the basis of that faith was not the layers of ritual and tradition that had come to dominate the Church of Rome, but the Scripture itself.

The scriptural focus of Protestantism was enabled by major social changes and in turn shaped and accelerated those changes, most of them doubtless unintentional. The Catholic Church had not encouraged widespread literacy, to say the least. It had reserved the right of interpretation of scripture to its own scholastics who knew the languages of antiquity, mainly Greek and Latin but sometimes also Hebrew. When the Bible became available to increasing numbers of literate people in a language they could understand—Gutenberg had introduced movable type in 1450, not coincidentally—a tremendous power was unleashed all over early modern Europe, not entirely unlike the role the Septuagint played in Greco-Roman times. Whatever one supposes its true authorship to be, the Hebrew Bible is a book of captivating interest and wisdom. Its narrative captures human nature, the intricacies of applied moral reasoning, and the sense of the sacred in history like few if any others. It was bound to have a major impact on those who could now for the first time read these powerful stories for themselves, and scripture-focused Protestants had and still have special incentives to do so.

Luther's Protestantism, after all, focused on the example of Abraham, on his direct encounter with God, on his willingness to leave his home and his family in search of truth. Early Protestantism was radically Abrahamic, and most forms of Protestantism still are to one degree or another. It is belief based on personal faith and on a personal relationship with God, without the need for intervening hierarchy or priesthood. It is therefore natural that early Protestantism became, if not Judeophilic, then at least more oriented toward Jewish sensibilities as defined in the Hebrew Bible. More than the Church of Rome had ever done, Protestantism interpreted the New Testament in the direct light of the Old.

Indeed, so Abrahamic and Judeocentric was early Protestant thinking that Martin Luther expected the Jews of Europe to flock to the Protestant banner and join his new church. When they did not do so, Luther became angry at the Jews and spewed forth some of the most hideous anti-Semitic invective in European history—which is really saying something. But Luther's anti-Semitism expressed the wrath of the suitor spurned. It did not affect his scripture-centered idea of Abrahamic faith. It merely led his followers to argue that just as the Church of Rome had superseded the Jews, so the Protestant way now superseded that of the Church of Rome. The Jews remained cursed, but now *doubly* so: they had not only spurned Jesus as savior, they had also spurned Luther as, in effect, his prophet.

This is more or less how the matter remained, theologically and historically, until roughly the middle of the nineteenth century. There was only Christian supersessionism, or replacement theology, as the stage shifts away from Luther's German-speaking Christian lands of Europe to the British Isles.

• • •

The notion of Christians restoring the idea of Jewish chosenness was inherent to some degree in the Protestant orientation to the Bible. It is impossible to read the Hebrew Bible or know anything about Judaism without being aware of the basic Jewish belief regarding the Jews' own future: Jews awaited redemption and return to the Land of Israel. Protestant Christians who understood this would naturally wonder whether the Jewish idea of the Jews' own redemption could be integrated in some way with Christian notions of the Second Coming.

These questions seemed to arise mainly in Britain, and the reason may have had something to do with an indigenous tradition of British "chosenness." The Christianization of Britain coincided roughly with a series of Nordic invasions. From the crucible of that violence some early British Christians fashioned a way to read their own historical narrative in parallel with that of the Hebrew Bible. The Epistle of Gildas, which seems to be a late-sixth-century work, pronounced Britain a new Israel, its battle against the heathen invaders comparable to Israel's struggles against Babylonians and Philistines. This theme was repeated in the Venerable Bede's *Ecclesiastic History* from around the year 735.[8]

Whether this theme lay dormant in the centuries thereafter— probably not entirely—we must leave to qualified scholars of that historical period to say. But whether it did or not, the idea returned after the Reformation. In 1585, an Anglican churchman named Thomas Brightman wrote a pamphlet called *Apocalypsis Apocalypsos* in which he suggested that Britain should support the return of the Jews to Israel. This, he argued, would hasten a series of events he believed were predicted in the Bible as leading to the Second Coming. This would not only hasten the return of Jesus Christ, but it would seal the role of the British people as God's vanguard of the messianic era.

It is not clear how many people took Brightman seriously. But not long after, in 1621, a leading member of Parliament named Henry Finch advanced a similar notion. The Jews, he said, "shall repair to their own country, shall inherit all of the land as before, shall live in safety, and shall continue in it forever." Such ideas then and afterward had an odd, bivalent appeal, insofar as they had any appeal at all. To those who looked kindly on such ideas, the Jews deserved a respite after all their centuries of wandering and persecution. To others, this was a convenient way to get rid of the Jews in England and perhaps elsewhere in Christian Europe. There had been no Jews in England when Shakespeare lived and wrote; they had been expelled in 1290. They had only a few years before Finch's birth been allowed back—in 1655–1656, under Oliver Cromwell—and already some Englishmen were sympathetic to any justification for getting rid of them again.

As with Brightman, few seem to have paid much attention to Finch. After the American and French Revolutions, however, and especially with the horrors of the Napoleonic Wars, a wave of premillenarianism shook the Anglican establishment and Protestant churches elsewhere in Europe. Many thought the Napoleonic Wars, the first ever mass-mobilization modern wars, complete with unprecedented massive casualties of both soldiers and civilians, fit the biblical description of Armageddon. Many expected the imminent return of Christ, and the idea of the Jews returning to the Land of Israel as part of a series of events leading to the Second Coming now became embedded for good in at least a British corner of Protestant thinking. An Anglican clergyman named Louis Way spread this notion through a journal called the *Jewish Expositor*; many well-known figures, among them the poet Samuel Taylor Coleridge, were among his subscribers.

By far the most important nineteenth-century figure in this drama, however, was John Nelson Darby. Darby, born in the year 1800, was the first to name and define dispensationalism, and he was the man who spread it to America. Like Way and Brightman before him, Darby was an Anglican priest—though an Irish, not an English, one. But Darby took Way's thinking far beyond where he had found it, systematizing it into a full-fledged theology. It was Darby who, basing himself on an interpretation of 1 Thessalonians 4:16–17, formalized the doctrine of "the Rapture," the idea that "born again" Christians would rise up into the sky when the Second Coming was imminent and be transferred directly to heaven, spared the sufferings of Armageddon.

It was also Darby who first specified how a reborn Israel would play pivotal roles in the series of events leading to Jesus's return. The Jews would be gathered again in their ancestral land, gain political independence, and be at the pivot of end-of-history convulsions. And it was Darby who developed the idea that the history of humanity from the creation of the world onward was divided into a small number of eras—just seven—each with its own particular characteristics and symbols, which Darby called "dispensations."

Above all, Darby challenged classical Christian replacement, or supersession, theology. He argued that the Church—any church— has never superseded the Jews as God's Chosen People. Rather, he argued, the Church was a "parenthesis" in earthly history, for it was not of this earth, but of Heaven. The Jews remain and always will be God's Chosen People on earth, while the Church is God's chosen vehicle for cosmic redemption. This dualism, which resembles ancient views that human time is unreal and only Eternity matters ultimately, seems to have been Darby's invention. As far as standard Catholic and Protestant theologians are concerned, it has no basis in Christian theology.

Through the idea of dispensations, Darby managed to combine prehistory, biblical times, postbiblical times, and all of Church history before and after the Reformation into one overarching narrative. This was utterly brilliant. In an age when people were first exposed to and persuaded by scientific evidence of geological time stretching back many millions of years, Darby essentially applied the same seamless method to religion, though, to be sure, only within the five-millennia-plus time frame consistent with a literal reading of the Bible. Through the invention of dispensationalism, Darby consolidated in Britain what we now recognize as premillenarian fundamentalism, a development that is now an integral part of evangelical and Pentecostal as well as fundamentalist Protestantism in the United States.

John Nelson Darby was a busy man. He not only invented an essentially new theology, he founded a movement: the Plymouth Brethren. He also exported the movement, finding post–Civil War America prime real estate for doing so. He made seven missionary trips to North America, growing more popular with each crossing of the Atlantic. He helped establish dozens of Plymouth Brethren congregations in America before his death in 1881.

Darby's residual influence on America today, not to speak of the policies and ways of the British Empire in the Near East (as we will soon see), is hard to underestimate. Yet almost no one who is not a dispensationalist, or otherwise a student in the history of nineteenth-century Anglo-American religion, has ever even heard of him. The reason for this seems obvious: we live in a time when social and intellectual authorities in the United States and Britain, almost to a man (and woman) secular people, are trained to think of history as being shaped by generals, politicians, inventors, entrepreneurs, and artists. It does not occur to them that any religious figure, let alone a semi-mystical, renegade Irish Anglican priest, could be relevant to our own times. Conceit blinds.

• • •

Darby's influence on British imperial policy in the Near East, with implications down to our own day, is improbable, perhaps, but unmistakable—if you know the history.

One of John Nelson Darby's followers was one Anthony Ashley Cooper. Ashley Cooper was Darby's contemporary almost to the year, born in 1801. Before Ashley Cooper became the seventh earl of Shaftesbury in 1851, he was already a disciple of Darby's. Born to nobility, Shaftesbury was a man in high places with a keen interest in foreign affairs. He took a particular interest in the affairs of the Near East after Napoleon's 1799 intervention in Egypt, the picturesque aftermath of which occurred in Shaftesbury's impressionable youth.

Muhammad Ali's 1831 rebellion in Egypt against the Ottoman Empire, during which Ali surged into Palestine and an area encompassing most of what was then called Syria, raised in Shaftesbury's imagination a combination of British imperial interests and Darby's religious visions. The Muhammad Ali rebellion enabled for the first time more or less unobstructed British travel to Palestine and helped reshape Anglo-French rivalries in the Near East as well. Acting on his religious convictions, but arguing other, more political, kinds of rationales, Shaftesbury helped to persuade the British foreign minister, Lord Palmerston, to send a British consul to Jerusalem. This Palmerston did in 1838, sending out William Young with instructions to "promote the welfare of the Jews." Darby was thrilled.

The very next year, Shaftesbury wrote an essay in support of the Jewish return to the Land of Israel. Entitled "The State and Prospects of the Jews," it was published in the January 1839 issue of a prestigious and widely circulated British magazine called the *Quarterly Review*. He also lobbied Palmerston to take a more active role in the idea, although to Palmerston, again, Shaftesbury stressed economic and other imperial arguments. Palmerston was receptive, leading Shaftesbury to conclude, rather typically for religious mystics who do not believe in coincidence but rather in Providence, that "Palmerston had been chosen by God to be an instrument of good to His ancient people."

Speaking of the impossibility of coincidence, it seemed to Shaftesbury that a necessary component of God's plan (that being more or less the same as *his* plan, of course) was that the Jews, too, should be leaning in the same direction—wanting to return to their ancient homeland, as even Napoleon had reportedly urged them to do in 1799 when he sought their aid against the Ottoman Empire.

Shaftesbury asserted this in his *Quarterly Review* essay. Palmerston, too, when he wrote to the British ambassador in Constantinople during the 1840 Damascus blood-libel affair, used language almost identical to that of Shaftesbury's essay, speaking of the "growing belief" among European Jews that the time was at hand for their return en masse to the Holy Land.

Shaftesbury and Palmerston were not the only members of British elite society who believed this. Such figures as Lord Lindsey, Sir George Gawler, Lord Manchester, Sir Charles Warren, Sir Laurence Oliphant, and the large-living, notorious Colonel Charles Henry Churchill, among others, understood the imperial opportunities inherent in Palestine's rebirth from the decline of the Ottoman Empire. Benjamin Disraeli, too, who probably should have known better, expressed some imperial mysticism of his own, although he at least had the sense to do it in fiction, mainly in his novel *Tancred.* So he expressed himself, too, however, in an 1851 letter to a young Lord Stanley, the fifteenth earl of Derby.[9] And then there is George Eliot's famous proto-Zionist novel, *Daniel Deronda* (1876), the finest of a subgenre of at least vaguely biblical and philo-Semitic Victorian literature. Many Jews knew all of this and read these books; surely they were moved by them to action, yes?

No, they were not. Zionist sentiment among the Jews of Europe had not yet emerged in a modern political form; it existed only in the old religious form, that of the prayer book, which implied that no action need be taken on behalf of any cause or movement. There had been stirrings of early political Zionism among Sephardim—Jews of Spanish-Portuguese descent—in America. In 1818, for example, Mordecai Manuel Noah made proto-Zionist remarks, and his correspondent John Adams affirmed them vigorously, hoping that the freeing of the Jews from the oppression they suffered in Europe would lead them to enlightened forms of Christianity. But the writings of the earliest pre-Herzlean Jewish Zionists—Moses Hess, Leo Pinsker, and others—were still decades in the future when Shaftesbury was a young man. So it is fair to say that dispensationalist Christians became political Zionists before many, perhaps *any,* European Jews did. Even Naftali Herz Imber, who wrote the lyrics to "*Hatikva,*" Israel's national anthem, seems to have been inspired by the man to whom he was travel secretary, the aforementioned Laurence Oliphant.

Taking his cue from Darby and his growing cohort of supporters, Shaftesbury kept pressing for British engagement in Palestine on behalf of the Jews. Ottoman authorities, naturally enough, took a dim view of the idea, but Shaftesbury did not give up. When, on the cusp of the Crimean War in 1853, it looked as though the Ottoman Empire might collapse, or at the least be made more pliable as a result of another battlefield defeat, Shaftesbury, by now an earl in his own right, again picked up his pen on behalf of the idea of a Jewish return to Palestine. Writing to Lord Aberdeen, then British prime minister, and speaking not just of Palestine but more broadly of geographical Syria, he argued that it was "a country without a nation," needing to be matched to a "nation without a country." Shaftesbury asked rhetorically, "Is there such a nation? To be sure there is, The ancient and rightful lords of the soil, the Jews!"

Those conversant with the lore and debates of Zionists and anti-Zionists will note something remarkable here. The phrase "for a land without a people, a people without a land" has been widely taken to be an ur-phrase of the Zionist movement, often attributed to Theodor Herzl or another of the Zionist founders. In fact, the Anglican clergyman Alexander Keith probably coined the phrase in 1843, enabling Shaftesbury to make it political and famous in July 1853—again, before there even were any Jewish political Zionists.[10] The phrase came down to the Zionists later on, through the British Jew and early Zionist Israel Zangwill, who first used it in writing in 1901, just four years after Herzl had founded the Zionist movement at the Basle Conference in 1897. Zangwill knew it was Shaftesbury's rhetorical calling card; in a 1920 essay he wrote as much.[11] By then, however, the phrase was already a source of controversy among Zionists themselves (of which more in chapter 14).

When John Nelson Darby began spreading his new gospel in the United States, he probably did not imagine the success he would eventually have. But just as the Napoleonic Wars had seemed to many devout Protestant Englishmen a harbinger of Armageddon, so did the Civil War seem to many Americans. The religious language used throughout the war by Lincoln, Robert E. Lee, and many others in and out of uniform surely did nothing to reduce those associations. The horrors of the war, the hundreds of thousands killed and maimed, and then the rapid economic dislocations and social changes that ensued left many Americans with strong feelings of uncertainty about the world and about their own future. The middle of the nineteenth century was still a deeply religious era for common and especially rural folk, even as the overlay of the Age of Reason thickened in some freer-thinking American cities. People everywhere turn to religion for comfort and bearings in unsettled times; why anyone ever thought that the Age of Reason could vanquish this deep human instinct in just a generation or two is surely a puzzle.

In any event, whatever the deeper sources, American dispensationalism needed advocates and it needed institutions to establish itself in the American free market of religious denominationalism. That it has done. It started with John Inglis (1813–1879) and his intermittently published "monthly" magazine, called *Waymarks in the Wilderness*, and a parade of influential and often colorful successors have followed—James H. Brookes and his Niagara Bible Conference of 1868, Dwight L. Moody and his theatrical evangelical entrepreneurship, and many others.

Of those others, consider William Eugene Blackstone, the author of the best-selling work *Jesus Is Coming*. This book, published in 1882, was one of the best-selling books up to that time in American history. In 1891 Blackstone enlisted 413 American prominent citizens to support a petition he presented to President Benjamin Harrison. Using the famous phrase about a land without a people for a people without a land, the petition sought the president's support for the establishment of a Jewish state in Palestine. Harrison ignored it and probably considered Blackstone some kind of crackpot.

Another major figure in the early advance of American dispensationalism was Cyrus I. Scofield. Born in 1843, Scofield created *The Scofield Reference Bible*, first published in 1909 by Oxford University Press. It is hard to overstate the influence of this book. Depending on John Nelson Darby's own notes, Scofield annotated the entire Bible. His commentaries systematized dispensationalist theology in a way that no one before had done. The fact that Scofield had put it all in writing was the key—that and the rapid spread of rural literacy in the United States through the nineteenth and into the early twentieth centuries.

Before long the Scofield Bible's commentaries took on an aura of authority equal to, if not greater than, that of the text itself. The reason is disarmingly simple: the Bible, particularly some significant stretches of the New Testament, can be rather cryptic; the text doesn't always say clearly exactly what it means. Scofield told readers what it meant, in plain, clear American English. He insisted further that the scripture was to be taken literally. Invoking Darby, Scofield wrote:

> Not one instance exists of a "spiritual" or figurative fulfillment of prophecy. . . . Jerusalem is always Jerusalem, Israel is always Israel, Zion is always Zion. . . . Prophecies may never be spiritualized, but are always literal.[12]

Among the literal meanings he made plain to his legion of readers was that the Jews, and only the Jews, were God's Chosen People.

Orthodox Jews, or at least those familiar with the ways of Orthodox Judaism, know exactly what this is all about—or they ought to. Scofield's commentary for dispensationalists is more or less what Rashi's Torah commentaries are for Orthodox Jews. Many Orthodox Jews do not distinguish the authoritativeness of Rashi's commentaries on the Hebrew Bible from that of the text itself. Many dispensationalist readers regarded *The Scofield Reference Bible* in a similar light, with the result that by the time Scofield died in 1921, his work had become the leading Bible used by evangelicals and fundamentalists in the United States, and so it remained for the next half century. It brought greater respectability to dispensationalism, which, before Scofield, lived in an ill-defined world suspended between an oral and a written tradition. Scofield changed that, and in doing so helped accelerate the institutionalization of dispensationalism.

The whole idea of a premillenarian theology embedding itself in institutions may seem a contradiction in terms, but it happens all the time. It's certainly very Christian and has been almost from the start. We should defer to psychiatrists to explain how this happens—although the excellent book *When Prophecy Fails*, by the social psychologist Leon Festinger and his associates, does a good job with the nineteenth-century American example of the Millerites (called today Seventh-Day Adventists). But it happens, and it is still happening, for in recent times dispensationalism has become further institutionalized through the wiles and ways of the American marketplace. For example, dispensationalist themes form the backbone of the enormously successful *Left Behind* book series written by Tim LaHaye and Jerry Jenkins. Even these pale next to the success and influence of Hal Lindsey's *The Late Great Planet Earth*.

And then there are the megachurch televangelists, almost all of whom are dispensationalists—Jack Van Imp and Jimmy Swaggart being cases in point. There are, too, the multidimensional empire-builders like Pat Robertson and the late Jerry Falwell, who famously claimed that God has been good to America because America has been good to the Jews. Above all, there is Billy Graham, confidant of eleven

U.S. presidents and one of the most influential men of the American twentieth century. Graham, in case you were in doubt, is a dispensationalist. He has also managed to be a closet anti-Semite, at least in his private sessions with Richard Nixon. But this should not be at all surprising once one understands what dispensationalists actually believe.

Dispensationalists love Jews in the abstract but are not particularly fond of individual Jews in the flesh unless they convert to Christianity. This is because dispensationalists know for an absolute certainty, and in detail, how it all ends. They know the Jews will be ingathered to Israel, after which there will be a great war, a great battle of Armageddon, and that only the "born again" will survive in the Rapture. They believe (although there are differences here among dispensationalists) that the anti-Christ will be a Jew, but that exactly 144,000 Jewish converts to Christianity will fight the anti-Christ and prevail, after which Jesus will return, imprison Satan, and establish the Kingdom of Heaven on earth—the final "dispensation" of history. All of this will destroy many millions of people and, they believe, all remaining Jews. The true believers, and the true believers only, will inherit the earth and live with Christ.

Dispensationalism has challenged, and may one day displace, more traditional forms of supersessionist or replacement-theology Protestantism in the United States. The old mainline churches still have a theology of dynamic religion, inherited from the cauldron of the English Civil War, but they have run low on octane in the past half century or so. They are being left in the dust clouds of dispensationalist empire-building in the South, the Midwest, and rural areas all over the country—precisely the places where American demographics and the weight of American electoral politics have been moving. According to the Pew Foundation's Center on Religion, more than 30 percent of American Christians define themselves as evangelicals, and of these, around 86 percent believe Jews are still the Chosen People; 67 percent believe the Bible is the word of God; and at least 36 percent believe that the foundation of the modern State of Israel is a harbinger of the Second Coming of Christ. Though what we might call orthodox dispensationalists may make up only 7 to 10 percent of the American population, their sphere of social influence is much larger than that. These are not small numbers, of course; even a 7 percent estimate of dispensationalists amounts to more than three times the number of all American Jews.

The political clout of dispensationalism is great, and its political juggernaut, often characterized as constituting the Christian Right, is arguably growing greater, too, at least within the Republican Party. If it were not, prominent opponents of the trend, like former senator Jack Danforth, an Episcopalian minister, wouldn't be sounding alarums about it.[13] Consider how far the dispensationalists have come in just a century: President Harrison dismissed Blackstone's 1891 petition as though the latter were a nutcase; would any American president today even consider doing the same?

There can be no doubt: many of the truest true believers among American Protestants today—and not only American Protestants— believe that Jews are still the Chosen People. They believe that the birth of the modern State of Israel is part of divine cosmic history being revealed before our eyes. They believe they must defend Israel lest the Jews have nowhere to go to fulfill their cosmic destiny. They believe the end of days is near, and they interpret contemporary political and strategic events in this context. All who believe this way believe, by way of foundational premise, that what Jews are and do, especially in Israel but all over the world, constitutes the core of the divine drama itself. God writes the script; the Jews and their enemies are the star actors; everyone else just sits in the audience, as it were, and watches it all pour forth. These people are Jewcentric—*very* Jewcentric.

3

Anti-Semitism, Properly Understood

Alcohol is perfectly consistent in its effects upon man. Drunken-
ness is merely an exaggeration. A foolish man drunk becomes
maudlin; a bloody man, vicious; a coarse man, vulgar.
                                            —Willa Cather

So Mel Gibson got hammered one day—July 28, 2006, as it
happened—and after being pulled over for drunk driving
started mouthing off to the arresting officer about the Jews
being responsible for all the major wars in history. Those who knew
something about Gibson's family background were not particular surprised at this, or by his film *The Passion of the Christ*. But, evidently,
few were aware that he was raised in a conservative, pre–Vatican II
Catholic home. Mel Gibson is a good to mediocre actor, depending
on his role, and a terrible filmmaker unless one happens to like gratu-
itous blood and gore by the bucketful. But is he also an anti-Semite?

That depends on the definition of anti-Semitism—negative gentile
Jewcentricity—and it is not an easy term to define. Not only is the subject fraught with emotion, but it is one that has been dissected and argued
over by historians, psychiatrists, sociologists, philosophers, and armchair
moralists for centuries. To say that the literature on anti-Semitism is vast
is like saying that a mature California redwood is a big tree.

But not to worry: no extensive review of literature is about to be inflicted upon you. Nor will we retrace the history of European anti-Semitism, engage in a lachrymose account of the Third Reich, or indulge more than necessary in inevitably inconclusive exercises in social Freudianism—my term, analogous to social Darwinism, for the impulse to plumb the subconscious of entire civilizations. For the purposes of our inquiry into Jewcentricity, a smidgen of etymology, a short definitional sojourn, and a humble meditation will suffice.

The consensus among scholars is that anti-Semitism can be defined as "the irrational hatred of Jews." This has led to a lot of jokes toying with plays on irrationality in their punch lines. As noted above, Jackie Mason used to say that anti-Semitism means disliking Jews "more than is absolutely necessary"; for the sake of argument, let us grant Mason's implicit premise as a way into the discussion.

Jews can be pushy, clannish, arrogant, ostentatious, and boastful to the point of producing irritation in others. That makes it possible to dislike Jews as individuals or as a group, even if disliking whole groups is not politically correct these days (or indicative of refined character in any days). This is not anti-Semitism, however, because it may not be irrational. It may be ignorant, mean-spirited, and small-minded, or it may be just a matter of taste. It may be all that and still not be irrational in the sense that psychiatrists use the term.

For example, early- to mid-twentieth-century American "country club" anti-Semitism, as it used to be called, had more to do with white racist chauvinism than with anti-Semitism. It is sad but true: racism can be so deeply embedded in a cultural idiom that those who inherit its biases need not be, and usually aren't, irrational or otherwise evil people. Quite the contrary: it is those who *refuse* to behave in prejudicial ways toward targeted minorities who are considered irrational by their peers. That is partly because racial prejudice is typically inculcated by parents into their children before the children can make a rational assessment of what they are being told. It is also partly a result of the way attitudes are conveyed by means of social networks; behavior by those we don't even know can influence us, as research on smoking, obesity, and other more easily observable traits have shown.[1]

Anti-Semitism is something different. It goes beyond mere dislike. It is a kind of disease of mind, the most elemental definition of which is twofold: that Jews are inherently judged according to a double standard, and that Jews are implicated in some sort of cosmic evil.

From this basic definition one can sketch a more specific model based on the observation that one can distinguish criticism—which may be fair or not, accurate or not—from irrational hatred by examining the logical premises of an argument. It works like this: If an argument takes the form, a Jew or the Jews are guilty of X because he or they did Y, where Y is something specific and subject to objective description, then you have a criticism. But if the argument takes the form, a Jew or the Jews are guilty of X because Jews are inherently Z, where Z is some imputed characteristic that is not specific or subject to observation ("disloyal" or "sneaky" or "dishonest" or "lecherous" or "criminal" and so on), that is anti-Semitism. With such broad categories of ill-doing set forth, almost any behavior can be interpreted as falling into one or more of those categories if the anti-Semite wishes to see it that way. In other words, a dislike can be based on seeing and then judging, but real anti-Semitism—and all other forms of genuine bigotry—is based on first judging and then seeing.

If, indeed, one is confronted with a case of bigotry, four phases or aspects of a bigoted narrative will usually follow. The first is selectivity: only "data" that are unfavorable to the targeted group will be acknowledged, and all other data will be ignored. The second is demonization: comparing the "guilty" to culturally embedded symbols of unarguable evil. The third is selective representation: finding the few members of the targeted group who are critical of their own and wildly exaggerating their relative significance. And the fourth is obsession: the idea that the targeted group is active virtually everywhere and is responsible for virtually everything evil or troublesome or problematic in the life of the bigot.[2]

It is thanks to the power of obsession that anti-Semitism ascends into the ultimate abstraction, in which the old medieval bias that what is Jewish is also evil gets inverted in more modern times to what is evil must be Jewish. It is also obsession that almost invariably gives rise to conspiracy theories. Obsession allows no ambiguity. All is unified, simple, monochromatic: there is one and only one source of the trouble and one and only one solution for it. As the infamous French anti-Semite Édouard Drumont put it in 1886, "All comes from the Jew; all returns to the Jew."[3]

If others do not see the Jewish conspiracy, it must be because the Jews are clever and manage to mislead the naive in service to their plan for conquest, however defined. The bigot's target is always guilty of conspiracy, of acting in secret, of planning behind the scenes, and the bigot is always trying to pull back the curtain and rip off the mask, revealing the hidden hand of conspiring evil. Conspiracy theories are thus convenient substitutes for ignorance. The world is complicated, but conspiracy theories address this problem in two ways. First, they make the truth simple for the believer, and second, they explain why the world seems complicated only to others. Conspiracy theorizers thus suffer from compound delusion.

By definition anti-Semitism is about distortion and exaggeration, and almost invariably it has a projected character to it: bigots are the ones doing the distorting and the exaggerating, but their accusations are precisely that the target of their hatred is responsible for conspiracies that distort and exaggerate. Not surprisingly, the proportions are often symmetrical: an anti-Semite's narrative about how the Jews manipulate and distort reality is likely to be roughly proportional to how much the anti-Semite is himself distorting reality.

All cases of genuine anti-Semitism are therefore examples of Jewcentricity. So when Mel Gibson gets drunk and runs his mouth, he is an anti-Semite right out of central casting. He is very Jewcentric. All the wars in history? Really? Oh, Mel.

So much for a working definition of anti-Semitism. But what causes people to engage in irrational behavior on a large scale?

This is not a simple question. One reason is that where one stands on a judgment about what is and is not irrational is a function of where one sits. Haitian voodoo and South African witchcraft seem irrational to most middle-class Americans. It appears differently to many Haitians and South Africans. A more subtle but equally important reason that the matter is not so straightforward is that what defines rationality and irrationality in an individual gets very complicated when one shifts to small groups and then to larger collections of people. The term "mob mentality" describes something scientifically real, as do less sinister phrases like "herd instinct" and "keeping up with the Joneses."

The upshot is that people think and do things in groups that they would never think and do on their own. The classic proof is an experiment in social conformity conducted more than half a century ago by Solomon Asch. Without describing Asch's clever experiment here, suffice it to say that he found that even very subtle peer pressure could cause normal people to misperceive simple sensory data. There were only two possible explanations for this behavior: either subjects did not want to stand out from others and draw attention to themselves; or their perceptions were so strongly influenced by the pressures of the group environment that they were really persuaded that wrong answers were right ones. Asch concluded that the latter explanation was the strongest—even though, at the time, he could not prove it.

Now we can. Neuroscience, which can measure brain function in a range of social environments, has proved Asch correct: just a wisp of doubt is all it takes for many otherwise normal and socially functional people to get even basic perceptual judgments wrong.[4] When perceptual judgment is not at issue, but rather far more abstract social judgments in which the evidence of the physical senses does not come directly into play, the influence of social conformity is magnified many times over.

Another factor affecting the nature of anti-Semitic manifestations is cultural in a deeper sense. Some societies value individualism more than communalism, some the other way around. In most Western societies, and in American society in particular, the ethos at large sees each individual as a free and autonomous agent, so conformist behavior is less frequent and extreme than in societies in which hierarchy and communal norms prevail. On the other hand, communally oriented societies tend to have stronger control mechanisms against antisocial behavior. The result is that individualistic societies tend to produce outlaws and one-off weirdos, while hierarchical or communal-oriented societies are better at producing mobs. Mobs are better suited for enabling anti-Semitic policies and attitudes. It is no accident that fascism set deeper roots in more communally oriented European societies—Germany, Italy, and Spain—than in more individualistic ones like Britain, Holland, and the Scandinavian countries.

The most important factor, however, in determining when latent anti-Jewish attitudes blossom into significant anti-Semitic politics is the presence of significant, disruptive social change. Historical and social factors produce a potential for bigotry, but, as we have seen, prejudice is not necessarily irrational in ordinary people who have been socialized into such attitudes. Irrational, violent bigotry erupts from latency into mass irrationality when cultures essentially lose their capacity to interpret reality effectively.

The practical point here is that anti-Semitism matters politically only when certain group dynamics kick in, establishing an atmosphere conducive to mass irrationality. The anti-Jewish prejudices of creative individuals—T. S. Eliot and Ezra Pound, for example—are hurtful to Jews because intelligent people are supposed to know better. But this is hurtful only in the abstract. The attitudes of social and intellectual elites usually stimulate mass behaviors when a society is already otherwise roiled, and when large numbers of people are unusually attentive to exotic explanations for their circumstances. Fortunately, one rarely finds active mass bigotry in normal times. Historically significant episodes of anti-Semitism, therefore, need to be understood as compound three-step phenomena involving preexisting cultural bias, leaders willing and able to come forward and legitimate that bias, and a level of social unease such that people are willing to accept and act upon that legitimation. Let's look at these three elements separately and then together in action.

First, there must be at least some anti-Jewish cultural bias and stereotyping in the society at large, or in significant subsections of it. How that bias got there—whether because of religious indoctrination, socioeconomic circumstances, or some combination of the two—doesn't really matter except that the more widely shared and historically deep this cultural bias is, the larger the reservoir for violent bigoted behavior.

Second, there must be at least some elite figures or groups who transform this latent bias into their own personal anti-Semitism. Research and reason alike suggest that this transformation tends to occur during a seminal emotional trauma for which someone blames a Jew or the Jews. It is well known that events that take place during times of intense emotion tend to remain most vivid in our memories. Research has established the reason: a hormone released during times of strong emotion enhances the performance of nerve cells that then form unusually strong memory circuits in the brain. The hormone norepinephrine—the "fight or flight" chemical—enhances memory by adding phosphate molecules to nerve cell receptors.[5] Bathed in the hormone, receptor cells are better able to insert themselves into adjacent synapses, increasing the wiring density for that memory. In other words, strong emotion imprints memories, and if a bigoted image is imprinted at a time of great happiness, fear, humiliation, or grief, it will tend to persist. Steps one and two therefore reinforce each other: emotionally excited or roiled personalities are more prone to hit upon a particular bigoted obsession to the extent that anti-Semitic stereotypes are widespread in the culture.

Third, there has to be enough general angst in the society, and enough sharing of anti-Jewish cultural bias, that a small number of anti-Semites can galvanize the combination into a weapon of mass bigotry—a WMB, as it were. The power of educated and well-regarded anti-Semites resides in their ability to elevate latent tendencies toward bigotry to the point of being socially acceptable. Anti-Semitic leaders norm hatred; they are catalysts that join cultural bias to the impulse for scapegoating in troubled times.

Scapegoating has historically taken two forms: spontaneous and managed. Sometimes social violence against the Jews (or other targets of bigotry) has welled up without much planning and organization. Much of the time, however, local authorities whipped up and encouraged anti-Semitism in order to deflect anger directed toward themselves. That defines the difference between a genuine riot and a staged one (a pogrom).

When authorities lead, or do nothing to stop, anti-Semitic violence, and when the Jews end up in no position to resist or seek revenge, it can have the effect of intensifying anti-Jewish cultural bias in the society, thus reinforcing and compounding the three-step process. Jews were often passive, low-risk victims of scapegoating in European history, for in most cases, resistance was not a viable option.[6] This is illustrated by the popularity of the famous tale of the Golem, a medieval giant made of clay who protected the Jews from their enemies. It was by legend the creation of the famous Rabbi Low—the Maharal—in the sixteenth-century Prague of Emperor Rudolf II, when conjuring a fictional protector was often the best the Jews could do—though, amazingly, many superstitious gentiles of that day believed that the Golem, like the Wandering Jew, was real.

Less fancifully, Jewish reactions to episodes of prejudice and violence directed against them made Jews fearful of non-Jews, but often led them to blame their own imperfections for the suffering they endured.[7] But while many tended to translate their weakness into the idiom of piety, others became ever more convinced of their own moral superiority to non-Jews, in rough proportion to their suffering at their hands. These two reactions were not always mutually exclusive, but could be phases of reaction over a lifetime, or among generations. Either way, their reaction to persecution provided incentives for Jews to develop more subtle ways to achieve protection and advantage against non-Jewish predators, a phenomenon classically illustrated, and not without a degree of sympathy, by Shakespeare in *The Merchant of Venice*.

And this, of course, tended to give credence to anti-Jewish cultural stereotypes already in circulation—that the Jews were secretive, sneaky, manipulative, sharp in business—and to both extend and deepen their pervasiveness in society. This set the stage for the next outburst, rendering the three-step process effectively circular.

If one were to tour the past two thousand years of Jewish history, one would find no shortage of episodes in which mass violence and other forms of persecution were directed against Jewish communities. But it is wrong to exaggerate anti-Semitism. Not all attacks against the Jews were anti-Semitic according to the definition we are using here. For example, as we have already noted, one of the most horrific of all attacks against the Jews was mounted by the Roman Empire in the aftermath of the Bar Kochba revolt. Nearly as large a percentage of Jews were affected then—about one out of every five or six Jews was killed—as during the Nazi Holocaust of the mid-twentieth century when, iconic round numbers aside, between 5.2 and 5.6 million were killed out of a world Jewish population of just over 18 million.[8] Yet what the Romans did was not anti-Semitic, despite the considerable dislike and resentment toward the Jews among the elite classes. In this case, a small nation had defied Roman imperial power and had confounded, harassed, and slaughtered Roman soldiers to a highly shocking and unexpected extent. The Jews had to be made an object lesson to the rest of Rome's subjugated populations. It was brutal and doubtless invited irrational individual behaviors, but in the context of the times it was not irrational as a policy.

Similarly, much resentment and violence against Jews in pre- and early-modern Europe erupted because Jewish communities, which, before the French Revolution, were organized into self-governing and separate corporate entities, got on the wrong side of peasant masses, though usually through no fault of their own. Especially in Central, and later Eastern, Europe, local barons invited Jewish communities to settle in order to stimulate trade and craftsmanship—the Jews were invited formally to certain areas of Poland, for example, in 1343. The Jews looked to these barons as their protectors. A vocabulary in Yiddish developed to describe these relations as they developed from the fourteenth century onward. The overlord, or baron, was the *poritz*; the Jews who served as liaisons were *shtadlan*; and later on, as relations matured, Jewish aides to the *poritz* were called *hofjuden*, or court Jews.[9]

These feudal and early-modern social arrangements were not set in anything remotely resembling a democratic or liberal context. These were not societies that credited equality as a social good, and the Jewish community sometimes got itself identified with rapacious rulers. When bad governments fell for one reason or another, the vengeance of the masses often targeted the Jews as having been accomplices of the deposed tyrant. This was perhaps the ultimate irony of Jewish history: the people of the anti-myth being punished for aligning with the medieval and early-modern equivalent of pharaoh.

This happened rather a lot over the centuries, and, of course, the pretext or justification for anti-Jewish pogroms may have sounded anti-Semitic to the Jews who were their victims. No doubt, too, anti-Semitic bias was latent in the society largely for reasons of religious indoctrination. This kind of violence and persecution, however, was not necessarily irrational from the perspective of mainly illiterate masses, though, again, it could give rise to individual irrational behaviors.

That said, many attacks against the Jews in European history were anti-Semitic, the major episodes, again, almost invariably coinciding with times of social instability brought on by war, disease, rapid economic and technological change, or combinations of the three. Thus, feudal times did not evoke much irrational anti-Semitism, even though latent anti-Jewish sentiment based on religion was virtually universal. But when the feudal system gave way to early capitalism, Jews, as an alien people detached from the fixed "estates" (social positions) of the local people, filled certain roles in the transition, particularly in the urban areas that began to form and grow. A degree of instability always accompanies what Joseph Schumpeter famously called "creative destruction," and in this case that instability became transformed into angst and was then directed against the most easily identifiable "other." In much of Europe that "other" was the Jew.

The first instance of mass violence against European Jews coincided with the Crusades, in around 1095, and mostly in the Rhineland. This was a time of significant social instability in that part of Europe, as a growing population exerted pressure on the dominant system of primogeniture. There were too many young men with too much time on their hands, and one way to get them to stop marauding the highways as freelance knights was to ship them off to the Levant to fight the Saracens. Alas, they took the opportunity to slaughter any Jews they found along the way and at their destination. Much mass violence against the Jews occurred next during and after 1348, when the bubonic plague terrified much of Europe and the

Near East. The Jews were frequently accused of having caused the Plague and were hunted down in revenge. The Chmelnitzky massacres, which began in 1648 and ultimately wiped out about three hundred thousand Jews, were occasioned by a breakdown of Polish and Ukrainian society in the face of massive Cossack invasions from the south. The Holocaust itself followed a period of very great disruption starting with the French Revolution and the Napoleonic Wars, followed by the horrors of World War I and the collapse of the Austro-Hungarian, German, Ottoman, and Russian Empires—in turn followed by massive social-technical change and the worst inflation and economic depression in modern European history.

Another unusual example concerns post–World War II Poland. Polish Jewry was destroyed by the Holocaust out of proportion to all others; both in absolute and relative terms, more Polish Jews perished between September 1939 and April 1945 than any other Jewish community in the world. One would have thought that with the liberation of Poland and knowledge of what had happened to Polish Jewry almost universal, the small remnant of that community would have been safe. Not so: there were sharp spikes of violent anti-Semitism in Poland in 1946. In Kielce, hundreds of Jews were murdered by Polish mobs spouting hysterical anti-Semitic nonsense. How could this be? Polish society suffered grievously under Nazi occupation, too. In their anguish and disorientation, they turned on the traditional most-prominent-other of Polish history—the Jews—almost as if from some kind of intergenerational habit. They blamed the Jews for the Nazi invasion and occupation of Poland, and all they had suffered during the war.

Then in January 1953, an increasingly paranoid Josef Stalin had dozens of Jewish doctors arrested and many executed, accusing them of plotting to kill Soviet leaders. The insanity abated only upon Stalin's death in March. Similar "plots" were soon uncovered in Czechoslovakia and Poland. Later in Poland Wladyslaw Gomułka hatched an anti-Zionist, actually anti-Semitic, hysteria in 1968 to shift blame for government failures onto a Jewish scapegoat. Here was the bizarre phenomenon of anti-Semitism virtually without Jews. Like amputee victims who feel pain in their severed limbs, Poles and Russians felt the unsettling presence of the Jews even after the vast majority of them had already been murdered.

This was a very Jewcentric reaction, but a different sort of social dynamic was behind it, one that did not incite mass violence—only highly selected, targeted political struggle. In much of Mitteleuropa and Eastern Europe, Slavic peoples historically resided in rural areas as farmers. Most of the larger cities were established later than in much of the rest of Europe and were largely populated by religious orders (many cities formed around monasteries) and by *Kulturvolk*—Germans, Jews, and a smattering of other itinerant craftsmen and artisans from further west. When with the tides of history the natives of the land acquired literacy and new skills and came to the cities to use them, they found people who were ethnically different in positions many thought should be theirs.

The Communist Party movements in this part of the world eventually took on the resentment bred of this situation and made it their own. Jews had been prominent in the early days of socialist and Communist movements because, at a time of rising romantic nationalism often associated with racial-purity dogmas and heavily tinged with anti-Semitism, Jews inclined toward doctrines of universalism, rationalism, and progress. But Communism did not make Polish peasants any less conservative or bigoted even when it organized them under the aegis of a Soviet-imposed and Soviet-supported regime. Those of rural origins who came after World War II to dominate second- and third-generation Communist parties in the Soviet Union (Nikita Khrushchev was a perfect example) and what became the Warsaw Pact countries were on the whole inclined toward anti-Semitism not despite but *because of* the major role Jews had played in the formation of those parties. Just as the rural folk who were now upwardly mobile and headed to cities had resented the *Kulturvolk* of the late nineteenth and early twentieth centuries, so they resented Jews still in any position of power in the party. That's how many Communists in Mitteleuropa, as well as the generation of local petty fascists before them, managed to become anti-Semitic, in their case even in the absence of many Jews following the Holocaust.

This happened much to the sad astonishment of those Jews who had really believed in the power of socialism to vanquish anti-Semitism. They mistakenly supposed that anti-Semitism arose from material, class-based sources alone. If only it had been that simple.

The irrational hatred of Jews has been going on for a long time, long before the term *anti-Semitism* was coined in 1879 by the "half-Jewish" Jew hater Wilhelm Marr, and long before Mel Gibson painted his face blue and pretended to have a clue about Scottish history. But it does not happen quite the same way each time, and it cannot be attributed to some single root cause, such as the idea that all anti-Semitism everywhere has its origins in the hatred of ethical monotheism.[10] Over the centuries anti-Semitism as one of the four forms of Jewcentricity has shifted contexts several times. It has proceeded in stages that reflect the underlying predispositions and preoccupations of given historical eras.[11]

First was the philosophical/religious stage, which goes back at least to Greco-Roman times. As we have already seen, the Jewish self-image as chosen, and Jewish attitudes and behaviors derived from that self-perception, have attracted the curiosity and the ire of psychologically vulnerable people for a long time. This first stage seems not so much to have ended but rather to have merged with subsequent stages.

The second stage is the one in which racial tropes replaced religious/philosophical ones. This is "modern" anti-Semitism of the sort that gave rise to the Holocaust.

The third stage is the postmodern, explicitly political stage in which we live today. The irrational hatred of Jews as a group does not identify religion or race alone as the source of Jewish "crimes" but focuses instead on material and political power: the Jews are evil not because they rejected and killed Christ, or because they have inferior "blood," but because they conspire to steal power from others and live parasitically on established, "normal" communities for purposes of their own aggrandizement. They pose as a people like any other, but they are not, and Zionism is the singularly deceptive and evil garb by means of which the Jews plot to execute their avaricious deeds.

In the first stage, anti-Semites said to Jews, in effect, you cannot live among us as equals (or at all) because you have the wrong philosophy or the wrong god(s). It was all about faith and belief, and it led to prejudice, expulsion, and violence. Most of the violence at this stage was not eliminationist in nature or intent, but some such intent did exist in German-speaking lands, of which the Rindfleisch massacres of 1298 and the Prague massacre of 1389 are particularly poignant examples. In the second stage, anti-Semites said, in effect, you may not live among us because you are racially inferior, which over time graduated to an extreme stage, from "You may not live among us" to "You may not live," during the Holocaust. After all, one can change one's faith, but not one's "blood." It was all about "science," in this case the pseudoscience of race. In the third stage, anti-Semites are saying, in effect, you cannot live in the world as a people according to your own definition of your nature and rights. In every other case the right to self-determination is predicated on the prior right to self-definition, but in your case, the logic of postmodern anti-Semitism goes, you and you alone do not have that right. A better example of "selectivity" could hardly be found. Postmodern anti-Semitism is thus based not on religious or racial selectivity, but on ideological selectivity.

Postmodern anti-Semitism seems to be a layered phenomenon, for remnants of the two earlier phases remain with us generally below the line of sight. This is why the postmodern anti-Semitic argument often gets so strange. Some contemporary anti-Semites characterize Jews as a race and therefore construe modern Jewish nationalism to be a form of racism: hence the "Zionism is racism" United Nations resolution affirmed by the General Assembly in November 1975 and rescinded in December 1991. This was an example of anti-Semitic projection, with racists falsely accusing Jews of racism—the theme, as it were, of the so-called Durban conferences on racism. At the same time, others insist that Jews constitute a religion and that religions are not entitled to territorial states in today's nation-state–dominated world. Postmodern anti-Semites therefore have the Jews in a kind of vise grip: only "peoples" or "nations" can legitimately have states, but Jews are either a race or they are a religion: hence the State of Israel has no right to exist, and Diaspora Jewish support for Israel is by association illegitimate.

Jews are not a race, however, and not "just" a religion. As we have seen, Jews are a people formed around the core ideas of a religious civilization. But in light of the unusual transterritorial history of the Jews, it is not hard to see how others might be confused by a modern identity that has come to conflate religion and national identity, as in a kind of identity double helix, like few if any others. It is in a real sense an identity frozen in time, revolutionary in its day but premodern in the sense that Judaism's identity formula does not accord with today's taken-for-granted divisions between citizenship and ethnicity. "Religion" and "race" are modern categories; Judaism's identity formula predates and yet in a way transcends them both. That explains why it makes sense in some regards to contrast Jew with Muslim or Christian—a religious comparison. It is also perfectly sensible in other regards to contrast Jew with Arab or Persian—an ethnic comparison. It is also understandable in the right context for someone to contrast Jew (Jewish Israeli to be exact, in this case) with Palestinian—a national comparison.

Clearly, then, since Jews don't fit unambiguously into the categories of contemporary identity that explain and define others, several anomalies about Israel as a Jewish state have arisen. Israel, while "Jewish," is not a theocracy. It allows non-Jews to become naturalized citizens, and endows native-born non-Jews with technically full democratic citizenship rights. It also makes it easy to show that the ideology of anti-Zionism is often a form of anti-Semitism. While many seek to delegitimate Israel on the grounds that Jews are either a race or a religion but not a people, when is the last time you heard a similar argument made with respect to Greeks, Armenians, Georgians, or Ethiopians, groups of people in which there is also significant overlap between religious, ethnic, and national identities? How about approximately never?

Obviously, not all anti-Israel criticism qualifies as anti-Zionism, any more than all dislike of Jews qualifies as anti-Semitism. But the Zionism-is-racism canard, as well as the delegitimation rhetoric based on the "religion" canard, are examples of anti-Semitism because they are never raised against any other country or people. If Zionism as the national movement of the Jewish people is inherently racist, then German nationalism, Japanese nationalism, and a dozen other ethnic-based nationalisms are racist, too. Indeed, bloodlines have played a far more obvious role in defining citizenship in these and other cases than it has in Israel. Until fairly recently, German citizenship laws were such that Turks living in Germany for generations could not become citizens, while Volga Germans could acquire instant German citizenship upon request by proving that at least one grandparent was of German blood. In Japan, Koreans who have been resident in the country for even five, six, or seven generations are not allowed to become citizens. Yet no one who focuses energy on delegitimating Israel on racist grounds ever talks about Germany or Japan.

Also anti-Semitic, on the same grounds of distorted selectivity, is writing critical of Israel that refers to Israeli government actions as "crimes," when the same authors use far less harsh language to criticize similar or even more reprehensible actions of other governments. Some Israeli government actions may be justifiably criticized; they are not, however, ever justifiably demonized by a priori presumptions about "the Jews" or about Zionism.

The same with religion as with "race." Israel was not founded as a religious state, and Jews were not defined in Israel's founding documents as adherents of a religion. The Jewish state was created and exists for the Jewish *people*. But Pakistan was explicitly created as a

Muslim state in 1947, and more than a dozen Muslim countries define themselves in their official names as "Islamic." Yet, again, no one who tries to delegitimate Israel on the grounds that religious groups are not entitled to states ever mentions Pakistan or Saudi Arabia. A case in point is Michael Scheuer's 2008 book *Marching toward Hell: America and Islam after Iraq*. Scheuer refers to Israel as a theocracy and to the idea of Israeli democracy as oxymoronic. He thinks that Jews are a race, so that non-Jews cannot therefore legally be equal citizens of Israel.[12] In fact, during more than two thousand years of Jewish sovereignty and autonomy in Israel, never was the country ruled by clerics—never was it a theocracy in the plain dictionary meaning of the term.[13]

The postmodern Judaism-is-racist and Zionism-is-racism argument, once its real premises are clarified, comes very close to the standard deviation, so to speak, of white supremacism arguments. What poses as "progressive" is therefore a lot closer in practice to what has long been a calling card of fascism. The former American Nazi Party leader William Pierce, for example, has asserted that Judaism is

> an ethnocentric religion, a racist religion. Whereas Christianity and Islam, for example, are universalist religions, religions for anyone who chooses to believe in them, Judaism is not. Judaism is a religion only for the Chosen People, only for the circumcised sons of Abraham. Jews are defined in terms of their bloodline, not in terms of their faith.[14]

No matter who asserts this view—speakers at United Nations Durban conferences, Louis Farrakhan, Michael Scheuer, or American Nazis—it is still exactly wrong. Anyone who sincerely wishes to convert to Judaism can do so, and a great many people over a great many years have done so—of which more in chapter 8. Jews are defined by membership in a religious civilization, a phenomenon wider than faith but closely related to it.

There is, however, a noteworthy difference between postmodern anti-Semitism and the reactionary American Nazi variety. Pierce calls Judaism a racist religion not to insult it, but to praise it:

> This tendency of the Jews to stick together, always to favor their fellow Jews over non-Jews, and to work for the interests of their tribe instead of just for their individual interests is a fact: a very enviable fact. . . . [T]he 14 million Jews of the world form a huge, self-conscious racial-interest group. They really are unique in this regard. I wish that our people had the same degree of racial consciousness the Jews do. The Jews understand the power of togetherness. Most of our people don't.[15]

Pierce's confusion is clear: he is comparing Judaism to other religions, and in that light it appears parochial. He should be comparing Judaism to the other proto-nationalisms of ancient times, for in that light it is anti-bloodline and anti-ethnocentric. The overarching proof of this, of course, is right before the eyes of anyone who cares to look. If Zionism and Israeli citizenship are based on a bloodline concept of nationalism, then it would follow that the Jewish citizens of the State of Israel today would form a fairly homogeneous population from a strictly genetic perspective. The reverse is true, however: Israeli Jews make up one of the most genetically diverse populations on earth, and Jews in general, living outside of Israel, are almost equally so.[16] And we know why.

In eighteen centuries of Diaspora, not to speak of what happened before in Babylon, the Jewish people, despite their largely endogamous mating behavior in premodern times, have both picked up and shed genes in more places over a longer period of time than perhaps any other group in history. Genetic analysis shows the pattern. The Jewish male (Y) chromosome can almost invariably be traced to the J variation that indicates West Eurasian and Near Eastern origins. The female (X) or mitochondrial DNA of Jewish communities is far more mixed and diffuse. The likeliest explanation is that Jewish males, as the young, unmarried extensions of Jewish families who set off to establish a trading post for the clan, often took wives from the local population and converted them to Judaism—to be members of the Jewish people.[17] After a while, once the community was of a certain size, Jewish men returned to the pattern of endogamous mating—cousin marriage, mainly—and through the dynamics of genetic drift, the community's genetic profile took on a characteristic shape different from that of the non-Jewish population. This explains the commonplace and commonsensical observation that, as Nicholas Wade puts it, "Jews often resemble the people of the host country, yet also in some respects resemble one another."[18]

Some people, obviously, have trouble distinguishing between group identity based on race and group identity based on a cultural concept of peoplehood. Jews are not a race, even though there is some genetic continuity among contemporary Jews, and Jews are not a religious group if by that phrase one means an entirely elective, self-selected group of believers. Jews are a hybrid of the two, a people based on a religious civilization. This is not just how most Jews define themselves; it is also an objectively accurate distillation of the historical record.

• • •

The old anti-Semitic formulae of religion and race from the first two historical stages of anti-Semitism are familiar to us because, as we have suggested, their vocabularies still echo in the third stage. Jews as believers in a religion could be hated for ostensibly theological reasons, and Jews as a race could be hated for ostensibly scientific racial ones. Jews as political actors, however, are harder to hate because the old vocabulary doesn't seem to quite apply. Postmodern anti-Semites have therefore substituted Zionists and Zionism for Jews and Judaism. At the same time, the State of Israel, along with its ties to American Jews, has become conspiracy central. It has all but taken the place of the widely dispersed Jewish people who were, nonetheless, presumed to have maintained some kind of conspiracy-hatching center in days of old.

Thus, to take just one example, during the brief but dramatic Russo-Georgian War of August 2008, many Russian nationalists adopted the view that the Jews were responsible for the war. Which Jews? Supposedly, they were Israeli Zionists who were advising the Georgian military, and the Russians went on to point out that the Georgian defense minister was himself a Jew—as Georgian president Mikhail Saakashvili proclaimed. Also supposedly involved were neo-conservative American Zionists, whom Vladimir Putin blamed for fomenting the war to help elect John McCain president of the United States. This is crazy, of course—very Jewcentric indeed; but that doesn't stop people from believing it.

One can grow weary of this, particularly if one happens to be a Jew. Just when one murderous form of anti-Semitism is discredited in the eyes of the world by its unprecedented excesses, another form arises to take its place. This reminds one of the host desecration accusations during the Middle Ages, in which Jews were accused of assaulting the body of Christ for a second time, when they had not done so the first time. It is also the sort of behavior that clinicians come to expect of addicts, who may kick one intoxicating, mind-addling substance only to take up another.

It must be said, however, that Jews themselves have played a role in the transmutation from the second to the third stage of anti-Semitism. Four or five generations ago, before the Holocaust and the birth of the modern State of Israel, most Jews identified themselves as members of a religious civilization, however attenuated religion might have become in the lives of many Westernized Jews. Zionism, or Jewish nationalism and Jewish "politics," broadly construed, was the *primary* form of Jewish identification for only a tiny minority. Before World War II, most religious Jews were leery of Zionism or downright hostile toward it. That hostility had a theological basis, as we have seen, that Jews should not force the end and redeem themselves from exile—that's God's job. But it was also reinforced by memory, particularly the memory of the disastrous Shabbtai Tzvi incident of the seventeenth century, when a false messiah promising that the day of redemption was at hand effectively destroyed the fabric of Jewish social life over much of Europe.

The Orthodox hostility to Zionism changed dramatically during and after the late 1940s. For many Jews who were born into religious homes in the 1950s and 1960s, Zionism and Jewish religion virtually fused. For those whose homes were not religious, Jewish politics became a more compelling motivating force than religion. For assimilated Jews in the West, especially in the United States, Israel and Zionism became substitute religious icons, although they would not have understood or articulated it in that way. For many and probably most religious Jews they became complementary and mutually reinforcing.

The same was true, though in a different way, for most Jewish Israelis. Their sense of being a Jew was even more strongly embedded in the fact of their being Israeli nationals in a Zionist political enterprise. Before the October 1973 Middle East war, and before the 1982 Lebanon War and its protracted aftermath, the image of Israel in the minds of young American and Western Jews—as well as Israel's own Jewish citizens—was of a heroic and morally superior small state beating the odds laid down by a still unfriendly world. Many Jews still feel that way, but others have become worn down and dispirited by the ways of the world. Ambiguity and even pain have joined pride and hope in what has become a mixed image of Israel.

As a result, many of those for whom the State of Israel, not God, was the focal point of their identification as Jews have found their enthusiasm for Jewish observance wane as the luster of their love for Israel has dulled. The old Orthodox anti-Zionist warnings come back to haunt: do not let politics pollute faith; nationalism is a temptation to idolatry. Just as Samuel tried to warn the people when they clamored for a king of their own and got Saul (in Samuel I, chapter 8), the state will requisition your resources and spill the blood of your children, they predicted. Faithless Jews in thrall to the idol of politics, like non-Jews in similar states of mind, will come to value material strength, cunning, and a certain coldness of heart. The service of God, rather, asks of us strength of spirit, humility, and compassion.

Faced with such counsel, a Jew who recognizes the religious authenticity of that message, but who can believe neither as an innocent in the God of earlier times nor anymore in Zionism as a substitute spiritual promise, has a problem. Such a Jew is beset by disappointments mostly of his or her own making, of which third-stage, ideological anti-Semites make the most they can. Every option seems to bleed potential tragedy, hypocrisy, and disquiet. It is not easy to turn a young idealist, a messianist in modern garb, into a mature and content realist. It is often impossible, and in a few cases it has led to visceral Jewish anti-Zionism of the sort we take up in chapters 10 and 14.

Not all Jews feel thus beset, and engagement between those who do and those who don't makes up some of the more interesting Jewish conversations of our age—as A. B. Yehoshua's newest book, *Friendly Fire: A Duet*, brilliantly portrays. There are, however, still unvarnished partisans of Israel and Zionism who refuse to acknowledge any sense of ambiguity about the enterprise, no matter what Israelis and Israeli governments do. Most are in America, for it is much harder for Jews actually living in Israel to ignore these uncomfortable matters. These more or less blind partisans, who have displaced the religious notion of chosenness from the Jewish people onto the State of Israel, unwittingly feed postmodern anti-Semitism, just as postmodern anti-Semitism feeds them.

Of course, anti-Semites have always needed for there to be Jews living and acting in certain ways in order for them to be anti-Semites. When Jews acted preeminently as carriers of religious ideals, anti-Semites hated them for that. When Jews were conceived, and to some degree conceived themselves, as embodying a certain racial essence, they were hated for that. Now that so many Jews conceive of themselves in postreligious and postracial political terms, anti-Semites hate them for that, too. There seems to be a pattern here: it's not that Jews "cause" anti-Semitism, but the ways Jews think and act shape the form anti-Semitism takes. Jews have shifted the context of their own chosenness, and so those who hate Jews have had to modify (but not moderate) their anti-Semitism along with it. The third stage of anti-Semitism has followed hard upon the latest era of Jewish history. Who expected anything different?

4

Jewcentricity Globalized

Exaggeration is a blood relation to falsehood, and nearly as blamable.

— Hosea Ballou

J ust as the history of anti-Semitism and philo-Semitism cannot be understood in the absence of their wider social contexts, so their futures cannot be divorced from the broader social and political context to come. So what does the future hold? Will it confirm the optimist's view, focusing on the defeat of communism by liberal democracy and the prospect of greater global rationality, or the pessimist's perspective, focusing on the threat of mass-casualty terrorism and the spread of religious zealotry? Is globalization falling apart, as earlier attempts at integration did, or just getting started, and hence encountering some inevitable bumps in the road? The answers have everything to do with the future of Jewcentricity.

Jewcentricity has been associated historically with places where Jews have lived in significant numbers for substantial periods of time, mainly in the lands of Abrahamic faith that we refer to as either "the West," the Christian-majority United States, Canada, and Europe (with outposts in Australia and New Zealand), or "Dar al-Islam," meaning those countries where Islamic civilization prevails. Today, however,

Jewcentricity in both positive and negative forms is spreading and growing more eclectic. It is being globalized, like most everything else.

The reasons for Jewcentricity's expansion are basically twofold. First, the Abrahamic world itself is growing. Both Christianity and Islam are spreading, gaining new adherents in places where neither has previously been widespread. In sub-Saharan Africa, for example, both Islam and Christianity have been gaining converts, Christianity even faster than Islam.[1] Much of this growth comes from new "low church" charismatic and Pentecostal Protestant movements, which tend to be philo-Semitic at least in the passive-aggressive way characteristic of dispensationalism. This means that the spread of Protestantism in places like Nigeria, South Korea, China, Mexico, and the Philippines generates at least vaguely philo-Semitic sentiments even in places where there are few if any Jews. Such sentiment may come one day to influence national policy, including foreign policy toward Israel and its neighbors, in these and other countries.

Second, even where Christian and Muslim missionaries are not particularly active, Jewcentricity hitches a ride on the transmission belts of globalization: increased trade, increased travel among and within countries, and increased cultural diffusion, particularly via globe-spanning television broadcasting and the Internet. What happens when a rerun of *Seinfeld* airs a "Jewish joke" or invokes a harmless Jewish stereotype to get a laugh—say, Jewish mothers pestering their children to call them on the phone and devising ways to make them feel guilty if they don't—when it alights in a town in Indonesia or a village in Botswana? What happens when news stories about Holocaust deniers in Europe, who break laws and are occasionally jailed in Austria or Germany for hate speech, make their way to places like Malawi and Somalia, where the history of World War II has never been taught in schools? What happens when a curious youth in Cape Town or Karachi, stimulated by such a story, tasks a search engine to find Web sites about Jews and comes across anti-Semitic invective, some of it made-in-the-USA, and some hailing from Cairo and Caracas? The answer is that we simply don't know.

What we do know is that stereotypes about Jews now have the potential to become "virtual." Just as increasingly larger numbers of people do not have to be in physical proximity to talk, teach and learn, engage in commerce, and otherwise exchange views, so images and storylines about Jews are no longer limited in distribution by where Jews actually live. But so what? Why should narratives about

Jews be expected to proliferate any more than other narratives in a globalized world? One reason has already been suggested: images of and interest in Jews travel wherever Abrahamic faiths proliferate. But narratives about Jews will proliferate for two other reasons, as well: the transmission belts of globalization now connect the Jewish image to America, and perceptions of global capitalism.

The global image of Jews is bound up with the image of America as well as with that of Israel, and the United States of America is considered an inherently interesting country in the world today by large numbers of people. Whatever its current economic afflictions, the United States remains the sole superpower. It is the wealthiest mass society on earth, and in all of human history. It is the freest and most egalitarian society in history, too, which strongly attracts some people and produces deep revulsion in others. America is a place where science and technology, married to the global market, generate change on a worldwide scale above and beyond that of all other sources. America is also the world's foremost secular evangelist, urging other societies to embrace freedom, experimentation, and change. And America happens to be, not coincidentally as many see it, host to the wealthiest and most influential Jewish community in the world.

There are almost as many Jews in the United States (about 5.4 million) as in Israel, more in New York City than in Tel Aviv and Jerusalem combined. The prominence of American Jews, particularly over the past half century or so, is manifest as well, whether in politics, science, business, or entertainment and the arts. Images of America that flow overseas cannot be easily separated from images of Jews in and as a part of America. It follows that if people abroad who have little personal experience with Jews have a basically positive feeling toward America, then they will, all else equal, probably not bear a negative attitude toward Jews. If they value equality, affluence, and individualism and are themselves upwardly mobile, they are more likely to have a positive disposition toward America, and Jews as well. But if they respect traditional hierarchies, value communal or corporate identities over individual ones, and see their own social positions as vulnerable to the new global forces that have insinuated their way into their societies, then, all else equal, they are likely to have a negative view of America, and of Jews along with it.

Obviously, however, all else is very rarely equal. How those abroad feel about America and "the Jews" as a conjoined phenomenon is influenced by many factors. If they live in countries where there are, or were, significant Jewish communities, that makes a big difference: in

Germany there were such communities, with rich and complex histories dating back centuries; in Japan there were none. That helps explain why vocal anti-Semitism in Germany today is legally and socially verboten, which is why every intractable antiestablishment minority element in the country—skinheads and all—is both anti-Semitic and anti-American. Lacking any Jewish communal history, anti-Semitism among Japanese intellectuals is surprisingly open, if rare; but it, too, is usually associated with anti-Americanism. It has taken the form of several books over the years, many of them quite popular, with titles like *The Next Ten Years: How to Get an Inside View of the Jewish Protocols*, *To Watch Jews Is to See the World Clearly*, and a particularly amazing piece of fakery called *I'd Like to Apologize to the Japanese: A Jewish Elder's Confession*. Jews in America play a role in all these books.

Indeed, Japanese anti-Semitism nearly defies categorization: it manifests itself in a subset of Japanese people who buy into wild conspiracy theories about Jewish power but who *admire* Jews for their outsized influence and wish to study and emulate them![2] The phenomenon seems to have its origins in 1905 when, after the Russo-Japanese War, the Japanese stumbled upon the *Protocols of the Elders of Zion*—the infamous early-twentieth-century forgery of the czarist secret police—and took it to be real. The fact that a Jew, Jacob Schiff (the selfsame Jacob Schiff whose letter to John Stoddard is quoted below in chapter 5) had helped the Japanese win that war by floating a bond for them just confirmed all their suspicions. That also explains why, during World War II, when the Nazis were asking Japanese authorities to round up and transfer all Jews under their control to the Germans, the Japanese instead arranged Jewish-Japanese friendship dinners in Japanese-occupied Shanghai (to which a sizable number of European Jews had fled).[3] The Japanese had concluded that it would be smarter to cultivate Jews than to murder them.

Japanese anti-Semitism has involved not only intellectuals. It is not widely known, but the terrorist cult Aum Shinrikyo, which launched a Sarin gas attack on a Tokyo subway in March 1995, was a rabidly anti-Semitic group. Not long before the attack it had published a ninety-five-page anti-Semitic rant, blaming Jews for everything from putting cryptic designs into Japanese currency to the Kobe earthquake that had occurred earlier that same year.

What goes for Germany and Japan goes for other countries, as well. South Korea is a good example. Korean attitudes toward Jews originally came from Japan, which colonized Korea and occupied it from 1905 through the end of World War II. There have never been many Jews in South Korea, and there are today only about half a dozen Korean converts to Judaism. Most of the few Jews Koreans have met have been Americans, with either the U.S. military or American businesses operating in Korea. Yet, as in Japan, the Korean popular image of Jews is distorted. There is Korean anti-Semitism. As Jason Lim put it, "There is a widespread belief that Jews supposedly control the world through shadowy governments and institutions, fanned by best-selling books and exposes."[4]

He is right. Conspiracy theories about Jews similar in trope to the *Protocols* are common. A popular comic book series by Lee Won Bok is a good example; millions of Korean children "learned" from these comic books that Arab terrorists attacked the United States because "Jews use money and the news media as weapons to control the United States." They learn, too, that the "final obstacle" for Koreans trying to make good in America "is always a wall called Jews."[5]

On the other hand, there are many books in Korean that qualify in one way or another as basically philo-Semitic. One item to be found in many Korean households is a book called *The Wisdom of the Talmud*, which was written originally in Japanese by a New York–born rabbi named Marvin Tokayer and subsequently translated into Korean. But other books have titles like *How to Succeed Like Jews*, and examples in them seem often to involve American Jews. The books are not so subtly racist in tone, and their admiration for Jews is based on stereotypes that would probably embarrass Koreans if they actually knew any Jews personally.

Anti-Semitic forms of Jewcentricity also exist elsewhere in Asia, even though, for the most part, overseas Chinese have played the role in many countries that Jews played in Europe, and have suffered similar forms of prejudice for so doing. But there is some. A recent Chinese best-seller called *The Currency War*, by Song Hongbing, describes how Jews are planning to rule the world by manipulating the global financial system, and this is why some in China believe that the current economic mess is in fact a secret Jewish conspiracy. A recent essay in a leading Filipino business magazine argues that Jews have always controlled the economies of the countries in which they have lived, including America today. It, too, implies that the current American economic crisis is the result of a deliberate Jewish conspiracy, and so on and so forth all over the continent.[6]

There is no obvious pattern to the way that conjoined contemporary images of America and Jews play around the world. The image of Jews in Singapore, for example, is partly shaped by the fact that its first chief minister was a Jew—the revered David Marshall. Other examples display less arbitrary factors. The image of America in, say, Morocco is influenced by the fact that U.S.-Moroccan ties are of recent origin and are based more on mutual interests than on cultural affinity. The image of Jews in Morocco has little to do with Jewish associations by way of America. Rather, that image is instead shaped by the very old and, on balance, positive communal history of Jews and Muslims living side by side; the fact that the Moroccan monarchy in recent decades signaled toleration, and even friendship and appreciation, for the still existing, now quite small, Moroccan Jewish community helps. Now contrast Saudi Arabia, an Arab country whose strategic relationship with the United States is several decades older. Never in its history as a modern state has Saudi Arabia had a Jewish community of any size; indeed, it has not had a Jewish community of note since the eighth century. Anti-Semitic, anti-Zionist conspiracy theories about U.S. and Israeli policies do not play so well in polite circles in Morocco; in Saudi Arabia, on the other hand, such theories are dominant among the elite. When, on October 25, 2008, the Saudi king warned his listeners that associates of Satan were waging a "veiled economic war" against Islam and the sons of Islam, he was almost certainly referring to standard Wahhabi conspiracy theories about Jewish money and Jewish power.[7]

To make the contrast yet more vivid, right next door to Saudi Arabia, on the island of Bahrain, Emir Hamad bin Isa Al Khalifa decided in the spring of 2008 to appoint a Jewish woman, Huda Nunu, as Bahraini ambassador to the United States.[8] The Bahraini royal court insisted that the appointment of Ms. Nunu was not a publicity stunt designed to showcase Bahrain's toleration. Since 2006 Ms. Nunu has been an appointed member of Bahrain's *shura* council— a group of advisers meant to represent all major constituencies in society, with some influence but no legislative authority—replacing her brother Ibrahim. Apparently, she simply impressed the emir with her intelligence and talent. The fact that the emir may believe that a Jew can have outsized influence in Washington, a belief no doubt based on a Jewcentric image about Jewish court power in the United States, probably did not hurt. After all, the same basic Jewcentric idea apparently convinced many principals of the Turkish government in the 1990s that a closer relationship with Israel, whatever its direct benefits, would help the Turkish lobby in Washington gain leverage over the Greek and Armenian lobbies there. If that is what they thought, it did not work out so well. (As we will discuss later on, American Jews do not really have that kind of power.)

• • •

The association of America and the Jews in the minds of foreigners is nothing new as a type, and the type has a great deal to do with global images of capitalism. In the nineteenth and early twentieth centuries, a form of global elite anti-Semitism was closely associated with Great Britain and British power. In those days, Britain was as prominent globally as America is now. The sun never set on its empire; it was the wealthiest, largest, and most powerful nation in the world. Its literature and architecture—if not its cuisine and fine arts—were second to none. The British Jewish community then was nowhere as large or as influential as the American Jewish community is today, but it was not negligible. A certain banking family named Rothschild was not an insignificant player, and that wealthy and influential Jewish name was only one of several in Britain.

It was not the number or actual influence of Jews in British politics and economy that really mattered, though: it was the fact that Britain was an agent of change, a proponent and catalyst of modernity, an avatar of the West for better or worse—all largely associated with capitalism. Those who feared such forces often saw the Jews as the vanguard of all that was frightening about the British. As Philip Zelikow has pointed out, John Atkinson Hobson, who seems to have mightily influenced one Vladimir Lenin, condemned economic imperialism around the turn of the nineteenth century by working a strong element of anti-Semitism into his materials, "seeing a cabal of Jewish bankers and merchants lurking behind Britain's excesses." After World War I "the same distasteful mixture of bad thinking" was at work: "Many writers in Europe, especially in the defeated nations, decried the new 'Anglo-Saxon empire' that they accused Britain and America—and the Jews, of course—of having created."[9] Indeed, the Jews were characterized as the leading edge of an abrasive and culture-shredding modernity that undermined Christian traditions so that they could exploit the confused and dispirited outcasts thrown helpless into a heartless capitalist world. Some accused the Jews of actually having invented the accursed scourge of capitalism itself, not least the German economist Werner Sombart in a well-known 1911 book (to which we shall soon return).

The astute observer may notice a certain parallel here to the dynamic of the Middle Ages, when impoverished peasants saw a sinister alliance between their tyrannical overlords and the Jews those overlords had invited into the villages and towns of the land. The distressed agriculturalists of the nineteenth century, their lives changed by new patterns of commerce and migration, blamed Britain (and often enough the Jews) for their discomfiture. The rich got richer in the mainly British-propelled European gilded age of nineteenth-century globalization, while the poorer urban classes got, if not uniformly poorer, then certainly more unsettled. A man of Jewish birth tried to explain their plight to them and lead them to salvation—Karl Marx. Marx saw the Jews of Europe as simultaneously complicit in and victims of capitalist exploitation; he knew that there were vastly more poor Jews in Europe than rich ones. But most non-Jews focused on the perceived complicity of the Jews in the ills of capitalism and, instead of becoming Marxists in the main, became human tinder for fascism, whose political hallmark was its anti-British sentiment and, of course, its anti-Semitism. Anti-Americanism was still a minor element as long as Britain held pride of place as the world's grandest liberal imperium.

The Arabs were soon brought into the general picture during the Great War—renamed World War I after the next world war became part of history. Haim Weizmann, the head of the Zionist Executive, played the *hofjude*, or court Jew, and Sir Arthur James Balfour, Britain's wartime foreign minister, in effect played the role of the *poritz*, or overlord, on a vast imperial scale. With the November 1917 proclamation of the Balfour Declaration, the Jews got the greatest power on earth to offer its support for the establishment of a Jewish national home in Palestine. As with the Polish, Ukrainian, and Russian peasants of earlier centuries, the combined efforts of Weizmann and Balfour looked to the Arabs of Syria and neighboring countries like a nasty alliance of the overlord and the Jews ganging up on them.

Now, perhaps, the same basic dynamic appears to some to be taking shape on a global scale: the American Jewish community and the State of Israel are conjointly the world's *hofjuden*, the U.S. government is the *poritz*, and the self-proclaimed downtrodden of the earth—the resentful Third World intellectuals, heirs of Franz Fanon, who dominate the United Nations General Assembly, in particular—are the victims of this conjectured alliance. Need an example? Here is a typical statement, this one from Fatima Hajaig, deputy foreign minister of South Africa, at an anti-Israel rally in late January 2009: "Control of America, just like the control of most Western countries, is in the hands of Jewish money."[10] Need another? Here is one from November 2008, when the U.N. General Assembly president, Miguel D'Escoto Brockmann, from Nicaragua's anti-American Sandinista leadership, likened Israel's conduct in the occupied territories to "the apartheid of an earlier era." Helped by the outrageous title of former President Jimmy Carter's 2006 book, *Palestine: Peace Not Apartheid*, Brockmann added, "We must not be afraid to call something what it is," although Brockmann showed no indication of any fear whatsoever when he demonstrably hugged Iranian president Mahmoud Ahmadinejad upon visiting the General Assembly for "Palestine Day" festivities.[11] Clearly, as Zelikow observed, "The same fetid intellectual waters seep from this old gutter" that once associated hated British power and anti-Semitism "into much anti-American commentary today."[12]

The new narrative of conspiracy differs in its details from the older versions, of course. For some, the Jews in Israel control the American Jews, who in turn control the American government. For others, Israel is just a cat's-paw of America, and America's own Jews are just willing servants of the American plan for global domination. Back in pre- and early-modern times, de facto alliances between Polish or Lithuanian barons, for example, and small self-governed Jewish communities were real, and arguably common folk were sometimes exploited by them in what were then assumed to be the normal ways of the world. But the idea that there was a conspiracy between nineteenth-century British imperialists and the Jews, the latter led by rabbis and bankers all meeting with the British in secret conclave somewhere, was just lurid, addled nonsense. The same is the case with contemporary conspiracy theories about Israel, American power, and American Jews.

That said, there is a basis for associating Jews with capitalism, both its benefits and its discontents. Pardon a short detour to illustrate what that basis is, and why it still matters to the future of Jewcentricity.

Recall the ten elements of the Jewish system for transterritorial survival. Part of the fifth element was the long-distance system of communication that was part and parcel of the Jewish infrastructure of Talmud-based self-government. Recall, too, that Jews had learned the caravan routes of international trade in the ancient world as long ago as the heyday of the Babylonian Empire, and that common folkways and languages enabled Jews to travel widely, knowing they would be welcomed by other Jews and thus made relatively secure in other places—not *at all* a common expectation in the premodern world. The upshot is that this fifth element of the rabbinical system helped Jews learn to manage and exchange money more adeptly than other peoples.

Figuring out how to securely exchange money over long distances, often using more than one intermediary, required innovation. It required, in effect, a primitive system of international finance. Over time, Jews also learned to provide one another with economically useful information: about markets, suppliers, transport, new technology, and new products. For their own uses, the Jews created a system of international banking to move value, whether in the form of specie, jewels, or whatever then passed for currency (bonds, personal notes, and so on). This helped Jews deal with the gentiles around them at a comparative advantage, for Jews had trained themselves not just in handling substance—things—but in managing relationships through handshakes and paper, which is to say, in effect, contracts.

The methods the Jews developed to move money and to write commercial contracts frequently enabled them to dominate trade among different states. Particularly in early medieval times, and particularly in Europe, where the Church forbade both usury and, most of the time, the right of Jews to own land, Jews were virtually the only ones who understood and practiced rudimentary banking. This has been popularly called moneylending, a rather sinister-sounding term; but when one breaks down exactly what services were performed and why, the distinction between moneylending and banking becomes a distinction without a difference.

That Jews were not only literate but numerate also provided obvious advantages. Since Jews could read and do basic math, they could handle a variety of business transactions. They could devise budgets, calculate investment ratios, set and adjust interest rates, even imagine the concept of insurance, which they in fact did. Thus, at a time when economic exchange was almost exclusively immediate and concrete, and was often barter-based, Jews created out of necessity the basic elements of an abstract economy.

That is not all they created. As these business practices evolved, they raised a host of practical and moral questions about what the Talmud calls "Damages" (Nezikin, one of the six books of the Talmud). Nezikin represents the development of an early, yet on balance quite sophisticated, form of international business or contract law that, in addition to discussing the elements noted above, also deals with the concept of torts, the definition and status of real estate, the sanctity of oaths (contracts), and more besides.

Simple literacy and numeracy do not sound like anything special to most of us today, but in the Middle Ages they were pretty special, numeracy particularly so. Before sometime around the year 1500, Europeans did not use Arabic numerals or have a practical way to apply the concept of zero—and calculating XIX percent of DCCLV is not all that easy, if you have ever tried it. The concept of zero did exist among Indians and Arabs nearly a thousand years earlier and was introduced in Spain, specifically in Córdova, in the tenth century during the reign of Hakam II. Many Jews were attracted to Córdova and its great library, so it seems reasonable to speculate that at least some Jews in Europe before 1500 did know about and use zero. If so, this would have provided significant commercial advantages.

In addition, Jews often operated in effect as joint stock companies at least in the sense that they sometimes combined their assets when necessary to make large transactions and to spread risk. They could do this because they had law—a law that engendered trust among them. That Jews could combine and move their assets when necessary also made it possible for them to amass more capital than practically anyone else. It is natural, therefore, that non-Jewish merchants often turned to them for loans, and for arranging to finance imports and sell exports.

It was natural, too, that rulers would turn to the Jews to finance public works, such as they were, and the implements of war. Jews were also in an advantageous position to supply luxury goods, like soaps, spices, perfumes, furs, and novelties of all sorts, at a time when the wealthiest ruling members of society did not have much to spend their money on in local markets. Financing government and those who governed is largely what enabled Jews to become court Jews in a later period of European history: There was simply no other reliable method of finance across political boundaries. Jews were the vehicle through which princes and barons managed to expand the range of their dealings beyond the limits of relatively small territorial units. This is the logic behind the social and political clout of the great European Jewish banking families like the Rothschilds, and also behind the great Middle Eastern merchant families like the Sassoons (who at most times made the Rothschilds look like paupers by comparison). And it is the reason that at the start of the modern capitalist era, this by then more mature distribution network (that is what we would call it in contemporary language) and facility in managing business relationships enabled Jews to often be first in the trade of new commodities such as wheat, wool, flax, textiles, dyes, sugar, tobacco, and distilled spirits.

With all this in mind, one will understand this vignette: In the fourteenth and fifteenth centuries, when the lingua franca of the eastern Mediterranean was Italian, Jews dominated the port and customs functions of their respective states on all shores of sea. They kept their records in Hebrew script, and often had not just one, but two or even three spoken languages in common with their counterparts.[13] No other groups had comparable advantages; naturally, the Jewish officials and their merchant relatives thrived, for then as now information is the most valuable commodity of all.

Vignettes are not enough, however, to explain what this Jewish aptitude for creating an abstract economy led to in due course. Some believe that out of the cauldron of the feudal age it was the Jews who created modern finance capitalism (though obviously not market capitalism itself, which took sophisticated forms in the ancient world, in the Near East, in the Far East, and arguably in pre-Columbian South America). Perhaps the most famous of such cases was made by the aforementioned Werner Sombart.

Sombart, an antimodern romantic who joined the Nazi Party in 1933, had at best mixed feelings about modern finance capitalism. He knew what he was talking about, however; in a six-volume 1906 work that remains an economics classic today, it was Sombart, not Marx, who coined the term *capitalism*. He also did not especially like Jews. His 1911 book, *The Jews and Modern Capitalism*, is full of subtle and not-so-subtle anti-Semitism, and is replete with factual errors of a Jewcentric sort—he somehow got it in his head, for example, that Robert Morris, the financier of the American Revolution, was a Jew.[14] Nonetheless, much of its analysis is brilliant, because Sombart noticed something that had eluded others. "Israel passes over Europe like the sun, at its coming new life bursts forth; at its going all falls into decay," he wrote. "Arm in arm the Jew and the ruler stride through the age which historians call modern. To me this union is symbolic of the rise of capitalism, and consequently of the modern State."

Sombart and others after him have pointed out that modern finance capitalism, or surplus-value capitalism as it has sometimes been called, requires the application of wealth to create more wealth; in other words, the ability to use surplus money, or profit, as capital to create more value. This kind of capitalism, which is relatively new to human history as opposed to earlier kinds of market systems, presupposes the existence of a basic financial infrastructure. Not only does it require a skilled wage-earning class of labor, it also requires labor and capital mobility along with some forms of credit, and the legal right both to collateralize property and to securitize and trade debt. It also requires reliable contract law. Above all, perhaps, it requires a certain level of abstraction and transferability, whereby financial instruments remain valid regardless of who holds them.

This may not sound like a big deal, but it is—or rather, it was, as Sombart understood. Under Roman law, which dominated European law for centuries, the concept of *obligatio* held that all indebtedness was personal and could not be transferred. Notes of indebtedness could not be sold to others. German law before the advent of the Napoleonic Code held specifically that a debtor did not have to pay anyone except the original creditor, and if the creditor died, the debt was void. Until the middle of the nineteenth century, even in England, a financial claim could not be transferred legally from one person to another.

By ensuring the inflexibility of economic exchanges, Europeans had managed to devise and maintain for more than a thousand years a nearly stagnant economic realm in which virtually the only way wealth could be accumulated was by plunder, opportunistic marriage, or trading with the help of the Jews. This was true not only for potentates, barons, and other nobles, but even for the Holy See. From about the tenth century through to the sixteenth, a succession of popes relied on Jewish bankers to finance the Church's enterprises. The abstract system of Jewish international banking and finance law raised the capital for a significant percentage of the cathedrals and monasteries of medieval Europe. Jewish banking services were so important that, as Dimont relates the tale,

> when the city of Ravenna . . . asked to be permitted to join the Republic of Venice, one of the conditions was that the Jews should be called in to open loan banks to assist the poor who stood on the edge of disaster. Florence, even as she basked in the sunshine of her Renaissance, begged Jews to come to the city to keep up its flow of capital.[15]

Sombart argued that the Jewish facility and experience with international finance, when conditions were finally right—when transportation technology had reached a certain level of development,

and when the early modern state had managed to create a rudimentary central administrative capacity—jump-started the whole modern
finance capitalist system.

Whether this is so must be left to specialists in economic history.
But the evidence suggests that the Jewish role in sparking the major
movements of early capitalism did grow with time. The modern formula first came together in the United Provinces, today called the
Netherlands, in the beginning of the seventeenth century, not long
after the Dutch had won their independence from Spain. Surely
the Protestant character of the Dutch counts for much in explaining Dutch success—Max Weber could not have been, and wasn't, all
wrong about the connection between the Protestant ethic and the
spirit of capitalism. But the fairly large number of Jews who had
come from Spain and Portugal (under curiously negotiated conditions having to do with an early Protestant version of freedom
of religion that need not detain us here) clearly had a galvanizing
effect. One might say that what the Dutch enabled domestically,
the Jews amplified internationally. By the end of the seventeenth
century there were over a hundred thousand Jews in Amsterdam,
which had become a major center of global trade. The Jews established new trade routes, introduced new products (like coffee, for
example), established banks, and made the United Provinces the
center of global commerce in precious stones and jewelry craft.
And as they built their schools and synagogues, they did something
else: they invented the first bourse—the first stock market.[16] It is no
coincidence that the two seminal theoreticians of securities and the
stock market were Iberian Jews living in Amsterdam in the seventeenth and eighteenth centuries, Don Joseph de la Vega and Isaac de
Pinto.[17]

What had started in the United Provinces blossomed next in
England. Again, Protestants were involved, not least Oliver Cromwell
himself, who invited the Jews back to England for the first time since
their expulsion in 1290. He specifically tried to attract Jews from
Amsterdam. The Dutch Jews sent an emissary to London to talk with
Cromwell about his invitation. His name was Rabbi Menassah ben-
Israel, best known to most of us perhaps from his magnificent portrait painted by Rembrandt. Ben-Israel was an extraordinary man,
learned but also practical. He appealed to Cromwell in terms of religious eschatology: Jesus could not come again unless the Jews were
dispersed in every land, including England. Cromwell agreed, and
that was that.

Except that it wasn't quite. Aside from the fact that Cromwell at first failed to persuade Parliament to let the Jews in, the initial movement of Jews from Holland to England was very modest. It grew far more significant only with the ascent of William and Mary to England's throne with the Glorious Revolution in 1688. William and Mary came from Holland, of course, and were already very familiar with Jewish financial services. The Machado and Pereira families had been the chief provisioners of the Dutch military for some years. William was friends with Solomon Medina, one of Machado and Pereira's agents. Medina dined with the king at his home on Richmond Hill in 1699 and, the very next year, became the first openly practicing Jew in England to be knighted.[18]

Jews later financed William Pitt's Seven Years' War against France and recommended (and shaped) the establishment of the Bank of England. How did England prevail in this war? Basically because it had access to more money than France, and that was largely thanks to the Jews.

This was no secret, of course; the French well understood it, and beginning with Louis XIV, French court Jews and financiers joined British and Dutch ones. But France never prospered in the same way that the United Provinces and England did. Thanks to the political strength of the French Church, it did not experience the requisite "religious" convulsions of the Protestant Reformation—which were anyway as much social as religious—to shuck off the vestiges of feudalism. French authorities instead persecuted, killed, and drove away talented Huguenots far too successfully for the country's own good. The result is that France experienced its Reformation and its Revolution together—with regard to France, the terms are functionally interchangeable—in one ghastly spasm in 1789, skipping the phase of Protestant belief and going straight to secular Jacobin fundamentalism. France (and Russia) were laggards in the process of European modernization compared to Holland and England, and that is why their convulsions, when they came, were so destructive and unsustainable. That is another story, however. For our purposes, it merely suggests why Jews prospered dramatically in Holland and England but not so well in France and hardly at all in Russia.

It is thanks in part to this history, and to Jewish achievement and prominence in the still early days of globalization, that we should expect a proliferation of Jewcentric conspiracy theories in our future.

After all, in Stalin's time Soviet agents in America were ordered by their superiors to wander the streets of New York and Washington looking for *the* building where the big capitalists (Jews prominently among them) met with and ordered the leaders of U.S. government to do their bidding. If the government of the Soviet Union at the height of its global influence could believe such nonsense at a time when conspiracy theories had to advance themselves without aid of the Internet, it is not hard to see how similar theories about Jews and the American juggernaut of destructive globalization can thrive today, as they already do in much of the Muslim world. The Internet encourages political pamphleteering on a global scale, particularly in a world in which more people than ever are politicized and motivated thanks to the rise of urbanization, literacy, and basic (often only very basic) education.

To the extent that the new political awareness of formerly passive groups corresponds to the anxieties generated by the "creative destruction" of globalization, they seek ways to understand what is challenging and bedeviling them. Unfortunately, many newly literate and politicized people are unable to grasp how things actually work, yet, as Charles Frankel once said, "simple-mindedness is not a handicap in the competition of social ideas." The infospheres especially of many non-Western peoples—that is, the cumulative total of the information available to them over the course of their lives—are limited by the fact that most countries do not permit complete freedom of the press, cannot afford a serious global news infrastructure, and have school systems that do not teach history as a subject that relies on facts. Ayaan Hirsi Ali, the Somali-Dutch and now, apparently, American apostate from Islam, described a few years ago a troubling encounter with her sister, in which the latter spouted the most outrageous anti-Semitic invective, replete with Holocaust denial and assorted anti-Semitic conspiracy theories. Upon reflection, Ali recognized that her sister's repugnant views had arisen from her social environment, one in which European history had never been taught.[19] The same revelation hit Judea Pearl, the father of the murdered *Wall Street Journal* reporter Daniel Pearl, when the Pakistani consul general showed up at his home in California after his son was beheaded. The elder Pearl relates how the consul reacted when he brought up the anti-Semitic aspect of the episode: "What can you expect of these people who never saw a Jew in their lives and who have been exposed, day and night, to televised images of Israeli soldiers targeting and killing Palestinian children?"[20]

As William James once put it, people will believe anything they can, and would believe everything if only they could, which is a way of saying that newly politically mobilized people are often ready to cling to the first emotionally satisfying explanation of a problem they encounter—the simpler, usually the better. And ready-made explanations with anti-American/anti-Semitic biases at their forefront are there to be had. After all, antimodernist anti-Semitic arguments have an old pedigree; many years and many hands have gone into polishing such arguments. *The Protocols of the Elders of Zion*, however ridiculous it sounds to any halfway educated person, is a skillfully written tract. Jews are living or have lived nearly everywhere, and one needs a very far-flung network to plausibly be held responsible for global, transterritorial evil. Jews frequently become prominent in a variety of fields, do they not? Practically everyone everywhere these days, far more than before, knows the name of a Jew who has had outsized influence, and knows that Jews as a group have achieved so far out of proportion to their numbers as to inflame the imagination of the Abrahamic world. Call it, perhaps, the Moses-Jesus-Spinoza-Marx-Freud-Einstein phenomenon. The ingredients for global virtual Jewcentricity are all in place.

So Jewcentricity seems to be spreading, and as it does, narratives and images from the past are mixing in peculiar ways. For the first time in human history, now that the real and the virtual walls of the Cold War have fallen, a fully global virtual society is emerging. Certain economic, cultural, and even epidemiological trends are for the first time nearly everywhere, and thanks to the technology in hand, the speed with which conversation about these global trends takes place is faster than ever. That is why we can now have episodes of anti-Semitism and philo-Semitism in places not only where there are almost no Jews—as in Gomulka's Poland—but where there *have never been* any Jews—as in Mahathir Mohammed's Malaysia.[21] It is also why modern Muslim anti-Semitism looks the way it does, having adopted many of its beliefs from the European anti-Semitism of the pre–World War II period (of which more in chapter 13).

Contemporary episodes of virtual Jewcentricity sometimes border on the bizarre, as when in April 2008 the Bolivian government, apparently under the influence of Cuban and Nicaraguan advisers, used the Star of David as a symbol of evil on new ID cards. The new cards apparently were given mainly to non-indigenous peoples in eastern Santa Cruz province, the center of opposition to the Morales regime, in numbers vastly larger than the tiny Jewish community in Bolivia. Another recent case concerns Turkey, where some secular fundamentalists now charge that Prime Minister Tayyip Erdogan, of the Justice and Development Party (AKP), is a secret Zionist doing the bidding of the Jews. A book by Ergün Poyraz, *The Children of Moses*, sports on its cover a huge Star of David encircling the Turkish prime minister and his wife.[22] The book is popular, and some Turks believe, too, that Erdogan's infamous spat with Israeli President Shimon Peres at the 2009 Davos forum was staged to deceive Turks into thinking that Erdogan is genuinely critical of Israel.

Will Jewcentricity keep spreading? Is more craziness of the Bolivian and Turkish sorts in our future? Well, that depends. If the world's population becomes more rational as modern economic processes spread, then, all else equal, episodes of mass bigotry, Jewcentric ones and others, will decline. If the pace of "creative destruction" overwhelms the capacity of given societies to adjust, again, all else equal, episodes of mass bigotry will multiply. A lot depends on the future of global capitalism.

If global capitalism survives and ends up making everyone richer, freer, and happier, then new manifestations of Jewcentricity need not be especially numerous or worrisome. It could be. Many argue that liberal institutions and even democracy are bound to follow successful applications of macroeconomic common sense. But others argue that contemporary global capitalism resembles old-fashioned carpetbagging on a planetary scale. If global capitalism is essentially "fixed" or crooked, manipulated so that a relative few gain huge wealth at the expense of the majority—and if Jews become prominent successes in it, as they were, for example, in the free-for-all grabfest that accompanied the fall of the Soviet Union—then global "virtual" anti-Semitism looks to be a growth industry. The role of the State of Israel in all this, too, whether it functions as a platform for Jewish global entrepreneurs or not, is clear: it will be blamed for being the global *hofjude* to globalization's *poritz* cabal, whoever they are imagined to be.

In most periods, the stresses of rapid change have produced apocalyptic religious movements, some of them quietist in orientation but others turned outward in explosive, suicidal, and insane violence. When certain societies came apart at the seams before—in the sixteenth-century Peasants' Revolt in Germany, in the nineteenth-century

Taiping Rebellion, in early- to mid-twentieth-century Germany—bad things happened. But even World War II, despite its name, was short of being fully global. Future outbreaks of collective psychosis may not remain segmented and localized, and the speed of their transmission may exceed the pace at which others can mobilize against them.

The globalizing world of the twenty-first century is so far a play without a settled plot; certainly it is a script without a conclusion. The players and the audience, however, seem to be merging into a drama heretofore unprecedented in scope. From the looks of the global economy as of mid-2009, the play seems more likely than not to end up a tragedy. Given the history of Jewcentricity, it would be strange if the Jews did not somehow play a starring role on that stage, one way or the other.

PART TWO

Jewcentricity
in
America

5

Jewcentricity Central

It is human to exaggerate the merits of the dead.

— MARK TWAIN

he United States of America is probably the most Jewcentric
society in world history, in a largely philo-Semitic way. Non-
Jewish Americans tend to exaggerate the influence of Jews,
and also their numbers (and American Jews, as we will see in chapter 6,
help them do it). That is bound to influence how American leaders and
average Americans see Jews in their midst and Jews abroad, how they
see Israel and the Middle East, and how they see other societies whose
views of such matters diverge from their own.

Whole books exist on American philo-Semitism, and there is
no need to recapitulate their contents here.[1] We need merely to
distill the essence of this literature and give some representative
examples to get a sense of it—including a few noteworthy ones that
for some reason the literature has mostly neglected. Don't worry;
this will be fun.

American Jewcentricity has several sources, but none is more important than the fact that Jewcentricity is inherent in the worldview of
the American Founders—and in "Founders" must be included not
only those who created the American republic in Philadelphia in July
1776, but also the earliest European colonists in the New World.

The Puritans saw America as the New Israel and themselves as a new Chosen People within a new Promised Land. They called their houses of worship synagogues, and their scriptural focus lay heavily on the Old Testament—the Hebrew Bible. Their feast and fast days were often modeled on Jewish traditions; even the quintessential American holiday of Thanksgiving seems to have been modeled on the Jewish autumnal holy days, a combination of Yom Kippur and the holiday of Succot, or Tabernacles. They interpreted American history, too, from dealing with the natives to speaking democratic truth to monarchical power, in the cadences of what they understood of the Old Testament history of the Jews.

In the generation of the Founders the association with Israel and the Bible continued virtually unalloyed. Benjamin Franklin and Thomas Jefferson, two of three Founders (along with John Adams) entrusted by the Continental Congress to craft a seal for the United States in July 1776, both suggested designs based on the Exodus from Egypt. Thanks to the Reverend Ezra Stiles, Hebrew had been taught at Yale for a long while, and some Founders knew at least a smattering of it.[2] And speaking of Yale, that university's coat of arms still features the words *urim v'tumim*, referring to the priestly oracle mentioned in the Bible. Not to be outdone, Dartmouth College's official seal features the Hebrew words "*El Shadai*"—God almighty.

It is therefore not surprising that the descendants of the Puritans in the generation of the American Founding had laudatory things to say about the Jews and their contribution to civilization. Thus America's second president, and the third member of the seal committee, John Adams:

> I will insist that the Hebrews have done more to civilize men than any other nation. If I were an atheist and believed in blind eternal fate, I should still believe that fate had ordained the Jews to be the most essential instrument for civilizing the nations. If I were an atheist of the other sect, who believe or pretend to believe that all is ordered by chance, I should believe that chance had ordered the Jews to preserve and propagate to all mankind the doctrine of a supreme, intelligent, wise, almighty Sovereign of the universe, which I believe to be the great essential principle of all morality, and consequently of all civilization.[3]

The Puritans made up only one of four "hearth cultures" to found early Euro-American society, but the other three were largely Protestant and, in the main, Jewcentric as well.[4] That is why the colloquial language of American politics, at least before the middle of the past century, brims with Jewcentric references. From the very beginning, whether one dates it from Jamestown or Plymouth Rock, the contents of sermons and of political language alike runneth over with Old Testament metaphors. In the earlier days these two forms of American meta-discourse were almost interchangeable; as time passed they separated, but not that much. Virtually everyone who was not a Native American saw America as a Christian country with a (Protestant) Christian mission in the world, and thus no one thought it at all odd that Herman Melville should write in his 1850 novel *White-Jacket*, for example, that "[w]e Americans are the peculiar, chosen people—the Israel of our time; we bear the ark of the liberties of the world."

Or that three years earlier a U.S. Navy captain by the name of William Lynch, motivated as much by religion as by the spirit of science and adventure, should want to lead a scientific team to investigate the hydrology, flora, and fauna of the Jordan River valley—and was in fact the first person ever to do so. Walter Clay Lowdermilk followed in Lynch's footsteps almost a century later. America's hydrology expert seconded to the Middle East following World War II, he set up the famous, if ultimately unsuccessful, Johnston Plan of the Eisenhower Administration. Lowdermilk and his wife, the daughter of a Christian minister, spent several happy years in Israel; both were fervent Christian Zionists.

Believing American Christians, Catholics as well as Protestants, regularly come up with Jewcentric praise for ancient Israel and its contributions to civilization. And the author or speaker does not have to be a dispensationalist or evangelical to wax excessive. Thus Thomas Cahill, in his abbreviated but still penetrating 1998 effort to assess the "gifts" of the Jews:

> The Jews gave us a whole new vocabulary, a whole new Temple of the Spirit, an inner landscape of ideas and feelings that had never been known before. . . . Because of their unique belief—monotheism—the Jews were able to give us the Great Whole, a unified universe that makes sense and that, because of its evident superiority as a worldview, completely overwhelms the warring and contradictory phenomena of polytheism. . . . The Jews gave us the Outside and the Inside—our outlook and our inner life. We can hardly get up in the morning or cross the street without being Jewish. We dream Jewish dreams and hope Jewish hopes. Most of our best words, in fact—*new, adventure, surprise; unique, individual, person, vocation; time, history, future; freedom, progress; faith, hope, justice*—are the gifts of the Jews.[5]

This is a thrilling claim, and it is not entirely false, as my own account of the historical impact of Jewish ideas in chapter 1 attests. It is, however, way overboard. Cahill claims that the Jewish "processive worldview" has now "taken hold in many (and, to some extent, all) non-Western societies," but the fact that non-Western languages have ancient roots for nearly all the concepts Cahill puts in italics suggests the possibility of separate if not simultaneous insight. Ancient Egypt came up with a notion of monotheism before Moses led the children of Israel out of that land, after all. The Jews are remarkable, and their history is, too; no need, however, to exaggerate.

American Jewcentricity has also been multiracial. Because the vast majority of white Americans have thought in expansive cadences about the Jews, Judaism, and its sacred literature, it was inevitable that black Americans would, too, and with a special intensity for an obvious reason. Most blacks in America came to profess Christianity, and the first book most wanted to read as soon as they learned how was the Bible. Naturally enough, blacks saw a parallel to their own circumstances, particularly into the story of the Exodus, of God delivering the Jews from slavery in Egypt. How could they not? That is, of course, why so many black gospel songs read as they do, from "Let My People Go" to "Swing Low, Sweet Chariot."

Later on, too, black gentile Zionism was reinforced by perceptions of European anti-Semitism. The Nuremberg laws stigmatized Jews in Germany in more or less the same ways that Jim Crow laws stigmatized blacks in America. Blacks argued during World War II against the incoherence of fighting against Nazi racism while condoning the homegrown American variety. Not for nothing did Paul Robeson learn and perform a number of Yiddish songs, some from America's largely Jewish-led labor movement. Harlem Congressman Adam Clayton Powell Jr. even raised money after World War II for the militant Zionist group the Irgun.

But we should not exaggerate. American society has been for most of its history about as reflexively anti-Semitic as most majority-Christian civilizations, for reasons already discussed. There have occasionally been anti-Semites in high places, too. The Jewcentric character of American Protestantism did not stop Ulysses S. Grant from banishing Jews from territories under Union Army control west of the Mississippi River during the Civil War, for example.[6] It did not stop some from caricaturing Jay Gould, a notorious robber baron of the Gilded Age, as a Jew, even though he was born a Presbyterian and was married in an Episcopal church.[7] It did not keep William

Jennings Bryan in 1896 from accusing William McKinley of being in league with the Rothschilds, highlighting the pervasive anti-Semitism of the Populist movement. And it did not keep Supreme Court Justice James Clark McReynolds from literally walking out of the room every time Justice Louis Brandeis spoke.

Well into the twentieth century, too, the gatekeepers of the WASP patriciate kept Jews, among others, away from the elite institutions that ran American society, from professional guilds for lawyers and doctors to the colleges of the Ivy League. It is true, too, that opposition to recognizing the State of Israel in May 1948 was motivated not just by strategic calculation but, as Richard Holbrooke has put it, by the fact that "beneath the surface lay real but unspoken anti-Semitism on the part of some (but not all) policymakers."[8] There has been plenty of anti-Semitism in American history, rising more or less proportionately with the rising number of Jewish immigrants.

Still, there is no doubt that American popular support for Zionism in the early twentieth century, and for the State of Israel in its early years, flowed above all from America's philo-Semitic founding and deep history, as well as from guilt about American "country club" anti-Semitism and then, of course, the enormity of the Holocaust. Harry Truman supported recognizing Israel because he believed it to be a moral necessity, and his domestic policy adviser Clark Clifford agreed with him. (Clifford wasn't Jewish either.) When in 1961 David Ben-Gurion told Truman that his support for Israel had "given him an immortal place in Jewish history," it brought tears to Truman's eyes—and Harry didn't tear up easily.[9]

The same is true of Lyndon Baines Johnson: Like Truman, Johnson had several Jewish friends and associates, not least Abe Fortas, whom Johnson appointed to the Supreme Court, and he had political reasons for not wanting to alienate Jews. But all that paled in comparison to a far deeper stratum of belief. "Take care of the Jews, God's chosen people," Johnson's Baptist grandfather—"Big Sam" he called him—had told Lyndon as a young man. And Johnson recalled an aunt saying, "If Israel is destroyed, the world will end." That aunt, Jessie Johnson Hatcher, who was a significant influence on young Lyndon, was a most unusual person. She did the astonishing thing—astonishing for a Baptist from Texas—of joining the Zionist Organization of America!

Johnson's parents and grandparents, it turns out, were deeply affected by the lynching of Leo Frank by a mob in Atlanta, Georgia, in 1915. Johnson's parents were so outspoken about anti-Semitism and anti-black racism that they had once to stand guard with shotguns on their front porch against menacing Ku Klux Klan mobs. Young Lyndon never forgot it, and unbeknownst even to most of his closest political associates in later years, in 1938–1939, as a young congressman, Johnson went out of his way to rescue endangered European Jews by supplying American visas to Jews in Warsaw. He also oversaw the technically illegal immigration of hundreds of Jews into Galveston, Texas. At the same time he warned his Jewish friends to try to get as many Jews out of Germany and Poland as possible; he saw clearly what was coming. And on June 4, 1945, he visited Dachau, an experience that, according to his wife, Lady Bird, changed him forever.

In May 1967 President Johnson remembered all of this, and if his own memoirs are to be believed, he likened Israel to the surrounded, besieged Alamo, and Gamal Abdel Nasser to the hated Santa Anna.[10] John Kennedy had been a friend to Israel, but not since Harry Truman had Israel had an American Jewcentric friend in the White House like Lyndon Baines Johnson.

Positive, mostly Protestant, Jewcentricity in the United States expresses itself in silly manifestations as well as sublime ones, in the trivial and—as we have seen in our portrait of the dispensationalists—the portentous. We will come to the silly, never fear; but first the somewhat more serious.

A long list of non-Jewish Americans beyond John Adams have commented on the Jews in one way or another, both Jews in general and American Jews in particular. Many, looking over the tapestry of Western civilization, have understood and lauded the role of the Jews and Judaism in that civilization, and in America as well. They have incorporated it into American letters almost from the start, and of course into politics. The most famous document in American history as regards the Jews is George Washington's letter to the synagogue in Newport, Rhode Island, establishing the principle of American toleration and religious freedom from the highest office in the land. But the Newport synagogue, the oldest in North America, resonates widely, too, in the world of American letters. No summary of this literature could be adequate if it failed to mention one of the great poems of the antebellum age, Henry Wadsworth Longfellow's poem "The Jewish Cemetery at Newport," written in 1852.

Longfellow's masterpiece is sixty lines long, and I will not inflict much of it on those with underdeveloped tastes in poetry. Suffice it to say that virtually every Jewcentric trope is represented somewhere in this poem, as the poet bends biblical allusions to his task in perfect pitch. Longfellow's tone is both sad and sympathetic as he describes Jewish suffering and sees the American refuge in the light of that history. Yet he ends, at a time when there were not many Jews in America, on a disparaging note:

> But ah! What has been shall be no more!
> The groaning earth in travail and pain
> Brings forth its races, but does not restore,
> And the dead nations never rise again.

Not so others, and the list includes the redoubtable Mark Twain, who, not surprisingly, had as complex an image of Jews as he had of many things.

Growing up in Hannibal, Missouri, the young Samuel Clemens was no different from his peers in having inherited negative folk stereotypes of Jews. When the Levys, a Jewish family, came to Hannibal, Twain joined other boys in hazing the younger members of that family, as any unwashed, loudmouthed backwoods banshee would. In 1857 he wrote a humorous article for a Keokuk, Iowa, paper that had unpleasant things to say about Jewish coal dealers. But as Clemens read, traveled, and matured into Mark Twain, his views changed radically. By the time of the Civil War, Twain had become the defender of the underdog in society—blacks and Indians as well as Jews—for which he is justly revered. He once told his daughter Suzy that the Jews were "a race to be much respected" and that since they had suffered so much, ridiculing Jews was like "attacking a man when he was already down." In 1879 he wrote in a diary that "the Jews have the best average brains of any people in the world" and that the Jews "are the only race who work wholly with their brains and never with their hands."

This was not strictly true, of course; Twain was waxing Jewcentric. Nor was it true, as he also wrote, that there were no Jewish beggars, tramps, ditch diggers, hod carriers, or day laborers. "They are," he concluded, "peculiarly and conspicuously the world's intellectual aristocracy." So Twain was not the slightest bit unnerved when his eccentric daughter Clara fell in love with a Jewish piano player named Ossip Gabrilowitsch. Twain liked Gabrilowitsch and told Clara that "any girl could be proud to marry him. He is a man—a real man."[11]

Twain went public, which is to say into writing, with his sentiments about the Jews twice, both times in *Harper's* magazine. During much of 1896 and 1897 Twain was in Europe collecting material for a book; he took note when Austro-Hungarian authorities resorted to anti-Semitic distractions to deflect attention from an unpopular decision to make Czech instead of German the official language of Bohemia. Twain wrote about this in the March 1898 issue of *Harper's*, in an essay called "Stirring Times in Austria." He defended the Jews in a shrewd analysis of Austrian politics, and the article attracted a great deal of attention and hundreds of letters to the editor. So Twain decided to write a sequel, "Concerning the Jews," published in September 1899 with the expectation that he would please no one.

He certainly displeased many. By writing that the "Jew is a money getter, and in getting his money he is a very serious obstruction to less capable neighbors who are on the same quest," he angered many Jews. It didn't help that he added that because the Jews exhibited an "unpatriotic disinclination to stand by the flag as a soldier," they had made no significant contribution to American independence. Twain also fell into a common trap: thinking that there were far more Jews than there actually were. Twain tells how he once wrote to the editor of the *Encyclopaedia Britannica* to contest its claim that the Jewish population in the United States at the time was only around 125,000. Twain believed the number was vastly understated because the Jews masqueraded as Christians either for business purposes or because they wanted to avoid prejudice and discrimination:

> Look at the city of New York; and look at Boston, Philadelphia, and New Orleans, and Chicago, and Cincinnati, and San Francisco— how your race swarms in those places!—and everywhere else in America, down to the least little village. . . . I am strongly of the opinion that we have an immense Jewish population in America.

For all his Jewcentric prejudices and his general tendency to exaggerate, Twain put his finger on the essence of Jewcentricity, not so much the idea of the Chosen People in this case, but the Jewish insistence on difference and the response it invariably evokes from the non-Jew: "By his make and ways [the Jew] is substantially a foreigner wherever he may be," wrote Twain, "and even the angels dislike a foreigner. I am using this word foreigner in the German sense—stranger. . . . You [Jews] will always be by ways and habits and predilections substantially strangers—foreigners—wherever you are, and that will probably keep the race prejudice against you alive."[12]

Yet Twain defended Jewish acumen and honesty in business. He also proposed that Jews concentrate rather than diffuse their political influence in Europe, which displeased liberal European Jews who considered themselves to be citizens of those countries and tended to avoid any actions that might lead to accusations of divided loyalties. And toward the end of his essay, Twain waxed lyrical to the point of mystical, in direct contrast to Longfellow's despairing realism. "The Egyptian, the Babylonian, and the Persian rule, filled the planet with sound and splendor, then faded to dream-stuff and passed away," Twain wrote,

> the Greek and the Roman followed, and made a vast noise, and they are gone; other peoples have sprung up and held their torch high for a time, but it burned out, and they sit together in twilight now, or have vanished. The Jew saw them all, beat them all, and is now who he always was, exhibiting no decadence, no infirmities of age, no weakening of his parts, no slowing of his energies, no dulling of his alert and aggressive mind. All things are mortal except the Jew; all other forces pass, but he remains. What is the secret of his immortality?

It is hard to get more Jewcentric than that, except that Twain did. The most enigmatic statement from his September 1899 discourse was not his closing, but an earlier comment on a new major issue of the day—that of Zionism. Twain asks his readers if they have heard of Theodor Herzl's plan for gathering the Jews in Palestine with a government of their own. His answer is perhaps tongue-in-cheek—one never knows for sure with Twain, one of history's most skillful leg-pullers:

> I am not the Sultan, and I am not objecting: but if that concentration of the cunningest brains in the world were going to be made in a free country (bar Scotland), I think it would be politic to stop it. It will not be well to let the race find out its strength. If the horses knew theirs, we should not ride any more.

Twain was not the only nineteenth-century American to be fascinated with the Jews and specifically focused on the new idea of Zionism. Here we must take a moment to appreciate that long-since-forgotten marvel of turn-of-the-century American highbrow entertainment, John Lawson Stoddard.

Stoddard, born in 1851 in Brookline, Massachusetts, attended Williams College and then Yale Divinity School. He left Yale, however, and traveled during 1874–1876 throughout Greece, Turkey, Egypt, and Palestine. After further sojourns in Europe and elsewhere, he returned to the United States in 1879, whereupon, at the tender age of twenty-seven, he embarked upon an extraordinary career as a public lecturer. Stoddard's success was enabled by a terrific gimmick: stereographs that he displayed on a screen with a huge stereopticon powered by large lanterns.

A stereograph consists of two photos taken from the same specially fitted out camera at the same time from slightly different angles. Mounted side by side in a stereopticon, a hand-held device with two lenses put up near one's nose, like opera glasses, the pictures display a sense of dimensionality. Even in standard sepia, stereographic photo display was a great novelty in the middle of the nineteenth century. Stoddard knocked 'em dead with his mega-stereopticon; audiences loved it, and he made good money.

Stoddard used his profits to finance more travel, which he undertook every year for the next eighteen. Before long, Stoddard had become a national celebrity, one of the most popular and influential entertainers of his day. He was so popular that he was invited in 1897 to lecture before a joint session of Congress. Stoddard was particularly popular in New York City, where his lectures sold out year after year. When he retired from the lecture circuit at the age of 47, Stoddard collected his texts and photos and published them in a multivolume work.[13] Stoddard sold more books, and made more money from them, than anyone before him in American history.

Owning to the firmly Jewcentric nature of American culture, Stoddard's Classical and Holy Land Lecture was always his most popular. Given his popularity, it is interesting to see exactly what Stoddard was saying to all these people about the Jews and Palestine, and what he wrote in his books. His lecture and essay on Jerusalem started with an unremarkable narrative about the land's physical features, its basic history, and its then-current filth and desolation. But then Stoddard launched into a full-throated attack on anti-Semitism, summoning his strength near the end for a plainly Judeophilic plea for justice and the future of Palestine:

> In a place so thronged with classic and religious memories as Palestine, even a man who has no Hebrew blood in his veins may indulge in a dream regarding the future of this extraordinary

people. Suppose a final solution to the "Eastern Question." Suppose the nations of the earth to be assembled in council, as they were in Berlin a few years ago. Suppose the miserly governed realm of the Sultan to be diminished in size. Imagine some portions of it to be governed by various European powers, as Egypt is governed by England at the present time. Conceive that those Christian nations, moved by magnanimity, should say to this race which they, or their ancestors, have persecuted for so long: "Take again the land of your forefathers. We guarantee you its independence and integrity. It is the least we can do for you after all these centuries of misery."

One can imagine Stoddard then pausing, sipping from a glass of water, and lifting his arms skyward toward a huge stereoscopic image of the Tower of David, and proclaiming:

At present Palestine supports only six hundred thousand people, but, with proper cultivation it can easily maintain two and half millions. You are a people without a country; there is a country without a people. Be united. Fulfill the dreams of the poets and patriarchs. Go back,—go back to the land of Abraham.

Stoddard's vision of what might happen when the "Eastern Question" shifted toward its historical answer was not far from Shaftesbury's ambitions and, indeed, not that far off the actual historical track. The Versailles Conference, confirming the Balfour Declaration of November 1917 in the provisions eventually ratified in 1920 at San Remo, Italy, bears a striking resemblance to Stoddard's proposal—even if he failed to predict the event that brought about the Ottoman Empire's full-blown collapse: World War I. In 1881, when the narrative that eventually ended up in print in 1897 was probably drafted, only Stoddard and a few far less well-known dispensationalists were saying such things. It is as if John Nelson Darby looked down from his heavenly abode to see British power advancing toward Palestine on the one side—Shaftesbury's dream—and Stoddard building on and advancing the cause of Christian Zionism in America on the other.

Of course, the vast majority of the American people to whom Stoddard spoke, and who read his books, were Protestant Christians. Some of these people had been hearing the dispensationalist message from members of their clergy—not all or even a majority of them, but from a lot of them—ever since the Civil War. Abraham Lincoln himself had said in 1863 that "restoring the Jews to their homeland is a noble dream shared by many Americans," and that the United States could work to realize that goal once the Union prevailed.[14]

Stoddard himself was not a member of the Plymouth Brethren in America, nor is there any evidence that he was attached to any formally dispensationalist congregation; had he been, his 1935 biographer Daniel Crane Taylor would have said so. But as a onetime student at Yale Divinity School, he surely understood it; he certainly knew who Darby was, and he probably knew of Keith, as well.

At least some Jews also heard and read what Stoddard had to say, and were stunned. Stoddard received hundreds of letters from American Jews, thanking him for his philo-Semitic and proto-Zionist views. One of the best-known and most respected Jews in America, Jacob H. Schiff, wrote Stoddard on April 6, 1892—when Schiff had almost certainly never heard of an assimilated Jewish journalist from Vienna named Theodor Herzl—as follows:

> My Dear Sir,
>
> I have listened with genuine pleasure to your lecture on "Jerusalem and the Holy Land" this evening, and I desire to express to you my appreciation of the tribute you have rendered to our race. It is gratifying and encouraging, that in the midst of the prejudice with which we have had to contend at every point, the debt which Christendom owes to the Jewish race is pointed out as forcibly as you have done it, by a prominent lecturer to his gentile audience.
>
> Believe me, dear Sir,
> Yours faithfully,
> Jacob H. Schiff

Jewcentricity in an America that was a seriously Christian country naturally took on serious hues. Whatever may be said about the differences in how John Adams and Longfellow and Twain and others saw the Jews, they saw, wrote, and spoke with the kind of reverence generally associated with the respect owed religion, and with the veneration associated with an assumption that history has meaning. There is still plenty of that in America, but there is also a lot of mass-marketed, pseudo-religious banality, a sort of Wal-marting of the collective social spirit. And that is why the Jewish contribution to world and American civilization sometimes gets reduced to mere positive superstition—a kind of omnibus good luck charm.

That seems to explain, for example, the phenomenon of *The Prayer of Jabez*, although its author, the Reverend Dr. Bruce Wilkinson, clearly depended on the existence of a widespread network of evangelical believers to sell his book (and sell it he has!). It also seems to explain Madonna's embrace of faux-Jewish mysticism and Britney Spears's Hebrew tattoo on her neck (of which more in chapter 7). In the many parts of the United States where Jews are scarce but celebrity culture flows freely through the channels of our electronic media, images such as these have had an unpredictable, but not necessarily trivial, influence.

Some black Americans, too, who have been raised under the influence of the African Methodist-Episcopal and Baptist churches, have adopted Judeophilic symbols—the Star of David, especially—as good luck charms worn as jewelry. Of course, there are genuine black Jewish converts to Judaism in the United States (and elsewhere). Sammy Davis Jr. was unique, true enough; but in this, anyway, he was not alone. Indeed, a significant segment of the African American community of Cairo, Illinois, converted to Judaism last year, for example.[15]

But a lot of what American blacks think about Jews and Judaism falls somewhere between superstition and calumny. At least a few blacks have developed a supersessionist theory of their own, which holds that the real Jews, the real chosen people, were and remain blacks. Some black Hebrews are serious Jews: they pray in Hebrew and study Torah, and some reach out to other, "white" Jews. The Israelite Church of God in Jesus Christ (ICGJC), however, argues that real black Jews used to rule the world and should rule it again. Those who say they are Jews today and who are not black are usurpers, says the ICGJC. Shakespeare, King Arthur, and Mozart, among others, were all blacks and all Jews.[16] This is very Jewcentric, and very, very strange. It is mostly harmless, however, because it is so small—much more harmless than the genuine black anti-Semitism of Louis Farrakhan and the anti-Semitism residing in many Black Studies programs in American universities.

Other Americans, too, think Jews are interesting and somehow consequential, whether for good or for ill. But this attitude, instead of relating to a semisacred context, as it once did, now relates mostly to a media-fed celebrity culture context that tends to create rills of mostly silly Jewcentricity when and where one least expects to find them. It came to light in September 2006, for example, that then-senator George Allen, Republican of Virginia, son of the late great coach of the revered (in Washington, anyway) Washington Redskins, was born to a Jewish woman—at least to a woman born and raised as a Jew, in Tunisia. According to Jewish law, that makes the former senator a Jew.

Only of course he was not (and is not) a Jew in any meaningful sense. He was not raised or educated as a Jew; he therefore does not see the world through the eyes of a Jew, exhibiting Jewish moral sensibilities or any sign of Jewish historical memory. And yet for weeks after this revelation, the local and indeed the national press spilled more ink on George Allen's practically meaningless Jewish origins, and on his parents' twisted story of love and denial, than on, say, genocide in Darfur. Why? Because as the old journalistic adage goes, Jews is news, and there are no Jews in Darfur.

What stirred my emotions was the elder Mrs. Allen's story of why she hid her Jewish origins and abandoned all Jewish practice after she arrived in the United States after World War II. Her father, Felix Lumbroso, she said, had been imprisoned and his life put at risk by the Nazis, and she wanted to spare her offspring the unspeakable fear of what being a Jew could, and often did, mean in this unpredictable world of ours. Of course, this is nothing unusual: the Holocaust evoked many such reactions among Jews. Some estimate that as many as 20 percent of all Jewish concentration camp survivors abandoned all association with Judaism and the Jewish community after the war. Some of these people became famous, like Bronisław Geremek, one of the men who liberated Poland from Communist rule and Poland's first post-Communist foreign minister. A surprising number became not just Christian, like Geremek, but Christian clergymen.[17] No one should presume to judge others, however, as few of us can really put ourselves in Mrs. Allen's shoes at that time and place.

Such stories strike many Jews as sad, but one gets used to this sort of thing. It was not so long ago that Madeleine Albright apparently made a similar discovery about her Jewish roots in Czechoslovakia. Her father, Josef Korbel, did something fairly similar to what Etty Allen did—but there are notable differences in the tales as told and understood. When Madeleine Albright told her story in February 1997, many observers found it impossible to believe that she had not known all along that at least three, and probably all four, of her grandparents were Jews. After all, there were, as many hastened to point out, her not-all-that-distant Jewish cousins, and there was the situation itself: the wartime exile from Europe and the two prematurely deceased grandparents, the most likely meaning of which no historically knowledgeable person could easily avoid.

Despite much insistence to the contrary, I do not think Madeleine Albright lied in any ordinary sense. We should all retain a healthy respect for a human being's capacity for self-deception, especially in a person born into parlous circumstances. Harder to respect is what sometimes follows the extreme cognitive dissonance evoked by such circumstances. With the revelations, Ms. Albright pronounced herself proud of her parents and called her father "brave" for what he did. But what did Josef Korbel do? He hid his own children's birthright from them, but, privileged as a Czech diplomat, he managed to take his family to safety before anyone could be imprisoned or harmed—an option Etty Allen's parents lacked. Indeed, Josef Korbel fled Czechoslovakia not just once, because of the Nazis, but a second time, because of the Communists. This was brave? Czech Jews who maintained their dignity and their identity, most of whom perished at Treblinka and other death camps, were brave. Brave, too, were those remaining few Czech Jews and many Christian Czechs and Slovaks who suffered half a century of Communist tyranny.

Stories of hidden Jews, "half-Jews," Jews deceived by their parents allegedly for their own sake, converted Jews, and, above all, colorfully confused Jews roll through American history. And it is the Jewcentric origins of American society, at base, that keep making them so interesting for so many people. Every story is different. Had it not been for an insensitive Orthodox rabbi in Maine many years ago, Senator, and later Secretary of Defense, William Cohen might have lived his life as a Jew.[18] There are the stories of the forebears of Barry Goldwater and Caspar Weinberger, and the newer story about John Kerry's paternal grandparents. James Schlesinger, a Jewish-born convert to Christianity in his relative youth, is, among senior American political figures of recent years, in a category of his own.

But *so what*? What have the Jewish origins of any of these people really to do with the way they have solved problems, made decisions, lived their lives? The answer is unknowable, but it probably falls into the broad category of "not much" nearly all of the time. Yet still the ink spills out by the bucket, and the fascination with these stories seems never to slacken. One reason for this, perhaps, is that a disproportionate number of the journalists and editors who write and present these stories are themselves Jewish. Still, it is odd that American newspapers, popular magazines, and electronic media are addicted to trivial Jewcentric fluff, but seem not much interested in where gentile Jewcentricity in America comes from and how it really matters.

Let's end with one last example—a recent one that seems to demonstrate that Americans, too, no longer need the presence of Jews in a story for the story to be Jewcentric.

In September 2008, not long after she became John McCain's surprise choice to be his running mate on the Republican ticket, Sarah Palin quoted an "anonymous writer" praising the tendency of small towns to produce "good people with honesty, sincerity and dignity." This writer turned out to be Westbrook Pegler (1894–1969), a man aptly described in a *Wall Street Journal* article as "the all-time champion of fake populism."[19] In his prime, Pegler railed against the New Deal and was, to boot, a virulent anti-Semite back in a time when that was still socially acceptable. So obsessed was Pegler with the Jews, whom he called "instinctively sympathetic" to Communism, that even the John Birch Society banned him from its publications in 1964, after the social acceptability of anti-Semitism had ebbed in the wake of the Holocaust.

Literally within hours of Palin's source having been outed, the blogosphere filled to its virtual brim with insinuations that Sarah Palin, too, must be an anti-Semite. Others pointed out that Palin probably did not research or write her own speech and had probably never even heard of Pegler. Moreover, as a dispensationalist Pentecostal who displays an Israeli flag in her Alaska governor's office, it seemed very unlikely that Palin would be a closet anti-Semite of the conventional, Peglerian sort. But others answered that Palin had, after all, supported Patrick Buchanan for president in 2000, a man not known for his fondness for Jews, and that the most likely source for the Pegler quote was a 1990 book by Buchanan.

On it went, until it became known that one of George W. Bush's former speechwriters, Matthew Scully, helped Palin write the speech—and then on and on it went again as investigative eyes focused on Scully. Things soon got out of hand, as they tend to do in the unfiltered electronic ether. The Palin-Pegler affair was not widely covered by the mainstream media, which these days means the electronic media, but it was covered, and it clearly generated millions of electrons shot around the country and the world, like so many sparks from a Fourth of July fireworks display. Why? Because it had to do with the Jews.

Pegler was not Jewish. Palin is not Jewish. John McCain, Barack Obama, and Joe Biden are not Jewish. Patrick Buchanan and Matthew Scully are not Jewish. And yet just mention the possibility of even a third-order taint of anti-Semitism in American politics, and otherwise serene souls find their pulses quickened. In due course words are spoken, keyboards clack, and ink gets spilled all over the place. In this case the manifestation was minor and evanescent, but note that in the first 2008 presidential debate and in the vice presidential debate, as well, McCain and Obama, Palin and Biden, all competed to project themselves as the most pro-Israel of their pairing. McCain proclaimed with some drama, and Palin repeated, that there must not be a "second Holocaust," and so Iran must not be allowed to acquire nuclear weapons.

Why did they do this? Many saw a domestic political motive in such remarks, and certainly there was one. But the Jewish vote in the United States amounts nationwide to less than 2 percent of the electorate. How then to explain the lengths the candidates went to in order to attract that vote? Perhaps Jews are concentrated in key swing states like Florida; perhaps Jewish campaign contributions outweigh Jewish votes as such; perhaps such remarks were really directed at Christian Zionist voters, mostly evangelicals, who are far more numerous than Jewish ones. All this might be true, but these stories are almost always accompanied by exaggerations of various sorts. Slice it or dice it any way you will, the Jews play an outsized role, far beyond any objective measure of their actual influence. This is Jewcentricity hard at work.

6

The Two Religions of American Jews

Exaggeration—the inseparable companion of greatness.
— VOLTAIRE

As a rule, Jews in the United States feel specially blessed, twice chosen, as it were, to live in America. Most preserve pride in their chosen status as Jews, and take pride as well in the universal ideals of American civilization. They see both heritages as exceptional, giving rise to a kind of stereoscopic exceptionalism. They see no contradiction between the two, and many see that serendipitous harmony as historically unique.

It could well be—in a sense it *has* to be—that the experience and situation of American Jewry is unique. But it is not singular. The Haggadah's famous warning has not always been true: Jews have *not* in every generation had to deal with evil on a massive scale, risen up against them. There have been places where anti-Semitism for all practical purposes did not exist, in which Jews were free to live a reasonably full life in society without sacrificing anything about their Jewishness. This may not describe the majority of Jewish circumstances in the long history of the Diaspora, but to deny that some existed is, well, an exaggeration.

Whenever Jewish communities have lucked out historically, a characteristic narrative has sooner or later come into being. At least some Jews, and often many Jews, have fused the idea of their own chosenness with that of the larger society in which they lived: "We" are chosen by God for a cosmic historical moral mission, and they, those among whom we live, are also chosen to be part of God's cosmic design. Together we are weaving a beautiful tapestry in time; we are complementing one another; we are allies against the hidebound and the reactionary, the vulgar and the vain. These are highly Jewcentric narratives, cross-eyed ones, so to speak, as they seek to share the glory of chosenness with selected special others. If Jewish historical and moral sensibilities can be likened to lenses that bring focus to an otherwise fuzzy reality, stereoscopic exceptionalism as a special form of Jewcentricity amounts to bifocals.

There are many examples of stereoscopic Jewish-gentile exceptionalism. The Jews who elected to stay in Babylonia rather than return to Judea to rebuild the Temple probably qualify. The same goes for the Jews of the eighth-to-ninth-century Abbasid Baghdad of Haroun al-Rashid, the Jews of Amsterdam in the sixteenth century, and the Jews of post–Glorious Revolution England as well. Perhaps the most prominent example from more recent times is the Jews of nineteenth- and early-twentieth-century Germany. German-speaking Jews revered German culture, literature, and philosophy, and many went to great pains to persuade themselves that German civilization, particularly modern German Protestant Christian civilization, was fully consonant with the very best in Jewish historical civilization.

But the most spectacular historical case of stereoscopic exceptionalism was that devised by the Jews of Spain. Ordinary Jews expressed intense emotional attachments toward medieval Spain over some three and a half centuries. Spain attained the status of a substitute Promised Land, one so beloved that affection for the Land of Israel was elevated for most practical purposes into a mystical, otherworldly frame of reference. It was not for nothing that Ibn Gabriol, one of the greatest philosophers, scholars, and poets of the age, excoriated the Jewish community of Saragossa for their neglect of the Holy Tongue, of the Torah, and above all of Zion. In modern parlance, Ibn Gabriol's complaint was that these Jews were too assimilated, that they had "gone native."

The love of Spain expressed by its Jews was manifest in song, poetry, and art. For example, one of Abraham ibn Ezra's greatest poems, written after the Almohad conquest, is a lamentation of praise for the Umayyad cities destroyed in the war.[1] In another poem, Moses ibn Ezra refers to himself as having had to leave "a land more pleasant than all other lands," referring to Andalus in general and to the city of Granada in particular. Hasdai ibn Shaprut's letter to the king of the Khazars speaks glowingly of Andalus as a land of wondrous temperate climate and lush vegetation.[2] And most vividly, Judah al-Haziri, in his book *Takhemoni*, refers to *Sefarad*—Spain in Hebrew—as "the Garden of God," its air being the "life of souls." This was a play on a verse from Yehuda Halevi's poem *"Tziyon halo tishali,"* where, based on a Talmudic passage, he attributes that quality to the air of the Land of Israel.[3]

While American Jewish cases of stereoscopic exceptionalism evince many differences from prior examples, there are similarities, too, which illustrate more general points about Jewish history. The key similarities can be summarized in three points.

First, the quality and the breadth of Jewish life in any host society tend to rise as those of the host society rise, and to fall as those of the host society fall. Even in self-enforced marginality, Jews never have been able to escape the vicissitudes of the larger society in which they live, and they never will be. Jews are invariably the dependent variable, as the social scientists like to say. Major turning points in history—the rise of an avaricious conqueror, a plague, some epoch-changing technological innovation—have had little or nothing to do with the Jews. Jews have been talented flotsam on the waves of history, usually managing not to sink and learning how to swim, but never controlling the currents or the weather. This is why the gentile purveyors of Jewcentricity are so annoying: they invert, utterly and completely, what has been most true about Jewish social and political life for the past eighteen hundred years—its helplessness. To construe a more or less successful response to a condition of helplessness as a plot to control the world is, well, crazy. On the other hand, for Jews to think that good times under the same basic conditions of helplessness are not likely eventually to end is, well, naive.

Second, resentment of Jewish achievement varies depending on the dominant modes of cultural expression in a particular time and place. If a host society is enlightened, resentment will be muted. But if things take a general turn for the worse, resentment will take a religious cast in societies defined by religion, often a racial cast in early modern and modern societies, and a political-ideological cast in postmodern societies. If such a thing ever happens in America, it will likely express itself in terms of politics and ideology.

Third, when things are going fine, Jewish life is expansive and integrative and tends toward a rational interpretation of its own texts and history. When things are not going so well with the host society, both it and the Jews within tend to draw back, to separate, and to move toward a more mystical interpretation of texts and history.

All the historical examples of stereoscopic exceptionalism had one other thing in common, of course: for one reason or another, they all ended, often in tears. Will the Jewish American example do so as well? It may, but for a genuinely exceptional reason: it won't be the fault of gentile society at large, but that of the Jews themselves.

The extent to which Jews "went native" in Spain before the sixteenth century, at a time when religious culture was dominant virtually everywhere and in a place where toleration was at best relative toleration, was modest compared to what has gone on in the United States during the past century. After only 50 years of relatively good times in the northern parts of the New World, compared to at least 350 in Spain, American Jews already far exceed in praise for America anything Spanish Jews ever imagined saying about Spain. The period within American history that might be called a kind of Golden Age for American Jews dates, generously speaking, from about a century ago. If we were more exacting in our definition—say, if we disqualified times when informal quotas limited the number of Jews who could attend Ivy League and other elite universities—then the Jewish Golden Age in America dates only from just after the time when Sandy Koufax dominated the mound in major league baseball. Yet even on the basis of this relatively brief experience, most American Jews today are persuaded of the uniqueness of their good fortune in America and its likely unlimited future.

Clearly, the Jewcentric nature of American society and the toleration that has allowed Jews to prosper have led American Jews to become on balance great believers in American exceptionalism. Like most patriotic Americans, most American Jews think that America has been, is, and will always be different from and better than other great civilizations. Others rose only to have fallen, but America rises only to rise further, into a universal civilization.

Sounds wonderful. But is it true? This is an impossible question to answer as such because American exceptionalism is a faith-based notion, not a reasonably objective reading of its own history or of how the United States is perceived by others. On the one hand, the citizens of the United States in November 2008 elected a black man president of the land. Given American history, that has to count as exceptional by almost any measure. Moreover, at least up to now, America appears to have extended an exceptional attitude toward the Jews. There is virtually no anti-Semitism in mainstream American culture. The freedom of Jews to work and prosper, as Jews and as members of the wider society, has often led eventually to envy, resentment, and anti-Semitism. In America, so far at least, this unnerving pattern has been almost nonexistent, a conclusion that seems to be borne out by the fact that not even a systemic economic crisis with Bernard Madoff as its poster child, combined with the most broadly unpopular military action the Israel Defense Force has ever undertaken (in Gaza in January 2009), managed to evoke any evidence of mass-appeal anti-Semitism in the United States.[4] (This is a statement, it bears noting, that definitely cannot be made about Europe or South America.) On the other hand, we do not know what American society will be like as two or three hundred years pass. If it falls on difficult times, as happened in Spain after the twelfth century, there is no assurance that American society won't become more narrow, brittle, and fearful, and there is nothing to stop some Americans from searching for scapegoats on which to blame the country's bad fortunes, as occurred in Spain and many other places.

Most Jewish Americans believe such a thing impossible, preferring to rely on their own version of stereoscopic exceptionalism. But that rendition is dissonance. Let us count the ways.

Even as mainstream Jewish Americans luxuriate in their twinned pride—and by mainstream I mean the majority who identify as Jews but are not religiously observant or Jewishly well educated by historical standards[5]—many still fear anti-Semitism and rising rates of intermarriage and assimilation. But if Jewish Americans are so lucky, why do they think they face these two serious problems? Doesn't stereoscopic exceptionalism rule out serious anti-Semitism by definition? And if Jewish values are so precious to them, how do they explain the high rates of assimilation?

Alas, most Jewish Americans are confused. They exaggerate the compatibility of the Jewish and the American ethos, having drastically reconfigured the former to align with the latter. By doing so they have thrown overboard the ben-Zakkai system of rabbinic Judaism. Most Jewish Americans may think they are still chosen in some vague theological or cultural-historical sense, but they don't act chosen in terms of Jewish religious practice. As a result, they have jettisoned their own studied social marginality and the long sense of history that attends it. This, obviously, is what is causing rates of intermarriage—more than 50 percent by most counts—and assimilation that, extrapolated out a generation or two, are destroying the community. There is no anti-Semitism in mainstream American society to push back against the Jewish American willingness to leave the fold, but Jewish Americans and the leaders of their secular organizations and nontraditional institutions of worship cannot admit this, and many blame instead supposed legions of anti-Semites who refuse to accept them as Jews, making assimilation seem a buckling to the pressure of bigotry rather than a free and open choice. You can't get much more confused than that.

When I used the locution "Jewish American" just now instead of the more common term "American Jew," I did it deliberately. For the purposes of this discussion, I refer to halachic, or Jewish-law-observant, Jews in America as "American Jews," and to non-halachic Jews as "Jewish Americans." It really does matter which is the noun and which is the adjective because, as it happens, Jewish Americans unwittingly have two religions—Judaism and Americanism. And the faith tenets of Americanism, which are far more predominant among the majority of Jews than those of Judaism, prevent the special Jewish facility for historical memory and unsentimental realism from coming into play. Jewish Americans have not only thrown overboard the rabbinical survival system, they have reversed its essence. Rabbinical Judaism, whatever else it is and has accomplished, is a system for transmuting politics into religion; in our age, the impulse is precisely the reverse, to transmute religion into politics. The rabbis learned the lessons of the Greek and Roman eras, which is why they chose to characterize the founding of the Hasmonean dynasty—the events that have come to be celebrated as Hanukkah—as a religious event rather than as the winning of an unconventional war. In the Mishnah, too, they warn against hobnobbing with the political elite.[6] The reverse impulse of our political age, on the other hand, has driven Jews toward the political in all things. Above all, this reverse impulse explains the rise of what has been called Redemption and Holocaust Judaism, which essentially replaces the rabbinical system and which is the very engine of contemporary Jewcentric confusion.

At first glance, I am well aware, Judaism and Americanism do not appear to be entities that can be compared to each other in a meaningful way. One is a religion, or so it is thought, and the other is a kind of nationalism, or so it is thought—and these are different, like proverbial apples and oranges. But they can be and are competitive because both are creedal systems, templates for ordering moral understanding and behavior. Both have to be taken essentially on faith, not a word to be used lightly.

The reason that Judaism and Americanism are incompatible as creedal systems is that they encapsulate mutually exclusive ways of conceiving authority and personal status. The intrinsic source of authority that flows from the latter—"of the people, by the people, for the people," said Abraham Lincoln—cannot be reconciled with the extrinsic source of the former—"the Lord was King, the Lord is King, the Lord will be King for ever and ever," says the siddur. And the primary principle of individual autonomy (or liberty) and equality before the law that flows from American sacred texts cannot be reconciled with the hierarchical, communal principles that flow from rabbinic law, from halacha.

The rabbinic view of authority derives from a line of revelation through time from God to Moses on Mount Sinai, to Joshua, to the Judges and the Prophets, to the Talmudic *tana'im*, to the sages after them down to the rabbinic successors of our own time. Halacha evolves in this procession through the process of text-based progressive articulation, as described in chapter 1, but the core principles underlying it do not and cannot change, for they are taken by in-the-tradition Jews to be divine and perfect. Authority rests on what is accepted as divine decree, as cumulatively interpreted by those competent to do so.

In Americanism, authority also resides in sacred texts: the Declaration of Independence, the Constitution, and the Bill of Rights among them. Just as the Mishnah has "extra" passages that illuminate concepts but are not formally part of the book, so Americanism has the Federalist Papers—very important material but of no specific legal standing. In theory, here too, principles do not change, but interpretations and applications can and must. The Constitution is like the Torah, the statutes are like the Talmud (sort of, since only a fraction of the Talmud is concerned with law), and the codes are like the Shulchan Aruch, the Code of Jewish Law. But the differences are more important than the similarities: Americanism rests on temporal authority, not divine authority; on confidence in an individual's capacity for rationality, not on divinely justified, rabbinically administered, communal authority over the individual.

Both Judaism and Americanism depend on belief in certain principles, and both generate encompassing universalist visions that arise from those principles. Judaism is less concerned with abstract theology than with worldly deeds, and the power of American values is not limited to the public realm but inhabits the heart as well. Name any consequential public policy issue, and both Judaism and Americanism speak to it with passion and a logic inherent in their distinctive approaches to their respective sources of moral authority.

This truth is obscured not only by the ostensibly apolitical character of Diaspora Judaism, but also by the ostensibly secular character of American public life. And American public life has been more secular than most by far. Protestant Christianity's emphasis on personal salvation and on intentions rather than on works and consequences makes a perfect fit with a governmental ethos that privatizes religion in order to protect religious belief from the state. Yet America is, nonetheless, like no other modern state, also a covenantal state: in its self-conception if not also in social fact, it is not a "bloodline" society, a commonwealth based on a dominant ethnicity, but one based on a public creed that comes from a general Protestant Christian ethos. That makes America at least a little bit like Israel and Americans a little bit like the Jewish people.

More important for practical purposes, however, since ethnicity is not the social center of gravity in American society, as it was in all European societies, Jews are not automatically marginalized in it; and since freedom of religion is a hallmark of the American creed, Jews are not marginalized on that count either. This makes it easy for Jews in America to imagine a perfect harmony between Jewish chosenness and American exceptionalism since, as everyone knows, the American creed owes more than a little to the heritage of Israel. It isn't true, yet wanting it to be true has led Jewish Americans to redefine Judaism to fit into the comfort zone of stereoscopic Jewish American exceptionalism.

The assumption that religion and politics in America are so separate that Jews do not have to make choices between Judaism and Americanism is false. Choices are made, but they are often not acknowledged. American Jews have two religions the way some people have both a spouse and a lover. It is a condition that can be managed, learned from, even enjoyed, sometimes for a long time. But it cannot be reconciled into true harmony. Think of it this way: while Americanism as a creedal system is about life, liberty, and the pursuit of happiness, Judaism is about light, love, and the pursuit of holiness. The words sound similar; the meanings really are not.

The Jewish American belief in stereoscopic exceptionalism has given rise to an informal cultural cottage industry whose job it is to harmonize traditional Jewish and American social and moral ideals. We know the products of this industry well. They begin with the ubiquity of broad-stroke phrases like the "Judeo-Christian ethic" or "Judeo-Christian values." They include regular proclamation of the identity of American and Jewish social values, and American and Israeli political values, democracy foremost among them.[7] Such supposed compatibilities have as their aim the harmonization of the Jewish embrace of what is universal about the American creed—the devotion to liberal principles and mutual toleration—with Jewish particularism, the indelible sense of Jewish peoplehood, and, yes, even the idea of being chosen.

Of course, there is something to the claim that Jewish and Christian moral principles have much in common—how could they not? It's true, too, as we saw in the last chapter, that the American Founders had enormous respect for the Bible and, some of them, anyway, for the Jews. And it's true that both the United States and Israel are democracies. It's even possible, if one tries hard enough, to close the yawning gap between what Christmas really is and what Hanukkah really is.[8] Things are not really so simple, yet superficial commonalities feed the illusion of a deeper one.

The underlying harmony between Jewish and American principles comes apart on closer inspection. Western visions of democracy and equality may derive remotely from the heritage of Israel as well as from that of Athens and the Roman Republic. Human dignity, the sense that humankind can improve its lot and is not stuck in cycles of rise, fall, and repeat drill, the belief in progress and a better future— yes, all these ideas arose from Jewish minds and were formed with Jewish ink and utterance. Judaism is a forward-looking, messianic belief system, and the Anglo-American outlook has been, probably

above all gentile others, infused with such sensibilities. But this outlook sits at a considerable remove from ancient Israel. It leaves out
thousands of years of European thought from Cato to Locke. It is all
very well for John Adams to have praised the Jewish contribution to
democratic civilization, but when the American Founders got down
to their real work of government design, they relied on Montesquieu,
not Moses. To claim otherwise is, well, Jewcentric.[9] Thus, for example, Thomas Cahill once again: "Democracy . . . grows directly out
of the Israelite vision of *individuals,* subjects of value because they are
images of God, each with a unique and personal destiny. There is no
way that it could ever have been 'self-evident that all men are created
equal' without the intervention of the Jews."[10] No, not directly—
indirectly, at best.

Most Jewish Americans also champion the connection between
Passover, "the season of our freedom," as the siddur puts it, and
freedom as understood by the American creed. Sometimes they do
so with special English readings and rituals devised for the occasion. But Passover is about the freedom of the Jewish *nation,* not
about individual freedom. Jews who understand what they are
doing—who know what matzoh is really about—try to deflate
themselves on Passover, try to make themselves humble in
preparation for accepting God's law seven weeks later with the revelation at Mount Sinai (the celebration of Shavuot, or the Feast of
Weeks). That is close to the opposite of the original American idea
of freedom, which was and remains antifoundational in the standard (not the postmodern) sense.

And yes, the Liberty Bell at Independence Hall in Philadelphia
quotes the Hebrew Bible (Leviticus 25:10): "Proclaim liberty
throughout the land, to all the inhabitants thereof." But that it does
so has to be one of the great ironies of American history, for some
of the Founders who were proud to see that verse put on the Liberty
Bell were themselves slaveholders.

The Bible is referring to the jubilee year in which indentured
laborers are set free and the balance of contracts and landhold-
ings returned to their original state at the time of the division of the
land according to the tribes and clans. The biblical idea here is that
the flow of business should not be allowed to upset permanently a
fair distribution of resources. Israelites did not make slaves of one
another, nor did their use of non-Israelite labor constitute slavery as
we think of it. People did not "own" other people as property and
did not have leave to do with servants as they pleased, as had been

their lot as slaves in Egypt. The Bible states numerous laws regarding the treatment of servants, and most are "captioned," so to speak, with the warning "for you were slaves in the land of Egypt." The message is clear: Don't do to others what the Egyptians did to you; you suffered and so you should know better. Indentured servitude is therefore a more accurate English description of the biblical concept, which derives from the assumption that everyone (except Levites, the priestly caste) possessed land for pasture or agriculture held in common by clan and tribe. When a person or family had to hire out to others, this was considered an aberration, an unnatural act in a preindustrial civilization. So the biblical verse on the Liberty Bell is about a form of manumission specific to a premodern context; it is not a direct precursor to the eighteenth-century Enlightenment notion of individual liberty.

Nonetheless, most Jewish Americans, and American Jews, too, are proud of the historical Jewish contribution to Western civilization, and proud to be part of the ongoing American social experiment defining and expanding that civilization. Much like Jewcentric American Christians, they see no conflict between the two; indeed, they see a convergence on all essential issues. Both Jews and Americans have seen themselves as chosen people—Jews as a "kingdom of priests" and a "light unto the nations" and America as a "City on a Hill" and "the last best hope for mankind" (for those keeping score, that's Exodus 19:6 and Isaiah 42:6, and Governor John Winthrop and Abraham Lincoln, respectively). Both see both nations as covenantal, and, what is more, each also tends to see the other as chosen. American Jews thus entertain themselves with the fiction that they stand at a cosmic nexus of chosenness. What a lucky community.

American Jews are lucky in many ways, no doubt. But about the basic compatibility of these two sorts of chosenness, again, they are mistaken. And real consequences flow from the abyss, which is not just between Jews and non-Jews, but between American Jews and Jewish Americans—that is, between the majority of Jews in the United States who tilt toward Americanism and the minority who remain connected to Judaism as it has been understood stretching back some eighty generations or so to the time of ben-Zakkai. A few frequently raised questions may serve as illustration.

Should women be ordained as rabbis? How about homosexual men? Halachic Judaism says no; Americanism says, "Sure, why not?; that's our understanding of the equality principle." What about tattoos and pornography? Judaism says no; Americanism says, in effect, "Oh, what the heck; freedom includes the freedom to have and express bad taste." Let the kids go trick-or-treating for Halloween? Most Jewish Americans never think twice about it; American Jews, on the other hand, do.

If we dig a little deeper, we find ourselves in more complicated territory. Should an individual Jew be entitled to make judgments about his or her own level of kashrut and Sabbath observance? Do obligations concerning *taharat hamishpahah*, ritual cleanliness as regards sexual relations between a man and his wife, still apply today? Should a Jew support abortion rights or the "right to life"? What about gene therapy and cloning? What about moments of silence in public schools? On each and every one of these questions, and others, too, rabbinic Judaism has a view based in Jewish law, and in most cases it diverges from what the liberal forms of Americanism embraced by most Jewish Americans hold in both principle and practice.[11]

So what does someone who wants to believe in the compatibility of the Jewish and the American ways of looking at the world do when they conflict? Jewish Americans often solve the problem de facto through ignorance; if they do not know what Judaism says with respect to specific issues, no conflict can arise. But it takes more than ignorance to manage the lack of fit. Most choose Americanism and then accept what amounts to redefinitions of Judaism to exclude any inconvenient elements.

This is nothing new, of course; it has been going on for a long time, for the conflict is not only an American Jewish one. The Reform movement arose in Germany to square precisely this kind of circle. It stripped away from what it deemed essential to Judaism all elements of observance and belief that separated Jews from other Germans: dietary restrictions, strict Sabbath observance, prayer in Hebrew, the wearing of head coverings, and so on. What this shows is that in general terms, the choice for Jews in America is not just one between Judaism and Americanism, but more generally between Judaism and the Jewish understanding of modernity.

The situation of Jews in America, however, is especially pointed, for nowhere is the worship of modernity as pure and as enthusiastic as it has been here. As a result of the choices most Jewish Americans have made, only a minority feel any dissonance over their own conduct as long as it aligns with what most Americans do most of the time. So kashrut, Sabbath observance, regular prayer and study, and family purity observance—four constitutive elements of what being

Jewish has meant for a dozen centuries and more—have simply been jettisoned from what it means to be Jewish. This process has been greatly facilitated by the conceit of contemporaneity—the general bias that assumes that old ideas are necessarily more primitive and inherently less authoritative than newer ideas. Most Jewish Americans thus affirm non-Jewish views on abortion, homosexuality, pornography, and so forth because the American version of modernity itself is taken to be authoritative. To reject kashrut, for example, it is enough to assume, quite mistakenly, that it had to do with health problems long since vanquished by science.

All this is of a piece with the instant-gratification mind-set of contemporary America, a society with what seems to be an ever-shrinking attention span. Contrary to Jewish Americans who claim that rabbinic Judaism is hidebound and reactionary, Jewish culture, civilization, and law surely evolve; had they not, they could not have survived. Jewish civilization today carries within it Babylonian, Persian, Hellenic, Moorish, Aristotelian, and other influences, as the ben-Zakkai system constantly translated diasporic social and political reality into the Jewish religious idiom. Despite the exertions of some genuinely reactionary forms of Orthodoxy, it is evolving still.[13]

These influences, however, were assimilated over a long and often enough self-aware process. The issue is not change, but how change occurs. Jewish adaptability over the years can be likened to a flowering vine that has wrapped itself around its environment. However difficult the process, the roots remained the roots, and the genetic material, so to speak, that produced the seeds for future generations passed essentially unaltered. But discarding the central tenets of Judaism in the deliberate manner of German Reformism, or in the absentminded manner of most Jewish Americans today, is more like doing random sequential genetic engineering on the vine sufficient to change the nature of the organism, and then tossing away the record of the changes.[12] To discard the halachic process as the basis on which to navigate the engagement between Judaism and the non-Jewish world is like trusting a toddler to know how to break a raw diamond into a jewel.

Halachic Jews in America, American Jews as opposed to Jewish Americans, also love democracy, but not for its own sake. They love it because of what it allows: they can invoke the authority of halacha upon themselves as they please because what society demands of them in that regard is modest. Still, halachic Jews put any secular system that claims moral authority at a distance. And since a great deal of what American freedom allows disgusts them—rampant materialism, disrespect for parents and teachers, promiscuity, and general indulgence, rather like Greek hedonism and the late Roman times of "bread and circuses"—halachic Jews tend to take a somewhat jaundiced view of modernity, seeing new "truths" as more often than not passing fads.

The aversion to modernity as faddishness helps explain why halachic Jews tend to be conservative in the context of American politics, while most non-halachic Jews are decidedly liberal, having concluded, not unreasonably, that the liberal vision of America is what has created the circumstances for their own acceptance and success in American society. In the 2006 midterm elections, for example, exit polling showed that the Jewish vote split 88–12 for Democrats, by far the most lopsided split of any group except blacks, which split 89–11.[13] The Jewish vote split 76–24 in the 2008 election, still the most pro-Democratic of any group aside from blacks. This result, one of the most stable in American politics, was once famously described by Milton Himmelfarb as follows: "Jews earn like Episcopalians and vote like Puerto Ricans."

There are of, course, exceptions, and they illuminate the range of Jewcentric phenomena. Some American Jews who are not particularly religious are nonetheless conservative in terms of American politics. These are often called neoconservatives, but the term is harder to define than it may seem for two reasons. One is that the label suggests far more homogeneity than in fact exists, and the other is that both the meaning of the label and the people it presumes to label keep changing. But the easiest way to summarize is to say that neoconservatives are hard-line idealists when it comes to American foreign policy who started out mainly as generic political liberals or leftists. Some neoconservatives have served in high government positions and most are Jews.

What does this mean? A whole genre of weird literature has arisen to tell us, a literature claiming knowledge of what amounts to a neoconservative cabal hard at work hijacking American foreign policy. The cabal theory bears a cousinly relation to the *Protocols*, and is not far removed either from theories about the hypertrophic power of the "Israel lobby," because one of the cabal's supposed discoveries is the systematic suborning by neoconservatives of American interests at the behest of those of the State of Israel (of which more in chapter 11).

A more useful way to think about neoconservatives is to see them as a special case in American Jewish political life. Neoconservatives are the purest expression of two phenomena simultaneously. First, they are an American Jewish example of the broad modern tendency for religious energies to attach themselves to politics, and second, they are an expression of stereoscopic chosenness, having filtered out the realism-inducing study of Jewish history and replaced it with the heroic narratives of American and modern Zionist histories.

A few examples can demonstrate what happens when American-ism replaces Judaism as a marker of political understanding. In their book *An End to Evil*, David Frum and Richard Perle wrote: "A world at peace; a world governed by law; a world in which all peoples are free to find their own destinies: That dream has not yet come true, it will not come true soon, but if ever it does come true, it will be brought into being by American armed might and defended by American might too."[14] If that is not vivid enough for you—a close approximation of the Jewish messianic ideal yoked to American tanks and fighter aircraft—here is one even more explicitly religious. David Gelernter has argued that U.S. participation in World War I prefigured "the worldwide realization of the American Creed"—that it was "her attempt to act like the new chosen people, to set forth on a chivalrous quest to *perfect the world*; to spread liberty, equality, and democracy to all mankind." That is a fair description of what passed for thought in the mind of Woodrow Wilson, and it led to an idealism so disconnected from reality that it helped cause World War II and thus lay the predicates for the Holocaust. Gelernter, however, *likes* this; for him, now as well as in Wilson's time, America is a global humanitarian cause, and Americanism a world religion "for the oppressed, the persecuted, and the simply idealistic all over the globe."[15] Neoconservatism as a form of stereoscopic Jewcentricity doesn't get any headier than this.

Neoconservatives tend to unite around the conviction that small, beleaguered groups of chosen believers can prevail over all odds if they stick to their beliefs. The more they are assailed from without as having wandered from some more moderate, more reasonable opinion, the more certain they are they're right. If this sounds like the sort of reaction one would have expected from Jews in centuries past who were assailed in their ghettoes and small villages by masses of threatening ignoramuses around them, that's no coincidence. There really is such a thing as the moral chauvinism of the downtrodden alluded to in chapter 3, a "we suffer, therefore we're better than you" attitude that is not always easy to dismiss.

There is such a thing, too, as intergenerational rootedness, which is simply to say that behavioral traits have a way of being passed on from generation to generation despite sometimes drastic changes in the environment. Jewish immigrants and their children who debated the fine points of socialism at the City College of New York in the 1930s, and a man like Leo Strauss closely reading ancient philosophers looking for esoteric knowledge, were all, whether they realized it or not, engaging in the morally infused method of the Talmudic dialectic—*pilpul*—only with different texts and (only sometimes) for different purposes.

Liberal, non-halachic Jews also play games with the interface of their Jewish heritage and their love for America. A good case in point concerns the Holocaust Museum, on the edge of the National Mall in Washington, D.C.

Many Jewish Americans seem compelled to synthesize and concretize their love for American universalism with their Jewish particularism. The act of concretization seems to assuage any doubts that may exist over the truth of the assumption. This has led to the bizarre idea that the Holocaust was somehow an experience so deeply and authentically American that it deserves a place on the National Mall.

The Holocaust was in fact a parochial event; it was above all about the Jews, notwithstanding the horrors that other groups hated by the Nazis endured in those terrible years between 1939 and 1945. But the Holocaust has since become the single central reason for many irreligious Jewish Americans to remain self-consciously Jewish. It works on an abstract collective scale the same way that some Jews go to synagogue only to say the orphan's Kaddish—a practice that smacks of superstition and distorts the Jewish concept of prayer almost beyond recognition. As Irving Howe, the author of the iconic book *The World of Our Fathers*, once remarked, "Israel has become the religion of American Jews, and the Holocaust their liturgy."[16]

Indeed, most Jewish Americans do not, for example, build their own succah every year and join with children and grandchildren in decorating it. Most do not dance with the Torah on Simchat Torah or join in the noisemaking and revelry on Purim. Most do not sing traditional hymns as families around the Sabbath table on Friday nights, do not praise their spouses or bless their children according to the ancient formulas before the blessing over the wine. Most Jewish Americans know little of the joyous aspects of their tradition, having instead made the Holocaust into a collective ancestor-worship cult that now masquerades as Judaism, along with substituting a virtual worship of Israel as a substitute for God. Assimilated Jews, who want to be recognized as full-fledged hyphenated Americans by other Americans in this age of multiculturalism, have then taken that faux Judaism and offered it up as the quintessential experience that defines their Jewishness: a mass murder, in which they and their immediate family were but marginally, if at all, implicated, that somehow affirms Israel's right to exist. And they do this for a reason that the original director of the Holocaust Museum project, Michael Berenbaum, could not possibly have spelled out more clearly: "What we are about is the Americanization of the Holocaust."

By Americanizing the Holocaust, Jewish Americans have completed the project of exorcizing the idea of *galut*, of exile, from their Jewish vocabularies. They have performed the ultimate act of stereoscopic Jewcentricity, and the ultimate act of bad faith. The leaders of their secular "ethnic" organizations, as we will see in chapter 9, have helped them do it.

Spanish Jewry flirted with affection for Spain and assimilated to a considerable degree in the general culture of the Golden Age. But there were two interactive limits on how far they could ever go. One limit was internal: there was at that time no such thing as non- or post-halachic Judaism. All that is a function of what was a yet-unborn modernity—modernity defined, in part, as the separation of aspects of life, not least art, from religious thought and discipline, and the triumph of individual over communal agency. The other limit was external: the Spanish were not ready to accept Jews into full citizenship, for in premodern Europe the very idea of citizenship was bound up with faith communities. The universal citizen of the American and French Revolutions did not yet exist.

Thus it came to pass that the erosion of Jewish circumstances over time, and eventually even the Inquisition and the expulsion, did not break the spirit of Spanish Jewry. Their remnant of 165,000 souls remembered what they had been chosen for and continued on in new climes. The expulsion took Jews out of Spain and Portugal, to the enduring impoverishments of both countries, but it never took Judaism out of Spanish and Portuguese Jews. American Jewry may never have to face such dire circumstances, but what if, in the fullness of time, it does? Will American Jewry, possessor of a politicized version of Judaism whose memory requirements are extremely small, survive as well?

One may doubt it. The data show unmistakably that Jewish Americans have already converted away from a reliably transmissible form of Judaism, and I am not speaking of literal conversion or disaffiliation. Droves of Spanish Jews converted to Catholicism in a religious age, and not just by force or from the pressures of anti-Semitism. Droves of Jewish Americans have converted to Americanism in a political age, and they have not needed to give up their nominal identification as Jews in order to do so. America makes it so easy, so inconspicuous, that most Jews are not even aware of the choices they have made.

In the past, in post-Napoleonic Europe, say, Jews could assimilate into non-Jewish society, but it took a conscious effort, and it was not always easy to achieve. In America, as Milton Himmelfarb first observed decades ago, assimilation requires no effort at all; Jews do not have to do anything except take the path of least resistance to the social environment open before them.[17] And that, exactly, is what most Jewish Americans have done. It's not the first time in Jewish history something like this has happened, and it won't be the last. It is part of a now two-millennia-old process of human filtering wherein some join the Jewish people and others depart from it. But have no doubt: that, exactly, is what we are seeing, and only the most robust Jewcentric conceits manage to hide the truth of the matter from those most affected.

7

Adjewlation: Jews in American Celebrity Culture

All cartoon characters and fables must be exaggerations, caricatures. It is the very nature of fantasy and fable.

—WALT DISNEY

Mel Gibson *had* to be drunk to spout anti-Semitic vitriol in a place like Hollywood. Not even a committed anti-Semite would say such things sober, for the American entertainment culture's manifest infatuation with Jews and Judaism in recent years is plain to see. Everyone, even Gibson, knows that many, even most, of the influential directors, producers, and agents in Hollywood, and in the bicoastal world of commercial television, are Jews.

It has been this way for a long time, too, although that was not so obvious several decades ago. Show-business Jews and Judaism were discussed mostly in undertones in the years before and just after World War II, and very few Jews were portrayed as Jews in Hollywood fare or on the radio—an informal taboo broken in 1947 by the film *Gentleman's Agreement*. Well into the 1950s efforts to portray Jews in films and in the new world of television as being "not too different" from other Americans abounded, to the point where iconic

Jewish TV personalities such as Gertrude Berg and Jack Benny were depicted embracing Christmas. From around the middle 1960s, Jews in the entertainment business have been openly acknowledged and freely discussed; hence Jerry Seinfeld never had to hide his Jewishness and could even flaunt its stereotypes, at least to a limited extent, on the air.

As of about a dozen years ago, however, it has not only been acceptable in American entertainment-culture circles to be Jewish, it has been so downright hip that many non-Jews even appear, at least, to take not just Jews but Judaism seriously. They do not always get Judaism quite right, however, but then neither do many of the Jews. In the film *Independence Day* Judd Hirsch plays a Jew—the father of the hero—who is so stereotyped that, as Carol Leifer, one of the *Seinfeld* writers, put it, "they might as well have given him a jar of gefilte fish and a box of matzohs just to walk around with."[1] One scene that does get Judaism at least clingingly right (and is my favorite Jewish film vignette of all time) is Walter's line delivered by John Goodman in *The Big Lebowski*, where he sharply reminds his colleagues that he does not bowl, does "not roll on Shabbas." (Goodman is not Jewish.) The point, however, is that there has been an explosion of such Jewcentric scenes since the days, back in 1974, when a young Richard Dreyfus first cavorted around in *The Apprenticeship of Duddy Kravitz*, flinging out stereotypes old and new with promiscuous abandon.

The American celebrity culture's recent infatuation with Jews is for the most part many miles wide and half an inch deep; but it has been very telegenic. "Everyone" in America, and just about everyone in the Western plugged-in world, knows that Madonna is a believer in kabbalah—Jewish mysticism—even though neither she nor most of them seem to have a clue about what kabbalah actually is. "Everyone" knows, too, that Britney Spears has a tattoo in Hebrew on her neck (not everyone realizes that it was originally misspelled). The revelation that Scarlett Johansson is Jewish—her mother is Jewish, and she has publicly described herself as a Jew—sent shockwaves from YouTube to Facebook when it hit the airwaves and the Internet a few years ago. Natalie Portman, sure; Gwyneth Paltrow, well, all right; but a blonde with a name that sounds like a Viking's, *Scarlett Johansson*? No doubt this particular revelation made a real hash of the fantasies of several young Queens-born male Jewish adolescents. All those nights spent lusting in their imaginations after the archetypal shiksa, and for what?

Where does this mile-wide, inch-deep infatuation come from? What does it mean? How could such ephemera have anything but ephemeral consequences? (Hint: It may have more than ephemeral consequences, or this chapter wouldn't be here.) The essence is this: Hollywood's infatuation with Jews makes Jews look good to non-Jews, and Jewish Americans love it. This is notwithstanding the fact that the way Hollywood depicts Judaism distorts reality either a little or, in the case of Madonna's "kabbalah," a lot. It is mostly but not entirely harmless as it exists now, but there is at least a chance that it could become a lot more harmful later on.

The best way to get at the subject is perhaps to briefly review some irrefutable facts about entertainment-business culture in the United States. The first of those facts is, as already suggested, that this culture has been and remains disproportionately, overwhelmingly, even astonishingly Jewish. This does not mean that Jews "run" Hollywood. No one runs Hollywood, and besides, "the Jews" are not a monolithic group that gathers secretly somewhere just off Santa Monica Boulevard to plot the moral downfall of America. "The Jews run Hollywood," whether spoken by a Jew or a gentile, either in pride or anger, is a Jewcentric statement. It is a bald exaggeration.

But Jewish prominence in Hollywood is a fact that impresses even when it is not exaggerated. The heads of nearly every major Hollywood production studio from the beginning were Jewish, as were many of the directors and not a small number of the cinematographers and actors. Jews have been only slightly less prominent in the New York theater business for nearly a century, and in many aspects of popular music, as well.

Just to summarize the matter, let a relatively few data suffice as evidence. Both the composer and the lyricist for the most famous song and musical film in American history, "Somewhere Over the Rainbow" in the 1939 film *The Wizard of Oz*, were first-generation Jews from New York: Harold Arlen and Yip Harburg.[2] The best-selling song of all time, Bing Crosby's "White Christmas," a classic icon of the denatured Christianity of the American civil religion, was written by a Jew: Irving Berlin. The first "talkie," *The Jazz Singer*, starred Al Jolson, who was the son of the cantor at an Orthodox synagogue in Washington, D.C. And it is hard to imagine what American satire might look like today without the meteoric career of Lenny Bruce.

Some of the most serious composers of modern American music—George and Ira Gershwin, Aaron Copland, and Leonard Bernstein, for example—were Jewish. Even rock and roll: what would modern music be like without Lou Adler's "wall of sound," without Jerry Wexler's having invented "rhythm and blues," without the genius of Brian Epstein, the British Jew who managed and guided the young Beatles? The first American film sex goddess, too, the "Vamp of Savannah" herself, Theda Bara, was Jewish, and so was perhaps the very first genuine American media celebrity—Adah Isaacs Menken, who in 1863 created the scantily clad title character in a play called *Mazeppa* and along with it a scandalous reputation that she cultivated for the rest of her life.

In a way, Menken, who was a convert to Judaism, invented modern celebrity in the sense that she deliberately effaced the distinction between her onstage and offstage personalities. As the poet and critic David Kirby put it, she was perhaps "the first to realize that she not only had to perform roles on a stage but also perform herself offstage and in print, much as Madonna does today."[3]

Plus ça change, as they say: everyone from Harry Houdini (Erich Weisz, a Hungarian Jewish immigrant) and Tiny Tim to Peewee Herman, Madonna, and Courtney Love has followed Menken in the deliberate blurring of stage and real life. One of the things that has changed, however, is that as twentieth-century show biz developed in the United States, many Jews used to change their names to fit in better with the American mainstream; many fewer do so today. Before World War II most Jews who adopted "show" names did not do so to hide their Jewish origins. Most were not ashamed of being Jews, and few seem to have been particularly worried about being targets of bigotry; like many non-Jews who also took stage names, they merely thought it would be better for their careers, and it enabled them to project an offstage aura that accentuated their popularity. But since few Jewish Hollywood celebrities have been religiously observant, the changing of names often had the effect of masking their Jewish origins to the celebrity-attentive American public.

Among the famous actors and actresses of Hollywood's golden era, and a little beyond, that the typical American moviegoer would not have recognized as having Jewish roots are (and this is by no means an exhaustive list): Douglas Ullman (Douglas Fairbanks), Emanuel Goldenberg (Edward G. Robinson), László Löwenstein (Peter Lorre), Catherine Conn (Kitty Carlisle), Issur Danielovitch

Demsky (Kirk Douglas), Betty Joan Perske (Lauren Bacall), Arthur Leonard Rosenberg (Tony Randall), Bernard Schwartz (Tony Curtis), Harold Lipschitz (Hal Linden), Eugene Maurice Orowitz (Michael Landon), Samille Diane Friesen (Dyan Cannon), Barbara Lynn Herzstein (Barbara Hershey), Joyce Frankenberg (Jane Seymour), Karen Zeigler (Karen Black), Winona Horowitz (Winona Ryder), and—well, you get the point. For those with somewhat earthier tastes in film, know that Harry Reems, Ron Jeremy, Jamie Gillis, and Nina Hartley are also Jewish.

Jewish entertainers have thrived not only in America. Take Simone Kaminker and Ivo Livi, for example—that's Simone Signoret and Yves Montand. But nowhere have Jews dominated entertainment culture as they have in the United States. It would be easy to list Jewish Hollywood directors, producers, agents, and writers by the score; magicians and songwriters, too; and above all, comedians. Here are some random, easy-to-recognize names that don't sound Jewish but, in fact, belong to Jews: Victor Borge, Arthur Murray, Rodney Dangerfield, Paula Abdul, Billy Joel, Carole King, Neil Sedaka, Peter Yarrow, Phil Spector, David Copperfield, and Geraldo Rivera. The comic-book industry pantheon is mostly Jewish, too.

There is little point in mentioning entertainers who everyone knows were or are Jewish—from the Marx Brothers and the Three Stooges to Paul Newman and Bob Dylan, from Henny Youngman, Milton Berle, George Burns, Mel Brooks, and Woody Allen to Gene Wilder and Billy Crystal—except to ask the following question: when we add up all these people, and hundreds more not mentioned, we have to wonder just how dull this country might have been during the last century without the Jews.

So much for some illustrative facts (and a little boasting): but *why* has the American entertainment business been so dominated by Jews? Part of the answer is that show business was one of the limited number of avenues of upward mobility, aside from the retail trade, that children of immigrants could excel in without a professional education. Not that first-generation American Jews did not occasionally distinguish themselves as scholars, scientists, medical doctors, and so forth, but most American Jews of the late nineteenth and early twentieth centuries did not have educational opportunities of that sort. And, as was not almost uniformly the case among upper-class WASPs, there was little stigma attached to show business among the Jews.

It is not just Jews, of course, who have followed this pattern in the history of American culture. All groups that started on the outside of the mainstream—blacks, Italians, Irish, and others—have contributed in major ways to American culture generally, and to American entertainment culture in particular. The overriding point here is that social marginality often enough generates energy, encourages unconventional perspectives, and focuses ambition. It also produces anxiety, and angst, widely and probably correctly said to produce art, is a Jewish speciality. Pierre Paul Leroy-Beaulieu (1843–1916), the French Catholic economist and philosopher, put it best over a century ago: "The Jew is the most nervous and, in so far, the most modern of men."[4]

Indeed, Jews in the Diaspora have become connoisseurs of angst. Religious Jews tend to pour their nervous energy into prayer, study, and career; nonreligious Jews pour it into their intellectual and artistic passions. In America, historically a prosperous, secure, and self-confident nation, the Anglo-Saxon and northern European peoples of the land have been, again by historical standards, stolid and calm. The contrast between them and the Jews could hardly be more vivid. As wealth and technology have created the potential for a mass-based and varied entertainment culture, Jewish creative energies have helped turn that potential into reality.

On top of all this, America is perhaps the most change-friendly society in history. When it comes to the arts, Americans have inclined to be innovators who scoff at boundaries, letting happenstance, new technology, and, above all, intermingling subcultures define what is popular and marketable. We let the market drive cultural change like no other nation ever has, for better and for worse. That rewards those who can adapt, innovate, and just keep moving. Jews in the Diaspora have had to be adaptable and quick on their feet to survive. Put into the modern American entertainment culture environment, intergenerational rootednesss has driven the Jews to thrive as they have in all relatively open cultures.

Americans also admire success. That is to some extent what the American Dream is all about, and Jews succeed: as Benjamin Disraeli once said, Jews "can do everything except fail." So it is no surprise that over time Americans would come to admire Jewish talent and creativity in the entertainment arts. What Hollywood and American music culture do, in turn, is to amplify and encourage that admiration. Thanks to generations of Jewish comedians, Jewish tonalities of speech and even some Yiddish expressions have made their way into mainstream American culture. Most Jewish Americans don't realize when they say "knock on wood" or when they cross their fingers for luck that these are references to the crucifix and hence not at all Jewish, but most non-Jewish American have no idea that when they use words like *nosh*, *kibitz*, *schmooze*, and *nudnik*, they are speaking Yiddish.

A perfect if utterly inconsequential illustration may be found in Stephan Pastis's popular comic strip "Pearls Before Swine." The February 24, 2009, three-box strip, without the drawings of course, goes like this:

> Rat: "Oy vey! Sorry to kvetch but this meshuginah's chutzpah has me pretty farklempt."
> Goat: "Why are you speaking Yiddish, rat?"
> Rat: "Because it's *the* language for ripping on the idiots of the world."
> Goat: "Yeah, well, I don't think I'd ever learn a language just so I could rip people."
> Rat: "Tough talk for a shabbes klopper schmendrick nudnick."

Whether you think this is funny or not isn't the point. The point is that most of the non-Jews who read this column probably understood most of these words well enough to get the gist, something that would not have been the case forty years ago. (The cartoonist himself isn't even Jewish!) Yet this is so despite the fact that these days almost no American Jews speak Yiddish and very few can read or understand full sentences when it is spoken. Somehow, through the American entertainment culture, Jews have managed, without actually meaning to do so, to inject into American English words from a language their own progeny doesn't know.

Does this mean that Jews have made America Jewish more than America has made and is making Jews American? No. As suggested above, America is making Jews very American: it is their "other" religion, and one that usually takes practical precedence over Judaism. On the other hand, it *is* striking, one has to admit, that the cultural influence of Jews and Jewishness is what it is, considering that fewer than 5 million American Jews are influencing more than 296 million other Americans. The most likely reason for the outsized Jewish presence in American entertainment culture is that the Jews live within a civilization that has itself recently become entertainment- and celebrity-crazy. If Americans were less obsessed with amusing themselves, this would not be the case; but Americans are thus obsessed.

There are negative as well as positive implications of Jewish pre-eminence in American entertainment culture, and one of the former has to do with the image of frivolity and even dissipation increasingly associated with America's closely related celebrity culture. Cultures that focus on entertainment and gratification instead of edification, productivity, or salvation are not unknown in history. Many a royal court in olden days, European, Middle Eastern, and Asian alike, succumbed to the softness and frivolity abetted by affluence. One of the reasons that frivolity and entertainment overwhelmed some political systems is that, as already noted, rich people did not have much to spend their fortunes on before the modern era of production and trade, so they "bought" people to serve and amuse them instead. We trivialize the notion of the court jester nowadays, but jesters and dancers and musicians and artisans were often of enormous importance in the royal cultures of ages past. It was sometimes a rather dangerous profession, as the tale of Scheherazade in *The Arabian Nights* suggests. When monarchs neglected their obligations to govern in order to pursue their desire to be amused, the wrath of those harmed by such irresponsibility sometimes fell upon the entertainers. Sometimes, too, shrewd governments used entertainment to lull the masses into a sense of apathy about their circumstances. This is what the phrase "bread and circuses" from imperial Roman times is all about: give the multitudes cheap food and relatively harmless diversions and you can do whatever you like with the power of the realm.

Does any of this apply to America today? That's a matter of opinion, of course: mine is that it does. Americans spend a staggering amount of money each year on entertainment; it came to about $725 billion in 2007, according to the Department of Labor's Bureau of Labor Statistics. That's roughly eighteen times as much as all the wealthy countries of the world put together spend on official development assistance in a given year. If we add the $40 billion Americans spend each year on their pets, then this number starts to look, as the late senator from Illinois, Everett Dirksen, once said, "like real money." The questions are these: Do Americans do this *at the expense of* maintaining a decent society and an honest, democratic politics; and do many (most?) politicians and corporate bigwigs conspire to market mass entertainment in part for that reason? The answer to the first question, it seems to me, is yes; to the second, maybe. Either way, the Harvard political scientist Robert Putnam is hard to refute when he asserts that we are increasingly "bowling alone" in this country, that the robust civic participation that has usually characterized American

society and democracy is in decline—even despite the eclectic energies
that went into the 2008 Obama presidential campaign. And television
and the aura of celebrity culture that it and the Internet deliver are
certainly among the main reasons for it.[5]

This bears on Jewcentricity in an obvious way: To the extent that
left-wing and right-wing critiques of American society flow into one
another in attacking what American popular culture has become—and
increasingly they do—there are Jews at every turn, in marketing, in
media, and, of course, in the entertainment business itself. Critiques
launched from the left, including by Jews writing in the adversarial
culture's Marxist-influenced tradition, often focus on business media
concentration, alleging that big business, through the enormous
power of advertising dollars, has deliberately turned what used to be
actual news into pasty, hollow entertainment. Others, not least the
late George Gerbner of the University of Pennsylvania's Annenberg
School of Communication, have argued that what he documented
as television's "mean world syndrome" is deliberately manufactured
to make it easier for politicians and plutocrats to control society for
their own security and profit. Scare people, in other words, and they
become easier to manipulate.

Critiques from the right are also varied. Some are Burkean in
character, arguing that the "creative destruction" fueled by American
capitalism has become so rapid and intense as to undermine the sin-
ews of community and family that are the bases for a good society. A
major theme in American conservative social thought for more than
half a century has been critical of the libertarian worship of markets.
This tendency has recently given birth to what is known as the
crunchy con: the community-minded, tradition- and religion-friendly,
granola-crunching, small-carbon-footprint conservative.[6] These are
conservatives, some urban but largely small-town and rural, who do
not like what the Wal-Marting of America has done to the stability of
rural and small-town life in the United States.

Many of the same people do not appreciate, either, the increasingly
salacious content of mass media or the apparent elevation of antipa-
triotic sentiment and homosexual lifestyles above more traditional
values. Hollywood has become very much a target of such critiques,
and an increasing number of Americans are ignoring Hollywood fare.
Some are homeschooling their children for similar reasons. Some are
even forming extended family communes—abetting a kind of retribal-
ization of Western society. They are doing a retake of Timothy Leary's
old advice to "tune in and drop out," only "tune in" is not an appeal to

LSD, speed, and morning glory seeds, but to God, community, and family. Some crunchy cons are even rereading Samuel Smiles, the nineteenth-century British Victorian moralist who preached on behalf of honesty, hard work, and, above all, self-sufficiency.

So cultural critiques of American mass consumerism are proliferating by type and in volume, but do any of the critics explicitly blame the Jews for what they loathe about contemporary America? Yes, some do; but among the most prominent critics are Jews themselves. There is, for example, no more vociferous critic of Hollywood than Michael Medved, who has accused its elite of wallowing in an orgy of postmodern nihilism and moral vagrancy. There is no more splenetic critic than David Mamet, who contends that, as the novelist and critic Walter Kirn has paraphrased him, "Hollywood movies are profoundly, genetically Judaic; the product, via the minds of their creators, of certain distinctive racial traits that arose in the ghettoes of Eastern Europe and transported themselves to Beverly Hills."[7] Kirn summarizes Mamet's view that two of these traits, indifference to wider social norms and high intelligence, combine with a form of autism known as Asperger's syndrome, which, in Mamet's words, "has its highest prevalence among Ashkenazi Jews and their descendants." This combination, writes Mamet, "sounds to me like a job description for a movie director."[8]

Despite Jewish criticisms of Hollywood, or maybe in a way because of them, at least some non-Jews have indeed singled out Jews as the source of Hollywood's supposed undermining of American morals. Some already disposed to anti-Semitic attitudes have made a big deal about Hollywood Jews hollowing out the moral fiber of America, an argument that is spread all over the Internet.

Visit the *Jewish Tribal Review*, for example, and you will see full-blown, classic anti-Semitism at work—essays by James Jaeger ("Hollywood's True Agenda: Mel Gibson and the Culture War") and by Mark Green and Wendy Campbell ("Hollywood Advances 'Soft Assault' on Christian Imagery"). The site's founder and operator, whose name is impossible to find on the site for reasons easy to guess, is the author of what he describes as a book in progress called *When Victims Rule: A Critique of Jewish Pre-eminence in America*. It includes chapters on Jews in the entertainment business and the arts, as well as the media, fashion, sports, pop music, and so on. They are not flattering. Special attention is given to sexual immorality and crime, in which the author claims Jews are especially skillful entrepreneurs. The author knows, for example, that some famous pre–World War II brothels in

New York City and elsewhere were run by Jews. He knows that Diane Silberstein is the president and publisher of *Penthouse* magazine. Not mentioned, of course, are all the brothels and porn entrepreneurs who have not been Jewish, by far the vast majority. One can easily imagine what he made of the fact that the brains behind the Executive Club VIP prostitution ring that led to the fall of New York governor Eliot Spitzer was a sixty-two-year-old man named Mark Brener, who had $600,000 cash and an Israeli passport in his home at the time of his arrest in March 2008.

By contrast, there is the popular site *Jew Watch*, run by Frank Weltner of the National Alliance, which also identifies Hollywood "trash" as a Jewish conspiracy to undermine Christian American morals. This is a typical semiliterate neo-Nazi site, and one of the ways to tell is that the material is not only less sophisticated and full of factual errors, but it is strongly antiblack as well. Africans are referred to as "the abominations of Noah."

In a country as large and diverse as the United States, and with the Internet being what it is, it is inevitable that material like this will end up on the Web. Just about everything else is on the Web, too, after all. That includes the venting of arch–cultural conservatives who belie no anti-Semitic past, but who sometimes now blame Jews for the moral insolvency that they believe, not without some justification, ultimately underlies the current financial insolvency. One observer pinpoints the beginning of America's descent into the slime pits of Babylon to December 1953, the date when the first issue of *Playboy* magazine was released, and insinuates that *Playboy*'s creator, Hugh Hefner, is or was a Jew. (Hefner was raised in a strict Methodist home, as it happens.)

Some others see the democratization of American licentiousness in the development of the birth control pill, and again blame Jews for this. There is at least some superficial support for this claim. The two scientists who did the key pioneering work involved were both Jewish—Carl Djerassi and Frank Colton. Of the team that took the science and actually produced the pill, one was a Jew (Gregory Pincus), one was Chinese (Min-Cheuh Chang), and one was an observant Roman Catholic (John Rock). But of course, even the Jews involved in this didn't do what they did because they were Jewish, and, certainly, none of those involved thought they were conspiring against Christian America.

Has any of this marginal thinking and material found its way closer to the mainstream? There is so far little evidence that it has.

There is the phenomenon of Patrick Buchanan and especially Joseph Sobran, former affiliates of William F. Buckley's *National Review*, who have drifted over the years toward extreme views of Zionism and Jews. They buy into the "slouching toward Gomorrah" argument, to paraphrase a book title of Robert Bork. But the only noteworthy attack on Hollywood in mainstream print that suggests even implicitly that Jews have defiled American culture, to the point where it has contributed to al-Qaeda and affiliated groups' loathing of the United States, is Dinesh D'Souza's 2006 book *The Enemy at Home: The Cultural Left and Its Responsibility for 9/11*.

D'Souza, who was born in India and is in no way anti-Semitic, argues that organizations like the American Civil Liberties Union, the National Organization for Women, People for the American Way, Planned Parenthood, Human Rights Watch, and Moveon. org have encouraged the rise of an atheistic, salacious, and immoral society that is a main reason "why they hate us." It does not take a rocket scientist to connect the dots: liberals are responsible for the dangerous debauching of our society, not least through vapid entertainment-culture garbage, and a disproportionate number of liberals who are doing precisely that are Jews. D'Souza provides a bridge from the author of *When Victims Rule* to at least the conservative mainstream if not beyond it, although that is certainly not his intention.

It would be nice to be able to dismiss D'Souza and others who think as he does; the problem is, he is in the main correct. Salafi Muslims, meaning those Muslims who take a radical, literalist, and historically nontraditional view of Islam, are repulsed by American sexual exhibitionism, promiscuity, what they see as the abuse of women, toleration for homosexuality, and out-of-wedlock sex and procreation. They believe these behaviors are, strictly speaking, evil. That does not make them hate us exactly; rather, it fills them with disgust. But disgust is a far more powerful motive for their occasionally violent behavior than the claim that Salafis "hate" freedom or democracy or free speech, as many, including former president George W. Bush, have alleged. For the most part, these are concepts that do not register with them much at all for reasons having to do with their distinctive history and culture; they are but minor and derivative themes compared to less abstract codes of social conduct.

It bears note, too, that *we* are ones whose sexual mores have changed in recent decades. Half a century ago most Americans agreed with present-day, standard Islamic attitudes toward these subjects. Many Americans still do, religious Christians and religious Jews among them. The result of the shift in Western mores and their active export to Muslim-majority societies through Western, and especially American, entertainment culture and tourism has been to drive Muslim asceticism to further extremes. Western and American exhibitionism and Muslim asceticism have been feeding on each other in a negative spiral for years now, each pole pushing away the other. This is not good.

None of this is the fault of "the Jews" as such, to be sure. Hollywood's Jewish movers and shakers are with few exceptions not religious people, either in practice or in education.[9] They certainly do not invoke religious rationalizations to justify what they do—rather the contrary. Still, many practicing Jews would be more comfortable if Howard Stern, Andrew Dice Clay, Sarah Silverman, Steven Hirsch, Al Goldstein of *Screw* magazine "fame," and Sasha "Borat" Baron Cohen had been born as, say, Presbyterians. Thank God, anyway, for the late George Carlin, a potty-mouthed lapsed Irish Catholic genius if there ever was one.

America's celebrity culture has become so Jewish that it has managed to become Jewcentric without involving Jews or Judaism. Take the case of Madonna.

Born Madonna Louise Ciccone in August 1958, she was raised in a lower-middle-class Catholic family in a Detroit suburb. Her artistic energies may have come from a seminal tragedy, as Madonna herself has suggested: the loss of her mother to breast cancer when she was five and a half years old. Leaving the University of Michigan in her sophomore year in1977, she came to New York to be a dancer. She was nineteen years old and had thirty-five dollars in her pocket; her trip to New York marked the first time she had even flown in an airplane. She burst on the American entertainment scene in 1982, and nothing has been quite the same since.

You would have to have been living in a cave or in the forests of Borneo for the past two decades not to know what I am now about to reveal: Madonna's success has depended not only on her considerable native talent for song and dance, but on a highly sexualized presentation of self, admixed with a host of seemingly random social themes that, one supposes, somehow made it acceptable. She scandalized deliberately with her lyrics, her gestures, and especially her clothing, which at one point featured breast adornments that looked like rocket nose cones. She appeared nude in movies, regularly used foul language, took off her underwear once on the David Letterman show, and frequently used the symbols of Catholicism as a kind of postmodern piñata. She often wore prominently a cross around her neck, and several of her song lyrics made explicit, but not particularly warm and fuzzy, references to her Italian Catholic origins. She was, in essence, vulgar, profane, and deliberately irreverent. Her audience loved it, for she gave them permission, in essence, to be the same. This proved once again the famous remark attributed to P. T. Barnum, that "nobody ever went broke underestimating the taste of the American public."

But not even Barnum could have predicted the profit margins of this particular form of tastelessness. Madonna's styles became very popular with young American girls, who started imitating her lacy tops, bleached blond hair, short skirts, and extreme-bosom look. Thanks to the Christian symbols she used in the stage decor for her videos, the pope was not amused. He suggested that good Catholics boycott her shows and her wares. Her shows were also protested by Orthodox Jews in Israel and even by Protestants in Germany—and it really takes something special to get them upset these days. Madonna loved the controversy and stoked it skillfully. Why not? It helped make her rich and famous; in fact, she is the most financially successful female song artist and actress of the twentieth century, to the tune of at least $325 million.

Alas, those who sell sexuality need to worry about what the inevitable depredations of aging might do to their appeal. Madonna has real musical and acting talent, so sex is not all she has been selling, but getting older and eventually becoming the mother of three children seemed to change her sense of what was important in life. Her political activism became more important to her, and social issues began to actually engage her time, instead of remaining mere offhand symbols in her acts. Nothing about her upbringing, her education, or her lifestyle into her forties suggested that there was anything like a deep thinker in there behind the lace and the rocket nose cones. So what's a girl to do when life starts becoming serious, and you've made your name and fame by insulting every traditional religious person on the planet? A girl—this girl, anyway—turns to Judaism.

Sometime in the late 1990s, signaled by her *Ray of Light* album, Madonna joined the Kabbalah Centre of Rabbi Philip Berg (born Feivel Gruberger) in Hollywood. She has been associated with the "kabbalah" movement ever since and has spent in excess of a half dozen years studying what Rabbi Berg tells her is "kabbalah." She takes it as seriously as she seems to be capable of taking anything outside of career and money, and thanks to her involvement in "kabbalah" millions of her fans have come to see what they think is Judaism as something cool. What is so weird about this is that, aside from Philip Berg and a tiny handful of others, *no Jews are involved in any of this.* This is an image transmission about Judaism mainly from famous celebrity non-Jews to not-famous ordinary non-Jews.

Madonna has influenced other celebrities to come along with her: Britney Spears, Demi Moore, Roseanne Barr (a rare example of someone born Jewish), Lindsay Lohan, David and Victoria Beckham, Ivana Trump, Naomi Campbell, and—*can it possibly be?*—Mick Jagger. She has invested large sums in an orphanage in Malawi and has charged its operators to teach the children "kabbalah."[10] She proudly proclaims her adopted Hebrew name to be Esther, and in 2007, during a Jewish New Year visit to Israel, she declared herself "an ambassador for Judaism." On that occasion she presented Israel's president and former prime minister Shimon Peres with a copy of the *Zohar*, reportedly inscribed: "To Shimon Peres, the man I admire and love, Madonna."[11] Wow, Shimon.

I have thus far put "kabbalah" in scare quotes for a reason: there is such a thing as kabbalah. It is the generic name for Jewish mysticism, based in large part around the *Zohar*, the *Book of Splendor.* For Orthodox or traditional Jews, kabbalah—and the esoteric philosophical-mystical text of the *Zohar*—is difficult and even potentially dangerous knowledge. Traditionally, no one was allowed even to study kabbalah until after having mastered the Bible, the entire Talmud, and the Midrash. So powerful and intoxicating was the kabbalah thought to be that only married men of even temperament were allowed to partake of it, lest it unhinge the student and drive him insane.

Not only was kabbalah for just the best of the serious and most emotionally mature students, there were no shortcuts to it either. It was hard, and there was no early or obvious personal reward for studying it. The study of kabbalah was not about or mainly for the student; it was about God and creation. The purpose of study was to attain knowledge and enlightenment; the point was intellectual and spiritual, as in any serious form of mysticism. If dime-store therapy has an opposite, genuine kabbalah is it.

It is not difficult to explain the essence of kabbalistic beliefs about God and creation, for anything truly profound is also simple in its own way. But I'll not do so here, because Madonna's "kabbalah" is to real Jewish mysticism what Thunderbird is to real wine. It's McMysticism—an outsized, distorted knockoff, a fake and worse, as any educated Jew who reads the Web page of Philip Berg's Kabbalah Centre can readily see.

Rabbi Berg presents "kabbalah" as esoteric knowledge separate from Judaism, rather than as an outgrowth or expression of it. In the Web site's question-and-answer section, the viewer learns that it is not necessary to be Jewish to study and follow kabbalah, which appears to make Madonna an "ambassador for Judaism" who is herself not an actual convert to Judaism. Berg's son Yehuda told Daphne Merkin of the *New York Times Magazine*, apparently in a moment of unguarded candor, that the center downplays the Jewish aspect of kabbalah, because it might alienate the clientele.[12]

It is indeed a strange mix that Berg and his family have come up with: Seating in the center for prayer services is segregated by sexes; adepts are enjoined to keep kosher; the weekly Torah portion is read from a *bima* (platform) on the Sabbath, yet no claim is made that any of this is Jewish! *Mitzvoth* (commandments) are not called *mitzvoth*, but "tools." What goes on in the center is never referred to as "religion," and in all discussions of the matter religion is always put in quotation marks to separate "kabbalah" from it—as if, as Merkin put it, religion "were another of those tossed-out, old-hat ideas, like fidelity." This is why we can be told with an apparent straight face that Sir Isaac Newton was an adept, for example. So was Giovanni Pico della Mirandola, the remarkable man who wrote the *Oration on the Dignity of Man*, which helped kick off the Italian Renaissance. This is a bizarre half-truth, like much of what the Kabbalah Centre proffers. Pico believed the *Zohar* predicted Christianity, and so he had the remarkable Jewish scholar Abba Hillel Delmedigo teach him Hebrew so that he could read it in the original. This, however, did not make Pico a master of kabbalah, for he came at it with a preconceived purpose at odds with its teachings.

So has Rabbi Philip Berg. Berg claims inspiration from genuine kabbalists like Rabbi Yehuda Ashlag, and this claim seems partly true. But to see how, we must know a little something about Yehuda Ashlag.

Rabbi Ashlag was a rather unorthodox Orthodox Jew. Born in Poland in 1885, he founded the Kabbalah Center in Israel in 1922. While others, like Rabbi Avraham Yitzhak Kook, were busy fusing Orthodoxy with nationalism, Ashlag tried to fuse his understanding of Orthodoxy with communism. There are stories of Ashlag's audiences with David Ben-Gurion that left Ben-Gurion complaining: "I wanted to talk about kabbalah, but the rabbi wanted to talk about socialism."

As it happened, one of Ashlag's students was a man named Yehuda Tzvi Brandwein, and Berg claims to have been a student of Brandwein's. But while Ashlag was influenced—or addled, depending on how one sees it—by the incandescent idealist currents of his day, Berg seems to have been affected instead by some elements of either New Age or standard hippie culture. His version of kabbalah bears little resemblance to Ashlag's, only two generations removed from that original, which was itself a departure from tradition. Berg claims that there is greatness inside everyone, and that only by subduing one's ego can one find this greatness. Berg's kabbalah is dime-store personal therapy, and an illogical one at that: one seeks greatness by extirpating the ego? Sounds interesting, er . . . but doesn't the very act of seeking personal greatness make that difficult?

In any event, the advertised motivation for Berg's "kabbalah" is not primarily to seek knowledge about God and creation, it's about helping the student. What does "losing" one's ego and aura of negativity mean to someone like Madonna? One can only speculate, but if I had done more to popularize vulgarity than any other woman in the twentieth century, I might want to slim down my ego and expel my negativity, too. And if all I have to do to accomplish this is tie a red ribbon around my wrist—a negative color, by the way, in real kabbalah—learn about the eighty-two names of God, drink expensive designer water, and buy costly books I don't understand, well, that's a super deal if one happens to have millions of uncommitted dollars on hand.

It seems that Madonna has another interest in "kabbalah," however: immortality. Merkin learned this when she interviewed Madonna for a woman's magazine. Madonna knew that Merkin had been raised as an Orthodox Jew, so she asked her if she believed in death. Wrote Merkin: "I answered somewhat bleakly that I did. When I turned the question back on her, she announced that she didn't because she believed in the concept of reincarnation as taught by the Kabbalah Centre."

Madonna was referring to the authentic, if exotic, kabbalistic concept of *gilgul neshamoth*, or the recirculation of souls. So Merkin asked Madonna why she didn't stick with Catholicism, since the idea of life after death is more prominent in Catholicism than in Judaism. Madonna's answer: "There's nothing consoling about being Catholic. There're all just laws and prohibitions." Merkin, who went to yeshiva as a child and understands full well what "laws and prohibitions" are *really* about, doesn't record her response to this astonishing remark because, doubtless, she was completely nonplussed.[13]

Perhaps the Kabbalah Centre has actually helped Madonna and others. Fine: lots of people think that mixing and matching aspects of different religions is amusing and harmless—hence the increasing acceptance of the Jew-Buh (the Jew who thinks he is a Buddhist) and the local (Washington, D.C.) joke that the private, elite Sidwell Friends School is a place where Episcopalians teach Jews how to act like Quakers. But Rabbi Berg's Kabbalah Centre has got nothing to do with genuine kabbalah, and the organization is anything but harmless. There are now fifty "kabbalah" centers worldwide, five in Israel, and there are far too many stories about the rip-off cults some of these centers have become for none of them to be true.[14] Some of these centers look to be a combination of kooky Scientology-like nonsense—teaching courses in "antimatter" and palm reading—and the social cohesion of the Moonies in the way they combine rank superstition with ego escapism. This is not Judaism, and it is certainly *not* harmless.

It could get far worse, too. It would be really very bad if large numbers of innocent but uneducated people around the world came to think that this cynical rogue operation was an authentic expression of Judaism. And that, unfortunately, is not so far-fetched. Imagine some impressionable seventeen-year-old in Detroit, or Malawi, hearing a rabbi say that the Berg Kabbalah Centre is a manipulative, money-making cult that has nothing to do with Judaism, and Madonna contradicting that claim and saying otherwise. Indeed, she already has, as has her former husband Guy Ritchie, who explained that the only difference between "kabbalah" and Catholicism "is the amount of people. You don't call Catholicism a cult." To this Rabbi Berg added, "Eventually, when there's enough people doing kabbalah, it won't even be an issue."[15]

So who is that seventeen-year-old going to believe? An international rock star who has cultivated an aura of social consciousness and given millions of dollars to charity, or some bearded schnook she's never heard of? When Britney Spears gets a Hebrew tattoo on her neck and claims that's cool and part of kabbalah, but some unknown educated Jew points out on a talk show that tattoos are forbidden by Jewish law, who is she going to believe? The "kabbalah" phenomenon exists separate from Hollywood, to be sure, but it is Hollywood and American celebrity culture generally that has vaulted it into the limelight and given it the potential to do such harm. That is why it is probably not such a great idea for people like Shimon Peres to appear in public with Madonna when she comes to Israel, as she did in 2004 and again in 2007. Peres may not realize how weird Madonna's version of kabbalah is, but neither he nor any other Israeli official has any business stamping a *heksher*—a seal of kosher approval—on it.

Thanks to the Internet, we live in a time when demagoguery, bigotry, fads, and foolishness of all kinds can carom around the planet at nearly the speed of light. There are no filters and few controls, enabling Jewcentricity to be expressed, magnified, and mixed within and across national borders as never before. Philip Berg does not (yet) qualify as a madman leading multitudes to perdition, as did the false messiah Shabbtai Tzvi of the seventeenth century. But stranger things have happened. Berg may be a precursor of who knows how many charlatans in the future who may try to take Judaism for a ride on a Jewcentric merry-go-round for fun and profit. It is even possible that in the fullness of time, forms of fake Judaism will take hold in the United States, and perhaps Israel too, that respond to a growing need for spiritual guidance in a psychically unstuck time, but that bear no resemblance to actual Judaism. With the sharp decline in Jewish education and the decline of Jewish historical memory and understanding, Judaism could face the challenge of mindless and destructive heresies as never before. That would not be either trivial or harmless. Just imagine what Shabbtai Tzvi could have done with the Internet.

8

Meet the JACs

Some folks never exaggerate—they just remember big.
—ATTRIBUTED TO CHI CHI RODRIGUEZ

There is a slightly odd and very Jewcentric flip side to prominent non-Jews' expressing respect for Jews and Judaism. It is watching mostly assimilated Jewish Americans bask in such adulation. Tell a typical assimilated, but still Jewishly conscious, Jewish American that Madonna and Britney Spears have come to kabbalah, and the likely reaction will be—assuming he or she has heard the term *kabbalah*—one of pride. They will be cast into virtual Jewtopia. Ah, so famous and wealthy non-Jews admire us! Well that they should, for we are special, we are smart—hey, we're "chosen." They say Jews are interesting; they're right. They say Jews are successful and witty; they're right. They say Jewish men make good husbands and sensitive lovers; oh, they are *so* right. This is Jewcentric chauvinism, and those Jews who exude it are JACs—Jewish American Chauvinists.

JACs typically express Jewcentricity of a mostly harmless sort, but it is too pervasive not to be occasionally irritating—and "mostly harmless" is not the same as entirely harmless. The irritation flows from a basic rule of thumb that, in my experience at least, defines this subset of Jewcentricity: All else equal, the less a given Jewish American knows about Judaism and Jewish history, and the less that Jew practices rabbinic Judaism, the more openly chauvinistic he or she is likely to be.

147

There is nothing exclusively Jewish about this, of course. Irish Americans celebrate Saint Patrick's Day in ways that would stun most real Irish—"real" defined as those Irish actually living in Ireland. The same goes for many other expatriate communities in America—Poles, Armenians, Italians, and so forth. But examples of Jewish American chauvinism truly abound, and I need look no further for examples than to my own extended family, including an otherwise delightful cousin for whom all Jewish holidays, about which she knows little, boil down to a simple one-size-fits-all formula: "They tried to kill us, we survived, let's eat." This cousin and others love to bombard my in-box with what I call adjewlations, electronic tokens, as it were, of Jewish American chauvinism. They also send jokes like nearly everyone else, but I often cannot readily distinguish between the two.

Let me give a few examples, broken down into the three essential categories of adjewlations: "Everybody is Jewish"; "Cool goyim are 'like this' with us"; and "Gosh, but we're smart." Toward the end of this chapter a more serious subject must be parsed, and the non-harmlessness of Jewish American chauvinism thus illustrated. But first, some sheer nonsense.

We have already traversed some of the "everybody is Jewish" category in reviewing entertainment industry celebrities. But that is not nearly good enough for true Jewish American chauvinists, who revel in pointing out remarkable Jewish jurists, inventors, scientists, sports figures and, for some, crooks. This is as easy as Louis Brandeis, Hedy Lamarr, Jonas Salk, Hank Greenberg, and Meyer Lansky. But easy doesn't suffice either, for true JACs can never get enough Jewtopic tonic. So there is a whole cottage industry of esoteric Jewish American history that is almost invariably self-celebratory in character.

Take, for example, Haym Solomon. Born in Poland, Solomon helped finance the American Revolution. He also happened to once talk himself out of Hessian captivity (in German, one of eight languages he spoke fluently) by professing opposition to the Revolutionary cause. I recently received an amazing JAC-mail from my lovable cousin Paula claiming that Solomon was responsible not only for saving Washington's army at Valley Forge—not an entirely insane claim—but also that the dollar bill bears symbols of Washington's orders to honor the Jews for their help. Here is the text:

During the cold winter of Valley Forge when American soldiers were freezing and running out of food, it was Haym who marshaled all the Jews in America and Europe to provide money in relief aid to these stranded American troops and turned the course of history. Without this help, our "Army" would have perished before they could have defeated the British.

If you take a one-dollar bill out of your pocket and look at the back at the Eagle, the stars above the Eagle's head are in the six point Star of David to honor Jews. If you turn the Eagle upside down you will see a configuration in the likeness of a Menorah . . . both at the insistence of George Washington who said we should never forget the Jewish people and what they have done in the interest of America.

Needless to say (I earnestly hope), this stuff about the design of the dollar bill is simply not true.

The outsized Jewish presence in the Old West is also a favorite topic among some JACs, especially those living west of the Mississippi. There were two Jewish mayors in Deadwood, South Dakota, in the 1880s, and a Jewish mayor in Tucson, Arizona, too. It's even true that Wyatt Earp's third and last wife, Josephine Sarah Marcus, was a Jew, and that the couple is buried in a Jewish cemetery. When Ashkenazi Jews got to the American Southwest from points east and north, they met Sephardic Jewish merchants in places like Albuquerque, New Mexico, who had come along after the Spanish more than a century earlier. So, as the JACs tell it, the Jews were everywhere in American history, even at the most remote spots, and were succeeding wildly there before other Americans even showed up. It's as though, in the JAC version of American history, a mere several thousand Moishe Pipiks won the West. This, folks, is a very substantial exaggeration; this is Jewcentricity.

It *is* true, of course, that Henry Morgenthau, Louis Brandeis, Felix Frankfurter, Benjamin Cardozo, and Bernard Baruch were prominent figures. Pre–World War II twentieth-century American political history is generously dotted with prominent Jews, with a variety of accounts and memoirs suggesting their considerable influence as, in effect, American *hofjuden*. The mere truth is not enough for JACs, however, who invariably stretch for more, as with the by now old presumption that Christopher Columbus himself was a Jew. That stretch has more recently come to implicate bona fide American Founders.

A few years ago the buzz among the JAC set was that Alexander Hamilton was a Jew. Alexander Hamilton is a genuine, first-class

Founder. Though he was never president, he was the first secretary of the treasury and coauthor of the Federalist Papers with James Madison, good enough to get him on several U.S. postage stamps over the years and, of course, the ten-dollar bill. The fact that he was money-wise and associated with the Treasury was, for a lot of Jewish American chauvinists, prima facie proof that he "had to be a Jew." This seemed to fit a pattern both European and Middle Eastern going back many, many centuries, after all. That fact that Hamilton did not claim he was Jewish and never acted as a Jew did not daunt them. What, exactly, is their case?

Hamilton was born, probably in 1755, on the Caribbean island of Nevis, which at the time was a fairly important commercial and shipping center among the British Empire's holdings in the Western Hemisphere. His father was James A. Hamilton, the son of a Scottish laird. His mother was Rachel Faucett Lavien, but Rachel was not James's legal wife, meaning that Alexander was born out of wedlock. Now, Rachel Faucett seems to have been of at least partial French Huguenot descent, but on the island of St. Croix she married a Danish Jew named Johann Michael Lavien, that name very likely a variant spelling of Levy or Levine. Possibly, Rachel converted to Judaism to marry Lavien, but there is no evidence of this. The marriage was unhappy in any event, and Rachel left St. Croix for St. Kitts, where she met James Hamilton. The couple then left St. Kitts for Nevis, where Rachel had been born and where she had inherited some property from her father. There Alexander and an elder brother were born.

Since James and Rachel were not legally married, the Episcopal establishment on Nevis denied young Alexander and his brother membership in the church, which meant they could not attend the church school. So at the appropriate time mother Rachel took Alexander to the Jewish school on the island, which was housed in the synagogue. The members of the Jewish community of Nevis had arrived in the mid-seventeenth century from other islands, mainly Jamaica, but they descended more remotely from Brazil, where some Jews had fled after the Inquisition and expulsion from Iberia in the late fifteenth century. In the synagogue school young Alexander Hamilton learned Hebrew as well as French. He also learned Bible and some Jewish history and philosophy as well as the usual fare of arithmetic, English grammar, and the like. From this he developed a lifelong respect for Jews and for Judaism, which we can see from the historical record of Hamilton's writings.

All of this is well documented by historians and is not contentious. But in 2007 along came Yitzchok Levine, a math professor at the Stevens Institute of Technology in Hoboken, New Jersey, who tied Hamilton's early years to the life of the Nevis Jewish community, which had been lost to history and rediscovered only in the 1950s.[1] Levine never claims that Hamilton was a Jew; he just lays out the facts of Hamilton's early life and those of the Nevis Jewish community side by side and lets others draw whatever conclusions they please, which, of course, the JACs did. Before long I was getting cousinly e-mails with attachments created by I-don't-know-who that were filled with factual errors and whimsical fill-ins—like the unsubstantiated claim that Rachel's father was Jewish, which is why she married a Jew in the first place and why she had property to inherit, and insisting that therefore Hamilton was a Jew.

It is fairly obvious from the factual context that, having been married to a Jew, mother Rachel was familiar with Jewish people and did not hesitate to bring Alexander to a Jewish schoolmaster. But we do not know that mother Rachel was a convert to Judaism, which would indeed make Hamilton Jewish according to halacha. We are certain, however, that Hamilton never thought of himself as a Jew, so what, after all, is the point of this claim? There is, of course, none—except to Jews who believe in the mystical powers not of Torah or kabbalah, but of "Jewish blood."

The JACs were not satisfied with claiming Hamilton, however. They had to claim as well one of Hamilton's political rivals, Thomas Jefferson.

Nicholas Wade reported in the February 28, 2007, *New York Times* on a study that suggested Jefferson might have had a Sephardic Jewish male ancestor. It seems that geneticists at the University of Leicester found in studying Jefferson's Y chromosome that it falls into the branch designated K2, which is quite rare among Europeans, and particularly among people in Wales, whence Jefferson's family came. K2 is found in a few men in Iberia, but it is far more common in the Middle East and northeastern Africa. Of the eighty-five British Jeffersons the study tested, only two had Y chromosomes of the K2 lineage. Since K2 is so common in the Middle East, and since the Jewish Diaspora is by far the most likely path by which that chromosome ended up in Britain, the researchers concluded that Jefferson probably had a male Middle Eastern ancestor, probably a Jewish one. Another researcher, at the University of Arizona, then compared Jefferson's Y chromosome to others in his database and found a perfect match to the Y chromosome of a Moroccan Jew. He found others, off by two mutations or markers, from a Kurdish Jew and a non-Jewish Egyptian.[2]

Now, what does this actually mean? Practically nothing, of course. Even supposing Jefferson had a male Jewish ancestor in, say, the fifteenth or sixteenth century, very little of that ancestor's genome would have come down to Jefferson, since each child inherits only about half of each parent's genes. Nothing on the female side suggests any Jewish genetic legacy. And Jefferson, of course, knew nothing of any of this. He never professed to being a Jew, or to having any Jewish heritage. JACs who muse with smiles on their faces about Jefferson being a Jew have too much time on their hands and too little properly focused gray matter in their heads.

It may also mean—and this is not so harmless—that despite century after century of rabbinic instruction based on the Book of Ruth (in which the key female forebear of King David and hence of the messiah, who the rabbis have concluded will arise out of the Davidic line, is a Midianite convert to Judaism), some JACs, including some misguided Orthodox ones, presume a "deep" racial definition of Jewishness. This is depressing. Indeed, for many Jews ignorant of rabbinic guidance, being Jewish is simply a matter of blood; not even someone as sagacious as Benjamin Disraeli avoided this snare, which was harder to do in the nineteenth century probably than in any other thanks to simplistic distortions of Darwin.[3] This is not a harmless error, because it is a form of Jewcentric philo-Semitism that feeds its opposite, Jewcentric anti-Semitism. It helps justify anti-Semites who argue that Zionism and Israel are racist because Jews define themselves by blood, when, as we have seen, the opposite is in fact the case: all other ancient civilizations *except* Israel defined themselves by blood, while Israel defined its peoplehood by creed. Again, go to Israel today and you will see Jews with blond hair and blue eyes, Jews who are black, and Jews of every shade in between. This doesn't happen among a people that defines its identity by blood.

Alas, claiming Hamilton and Jefferson is not even enough for some JACs. Abraham Lincoln, too, was Jewish, didn't you know?

This is not as new a claim as those about Hamilton and Jefferson, nor is it quite as fanciful. There is some circumstantial evidence to warm the imagination of the credulous JAC.

It is true, for example, that Lincoln was the only American president not to express a formal religious affiliation. He was not raised in any church, although his father was a Baptist, and he never belonged to any church, although he did regularly attend the New York Avenue Presbyterian Church in Washington during his presidency. When asked about his religious beliefs, as he often was, Lincoln's stock answer was to point to the twentieth chapter of Exodus—where the Ten Commandments are written—and recommend that the questioner study, learn, and follow those rules. Lincoln read and knew the Bible well, particularly the Psalms, Isaiah, and most of the New Testament. All this amounts merely to evidence that Lincoln was not a conventional Christian of that era. But neither was Jefferson a conventional Christian in his day, so it proves nothing about Lincoln's being Jewish. The "positive" evidence for the case comes from two other sources, one historical, one hearsay.

The town of Lincoln in eastern England, where Abraham Lincoln's ancestors came from, has a noteworthy Jewish history. A Jewish community dates from before 1150, and, as the accepted narrative goes (accepted does not mean accurate, but never mind), the sheriff of Lincoln protected the Jews from riots during the period of the Crusades. Saint Hugh, the bishop of Lincoln, was also a protector of the Jewish community, whose members flourished in the typical medieval trades. Apparently, an Aaron of Lincoln was a financier whose operations extended far and wide; Lincoln was host to one of the five wealthiest and largest Jewish populations of the period in England.

All this is historical fact, not in doubt. In the JAC e-mail I got summarizing this case, however, there appears a genuine howler. "Rabbi Joseph of Lincoln," it says, "was a scholar mentioned in the Talmud." Now that would really be something, for a post-twelfth-century scholar to be mentioned in a book whose contents were canonized several hundred years earlier—but again, never mind. As the tale is told, Lincoln's Jews were accused of ritual murder in 1255; ninety-one Jews were put on trial in London, and eighteen were executed. The entire community was expelled, along with all other English Jews, in 1290. Ah, but the JAC e-mails suggest that just like the secret Jews who remained in Spain after 1492, secret Jews remained in England, and in Lincoln, after 1290—"passing the secret from generation to generation." Clear presumption: Abe Lincoln knew and carried "the secret."

The hearsay that makes this speculation plausible in the eyes of many JACs is the testimony of Rabbi Isaac Mayer Wise. Rabbi Wise was the pioneer of Reform Judaism in the United States. He had met Lincoln on several occasions, including once as part of a special delegation that pleaded with the president to overturn General Ulysses S. Grant's banishing of Jews from a particular zone of Union occupation during the Civil War. When Lincoln was assassinated, Wise eulogized Lincoln, saying, in part, "Brethren, the lamented Abraham Lincoln believed himself to be bone from our bone and flesh of our flesh. He supposed himself to be a descendant of Hebrew parentage. He said so in my presence." On the basis of this eulogy, whole communities of American Jews sat shiva, as the communal mourning ritual is called, for Lincoln after he was killed on Good Friday, April 14, 1865.

Did Lincoln really believe this about himself, or was he just trying to butter up Rabbi Wise? Did he really even say it to Wise? Perhaps Wise heard wrong, or perhaps he made it up for oratorical effect. We'll probably never know the truth of the matter. But to many a JAC, the "fact" of Lincoln's Jewishness is irrefutable. One can only imagine who is next: Washington? FDR? John Kennedy? Barack Obama? I continue to watch my in-box with rapt attention.

Still, I am fairly sure that even the most creative JAC will never be able to match the imagination and zeal of the true lunatics of the racist and anti-Semitic American right wing. A right-wing account of Lincoln's Jewishness has been around since a few decades after the Civil War. According to it, as relayed by Alex Christopher in an essay called "Pandora's Box," Lincoln was the illegitimate child of a Jew named A. A. Springs (really Springstein, they say) and an unwilling mother named Mary Hanks, from Lincolnton, North Carolina. Lincoln is also alleged to have had an affair (and two illegitimate daughters) in the 1850s with some Hapsburg princess; when Mary Todd Lincoln's drug pusher, John Wilkes Booth, told her about this in 1865, the irate wife killed Lincoln in Ford's Theatre, and Booth took the fall. Hard to beat that for creativity, isn't it?

As for the "Cool goyim are 'like this' with us" category, this mostly has to do with personalities in the music and entertainment industry, and its attention often focuses on the close ties that Jews have had with blacks going way back to the days of vaudeville and the emergence of jazz. Al Jolson went blackface in *The Jazz Singer*. While blackface is considered an insulting gesture nowadays, that is not how it was necessarily understood at the time. Some Marx Brothers films included black actors, most spectacularly the musical number within the movie *A Day at the Races*. That scene can be criticized today as having displayed stereotypes by the bucket load, but in the Hollywood of 1937 the depiction of blacks as having sophisticated personalities and surpassing talent was very rare.

Probably the most vivid and artistically impressive example of Jewish-black musical synthesis is George and Ira Gershwin's *Porgy and Bess*. Staged in 1935 with an all-black cast, it was, to put it mildly, a daring thing to do at the time, even in New York City. Todd Duncan and Anne Brown in the lead roles were so spectacular that even racists had to admit their talent, but by and large the reception was cold. The show was a financial flop. Many thought that bringing Negroes onto the New York stage was an abomination, particularly since the story depicted Negro characters with sympathy and sophistication, and presented Negro musical traditions with operatic reverence. And many blamed "the Jews" for this.

Most Jews, on the other hand, were proud that Jews had been instrumental in what they saw as a cultural breakthrough. In his old age, after his two strokes, my father, who was born in 1905, used to tear up every time he heard a Gershwin tune from *Porgy and Bess*. (I used to tear up, too—with fright—every time Dad fixed to belt out "I Got Plenty of Nuttin'," because as a singer that's exactly what he had.)

Well below the artistic achievement exemplified by Gershwin and *Porgy and Bess*, it was a simple fact of pre–World War II American life that Jews and blacks were often thrown together, and this led to a plethora of stories about their interactions, some of them even true. Probably the favorite JAC story in this genre has to do with Louis Armstrong.

It was well known among Jews of my parents' generation that Satchmo had a strong connection to the Jews. He wore a Star of David around his neck for most of his adult life, leading some to wonder, or to think, that he was a convert to Judaism. That was not the case. What is the case is that in New Orleans, where Armstrong was born as an illegitimate child into acute poverty in 1901, he was fortunate enough to be taken under the wing of Joe Oliver, a cornet player and one of New Orleans' premier black musicians. But he was also aided, and encouraged to sing, by an immigrant Jewish family from Russia, the Karnofskys.

The Karnofskys had a junk business and often gave Louis odd jobs to earn money. Louis learned a little Yiddish, pretty much the same way that Colin Powell did working as a kid for the Sicksers' children's furniture store in the Bronx.[4] Since Armstrong's mother frequently left young Louis with her parents, who had little themselves, the Karnofskys often invited him to their own table, sometimes on the Jewish Sabbath, when religious hymns were sung during meals. This doesn't seem like a particularly big deal at first blush until one stops to understand, as Louis surely did, that black people eating at the table of white people was not exactly a common occurrence in New Orleans in those days. When Louis yearned to buy his first cornet, the Karnofskys ponied up the money, which Louis insisted be a loan. As Armstrong himself wrote: "They really wanted me to be something in life. . . . It was the Jewish family who instilled in me singing from the heart."[5]

All of this happens to be true, so it is not Jewcentric to say so. But from listening to the way some JACs tell it, you'd think *they* were playing the cornet and singing "What a Wonderful World." JACs loved it, too, when Nate Bloom reported in the *Jewish World Review* how Billy Crystal told of Armstrong once attending a Passover seder at the house of Crystal's uncle, the famous music producer Milt Gabler.[6] You'd think that were it not for the Karnofskys, Louis Armstrong never would have hit the big time. It's hard to imagine that talent like Armstrong's could be repressed or for long misdirected—unless you're a JAC.

Jewish American chauvinism with regard to blacks expresses itself in other ways, too. There is genuine pride in the role Jews played in the civil rights movement. American Jews of a certain generation know that Rabbi Abraham Joshua Heschel marched many times with Martin Luther King Jr., and they know that many Freedom Riders were Jews, including a few who gave their lives for the cause in Mississippi. Many Jews therefore feel a special bitterness at post–Black Power anti-Semitism, which need not be exaggerated to be noted.

This is not necessarily born from a sense of Jewish chauvinism, but it does suggest that many Jews have not understood black anger in officially post-segregation America, because they have been too quick to analogize the Jewish experience with the black one. "We" were slaves, so were they; "we" pulled ourselves up by our own bootstraps, so "why don't they stop making excuses and do the same?" is a common plaint. But it is a plaint that fails to appreciate that Jews had their families and traditions intact in Diaspora thanks to the genius of the ben-Zakkai system, while blacks who were sold into slavery, their families torn apart, and who were later freed without much notice and with few resources, financial or otherwise, generally did not. It is also a plaint that fails to appreciate that were it not for blacks being America's most prominent historical "other," American anti-Semitism might have been much worse. The "favors," as it were, have worked both ways.

In the "Gosh, aren't we smart?" category, Nobel Prize winning seems to be the most popular JAC e-mail topic as of late. I received one of these last year, via my wife, from an Israeli who is a longtime resident of the United States. Titled "Interesting Statistics About Muslims and Jews," it starts off matter-of-factly enough. It points out that since the Nobel Prizes were instituted, Jews from different countries have won a disproportionate share of them, particularly in medicine, chemistry, physics, and economics. The e-mail conveniently lists all Jewish Nobel laureates in every category. It points out, however, that the global Islamic population, some 20 percent of the world total, has won only one prize for literature, compared to ten for Jews; four for peace, compared to eight for Jews; none for economics, compared to thirteen for Jews; and two for medicine, compared to forty-two for Jews. The not very subtle basic message: Jews are smart, Muslims are not.

That is one way to explain the numbers, but it is hardly the right way. The natural sciences and medicine have advanced largely under the aegis of Western civilization, and that is where the Jews who have won these prizes have lived and worked. Muslims for the most part have not lived in that environment. This is not, however, how the e-mail explains the discrepancy. Rather, it informs the reader as follows: "The Jews are *not* promoting brain-washing the children in military training camps, teaching them how to blow up and cause maximum deaths of Christians and other non-Muslims! The Jews don't hijack planes, nor kill athletes at the Olympics or blow themselves up in German restaurants. There is not a single Jew that has destroyed a church. There is not a single Jew that protests by killing people . . . ," and it goes on, and on—hey, electrons are cheap. The conclusion? "Perhaps the world's Muslims should consider investing more in standard education and less in blaming the Jews for all their problems."

One can sympathize with the sentiment, but what it has to do with winning or not winning Nobel Prizes is not at all clear. Just as not all Jews end up winning Nobel Prizes, not all Muslims by a long shot aspire to raise their children to be terrorists or blame their problems on Jews. Whosoever can convince the JACs of this simple truth probably deserves a medal, if not a Nobel Prize.

• • •

A great many Jewish Americans, not least the most assimilated ones, really do believe that Jews possess superior intelligence, and that because of their superior intelligence they have proved to be superior achievers in so many fields. It is an easy leap for some JACs to conclude that Jews are superior by blood, particularly since, as we have mentioned, so many mistake Jewish peoplehood for a bloodline phenomenon in the first place.

This is not a straightforward matter by any means, however. Psychometric data suggest that, yes, Jews are of high general intelligence, and data of other sorts show disproportionately large Jewish professional and intellectual achievement, not just in the United States, but wherever Jews have been allowed to compete on a reasonably level playing field. But the actual reasons for this have never been entirely clear, and they still aren't. The only thing we know for sure is that the processes involved—genetic, cultural, and historical—interact in complex ways. The matter is anything but simple, and oversimplified accounts and exaggerations about Jewish intelligence are the basis for some of the most frustrating and dangerous types of Jewcentricity in existence.

So complex and elusive are the explanations for Jewish intelligence that whole books can be and have been written about it. Our aim here is not to solve the mystery once and for all, but simply to dispel some myths and outline the factors that must be taken into consideration to attain real understanding. Once we do, it will become clear how harmful Jewish chauvinism can be.

The beginning of wisdom in any discussion about Jewish intelligence is that there is more than one kind of intelligence, and that no kind of intelligence is the same as either knowledge or wisdom. Intelligent people can do very foolish things, after all, and not particularly intelligent people can act very wisely. The rabbis never praise intelligence as such; they do praise knowledge and wisdom because they have seen them not as ends in themselves, but as means to perfect a person's capacity to serve God.

All that said, there isn't much doubt that Jews, and among Jews particularly Ashkenazi Jews, are significantly more intelligent by conventional measures relative to almost all other groups. Longitudinal studies of intelligence testing show consistently that two groups end up in the highest percentiles: Jews and Japanese, with other Asian groups close behind. The same tests consistently show certain other groups near the bottom. The mean IQ for Ashkenazi Jews is some-where between 110 and 115, depending on which test one cites.

As noted, overall scores are highest for Ashkenazi Jews and Japanese, but not in the same way. Japanese do better on spatial intel-ligence, Jews in language ability. Those expert in psychometrics are sure that group differences are real, and that finer differences among groups are real, too. There is nothing fatally wrong or culturally skewed about the tests, at least not any more. No one who under-stands the science doubts that these differences—and not just in intel-ligence but in, for example, natural aptitude for some kinds of sports, of which more in a moment—are rooted ultimately in differential genetic endowments.

Obviously, it makes a lot of people uncomfortable to credit a definite link between genetic endowments and both intelligence and achievement. But it should make these same people more uncomfort-able to deny plain scientific facts. Besides, it is in fact very comfort-ing to know that the wider science of intelligence measurement and explanation, as best we understand it, strongly suggests that genetic endowments are not *the* most significant factors explaining differen-tial intelligence and achievement among groups. Part of the reason is that we know that several nongenetic factors shape intelligence (such as body weight at birth, sibling order, early nutrition, and particularly the "imprinting" patterns of speech directed by parents to infants). We also know that cultural factors more broadly understood than just early socialization patterns, such as occupational selection, for exam-ple, make a big difference over time.[7]

Whatever the complex mix of sources that make up intelligence, we can see that, extrapolating from the data, if the American Jewish intelligence mean is around 115, that puts the average Jew in the 75th percentile of intelligence; even higher—around the 95th percentile—in the area of verbal and abstract reasoning skills. That's way up there. Now, as just stated and as should be obvious, innate intelligence is only one factor—necessary but not sufficient—in explaining why some people do well in school and in their careers. But exceptional innate intelligence is beyond doubt a key factor in explaining exceptional achievement—like winning a Nobel for medicine, math, or physics, say. If the mean Ashkenazi Jewish IQ is around 115 and the standard deviation is 15, then the proportion of Jews with IQs around 140 or higher will be about six or seven times that of the rest of the population. That starts to look like the right kind of math to explain the Nobel Prize puzzle.

The same basic reasoning and mathematics apply to phenomena like the domination of certain sports at their highest, "Nobel" level by specific groups. Average abilities among members of different groups will overlap very substantially, but in a contest designed to select the very best, the law of standard deviations will wash away averages and one group will dominate the winners' circle. Kenyans of the Kalenjin-speaking Nandi people of the Great Rift Valley hold the top sixty world times in the three-thousand-meter steeplechase.[8] Yes, that's right—*all sixty*. If anyone is so politically correct as to insist that this must be some kind of coincidence, then there is a certain bridge in Brooklyn I would like to sell him.

These and related facts about Jewish intelligence do not answer the key question, however; they only recast it. The trick is not to figure out *whether* Jews are smart—here the JACs are not mistaken—but to explain *why*—and here the JACs are clueless. The old folkloric explanations—that either the wages of persecution or the tradition of marrying off the best and brightest children to wealthy merchant families—do not make logical sense upon reflection or even come close to an adequate social science explanation. So what is the explanation?

As we have already suggested, this is not a case of determining nature *versus* nurture, but rather of nature *and* nurture, heredity and culture as co-dependent variables. Those unfamiliar with current research in genetics may have a hard time with this idea at first, so let me help by way of a highly summarized example.

We know that the human genetic code has a kind of switch that allows infants to digest lactose, and after weaning the switch turns off. But in northern Europe around six thousand years ago, people domesticated cattle—a cultural behavior—which was *followed* by a change in the genome of that group to enable most of them to be able to digest lactose well into adulthood. So here is a clear example of a causal co-dependency, of a cultural development doubling back and affecting the genetic makeup of a group. We can see, too, that while this sort of thing does not happen overnight, it does not take more than a dozen or so generations to occur. This suggests the likelihood that Jewish intelligence is explained by a convergence of natural selection and cultural selection, wrapped around one another in a kind of social-historical double helix.

As to the natural selection angle, Jewish history tells of two, and probably three, acute demographic bottlenecks that produced the rough equivalent of what geneticists call genetic drift—the tendency for isolated or pressured populations to reduce genetic diversity. The first of these bottlenecks was the Babylonian Exile (for only the national elite was carried into exile and remained as Jews), the second was the catastrophe that followed the failure of the Bar Kochba revolt, and the third, little known but possibly crucial, could well have been Justinian's Plague, which first hit Asia Minor and the Levant hard in 540 CE. That plague, similar to but not the same as the bubonic plague of the fourteenth century, killed a higher percentage of people than any other known pandemic in history, even including the Black Death. Since Jews were mainly city people and traders, the plague, which arrived and spread primarily through ports, probably drove Jewish numbers down disproportionately to the population as a whole. It may also have played some role, indirect if not direct, in generating Jewish migration northward, away from the sickness, into northern Italy and subsequently the Rhineland, thus creating or reinforcing the social separation that led to the development of Ashkenazi Jewry roughly fifty generations ago.

Part of the natural selection story involves a mutation as well as genetic drift. There is a mutation in Ashkenazi Jews, genetic research tells us, that occurred probably within the past eleven hundred years, but possibly earlier, that both enables a higher concentration of neurons in the brain and, if two recessive genes combine, a set of Mendelian diseases the best known of which is Tay-Sachs. (This mutation is called Mendelian because it can occur at random anywhere in the genome.) Like the mutation that causes sickle cell anemia in some black populations of West African origin, the Ashkenazi mutation may have arisen as a defense against environmental pressure—perhaps repeated exposure to varieties of plague—but hard evidence for this speculation is not yet in hand.

The cultural selection piece of the puzzle is even more complex. It probably involves occupational selection over many centuries, flows of less intelligent apostates out and more intelligent converts (mainly females) into the Jewish people, and the equivalent, too, of spiritual wills that linked the generations one to another in ways that fostered morality (including marital loyalty), discipline, and the continued fusion of piety and learning. Families that maintained these intellectual and spiritual traditions, and that built child-rearing customs around them, tended to remain in the fold of the Jewish people, while those that didn't did not. A three-step process thus seems to have been at work: a genetic endowment embellished by cultural factors that have been in turn successively filtered, culled, and recast by experience such that the group's genetic signature still resembles but also differs from what it was two millennia ago.

This is not the place to detail the interaction among all these forces, or to review the various scholarly debates about them. Suffice it to say that the sociological and cultural aspects of all this, spread out over thousands of years, can explain not only Ashkenazi intelligence but also the differential intelligence rates of Sephardic Jews and Oriental Jews—Jews who came to Israel mainly from Middle Eastern countries. Reverse occupational selection particularly among Oriental Jews, not anything genetic, seems best able to explain differences among the three groups.

The point of all this it that whatever role genetic endowments and mutations have played, it is relatively modest compared to the role of culture in the interdependent dance of nature and nurture. Where JACs see chromosomes and race, some sort of inherent, animalist bloodline superiority, wiser observers see the intergenerationally enforced traditions of Jewish peoplehood as the driving force. Even Sigmund Freud, never a religious Jew, realized late in life, for example, what the protracted, cumulative intellectual consequences of conceiving an abstract, immaterial God could be.[9]

So yes, it's true that Jews, and America's mostly Ashkenazi Jews, as a group are smart. But they are smart for reasons Jews should not rush to boast about. It's true because of a hard history that, unbeknownst to those who lived it, resulted in the improbably diverse Jewish gene pool that exists today. After all, excessive inbreeding is hardly known for its *favorable* effects on intelligence—so much for a "blood" interpretation of Jewish intelligence.

Indeed, with just a slight exercise of the imagination, one might say that this complex process of assembling the Jewish people over the centuries amounts to a redefinition of the very idea of the Chosen People: that Jews are "chosen" in the sense of being self-selected, of having assembled a unique genetic signature, linked back long into the past, but nevertheless very diverse by dint of cultural choices based on a single-minded adherence to a faith and a mission. Might "chosen" thus one day be understood to mean a genetically diverse "universal man," arguably the future of humanity on earth? Did the Jewish genome get there first because history scattered and pushed the Jews to it? And if so, did this just happen as a random fluke of history, or is this God's idea of wordplay wit on a cosmic scale?

We'll probably never know. What we do know is that the Jewish people are what and who they are today because many Jews over the centuries proved unable to rise to the level of learning necessary to be a good Jew, and thus proved unable or unwilling to raise their children in a manner that would enable them to carry on. Isn't it peculiar that Jewish American chauvinists, those often to be found in the vanguard of the process of culling their progeny right out of the rest of Jewish history thanks to their general disregard for religious tradition and education, should be the ones most boastful of Jewish "genius"?

Peculiar, maybe; surprising, no. Tell someone they possess a treasure, but give them no chance to understand it or earn it for themselves, and they will squander it. Happens all the time, and not just to Jews.

9

Professional Jews

There are people so addicted to exaggeration they can't tell the truth without lying.

—Josh Billings

Jewcentricity, by definition, always involves exaggeration and hence distortion of some sort. When non-Jews engage in negative Jewcentricity, they generate anti-Semitism and lesser forms of delusion. When non-Jews engage in positive Jewcentricity, as do dispensationalist Protestants on one side and reality-challenged celebrities like Madonna on the other, they can generate a host of misleading and sometimes harmful effects, as well.

Jewish American chauvinists manufacture their own, deceptively dangerous form of Jewcentricity that generates "racial" fuel for anti-Semites, which they in turn almost invariably exaggerate. Indeed, perhaps the most unfortunate expression of contemporary Jewish Jewcentricity is the unsupportable assumption that everyone hates the Jews. It's simply not true. As we have seen, some non-Jews like Jews and admire Judaism, and rather a large number have better things to do with their time than to care one way or the other. Imagining that everyone hates you and your kind is itself a kind of conceit, after all, albeit a warped one.

It is not hard to understand why this is so, however. Several reasons come to mind. There is, of course, the morbid character of the twentieth century. The Zionist narrative has also exaggerated the trials and misfortunes of Diaspora. But a cluster of secular American Jewish organizations have also played a major role in this. As we saw in chapter 6, most Jews in America have fallen away from the long-established traditions of rabbinic Judaism, subtracting in the process both Jewish memory and joyousness, leaving behind only the dour remains of what secular Jewish image-makers, fund-raisers, and political functionaries have wrought. And here we enter the domain of those image-makers, fund-raisers, and functionaries—the domain of "professional" Jews.

By "professional Jews" I mean principally the leaders of secular Jewish American advocacy organizations. To get at the essence of the novelty represented by professional Jews, one needs yet again to understand just a little history, in this case starting with the French Revolution and one Napoleon Bonaparte.

Before Napoleon, the Christian states of Europe from Iberia all the way to Russia defined their dealings with Jews on a communal basis, not an individual one. Jewish communities ruled themselves within the sufferance and boundaries of the larger political community. The leaders of the Jewish community, rabbis and some laypersons, spoke on its collective behalf. This relationship was founded in the original arrangement, as already described in passing, in which Jews were either allowed or invited to live in Christian lands, most often with the status of *servi camerae regis*, servants of the royal chamber. The Jewish community gained from the *poritz* residency rights and protection, in return for which their economic activities were taxed to help finance the various needs and ambitions of the court.

The Declaration of the Rights of Man, the fundamental document of the French Revolution, marked the rise of the concept of individual, as opposed to communal, agency and responsibility. Universal principles of citizenship replaced communal arrangements based on sectarian affiliations into which people generally were born. As a result, the control that had been exercised by Jewish communal leaders weakened; individual Jews could now choose to become part of the broader society, theoretically as legal equals, and still be Jews privately as a matter of personal religion. This is how Judaism came to be considered, in the West at least, as a religion as opposed to a religious civilization bound to a particular people. And what was true for France and the areas into which Napoleon spread such ideas was true, too, in America from the very start. Religious freedom is the hallmark of the American creed, and individual agency the vanguard of American civilization.

Before the advent of universal citizenship and the rise of individual agency as cardinal principles of government, Jews rarely saw any blue sky between their identity as a people and the practice of their religion. Now that Jews as individuals could become part of a national group defined separately from sectarian affiliation—Frenchmen, Dutch, Germans, Britons, Americans, and so forth—a previously nonexistent separation between Jewish peoplehood and Jewish civilization, with faith at its center, became possible. Religion, a Western term that drew its meaning from the post-Reformation containment of religion within the confines of state power and authority, was now applied to the faith and rituals of the Jews by both non-Jews and Jews alike. Thus the term Judaism, to mean the Jewish "religion," was born.

Just as it became possible in a liberal Western polity to be Jewish by religion without being a member of the Jewish people—the bifurcated identity pioneered by Reform Judaism—the reverse also became possible: one could in theory be a Jew ethnically, as the term we use today defines it, within the great social vault of abstract citizenship, without any necessary connection to Judaism. It is on the basis of this possibility that "professional" Jews in the United States may be understood.

In practice, it has never been easy in European states, even democratic ones like France and Britain, to keep the lines between citizenship, ethnicity, and sectarian affiliation completely clear. And different countries have gone about the matter in different ways. One can see this in the vestiges of the pre-Napoleonic system still extant in Europe. Again, while details differ from country to country, in general the main religious communities are recognized by the state, subsidized, and required to appoint someone as lead clergyman to serve as liaison to the state. For the Jews in Britain, France, the Netherlands, and elsewhere this position has usually been known as that of the chief rabbi. That is what the aforementioned Jonathan Sacks is today in Britain—the Chief Rabbi of the British Commonwealth.

This kind of system, of course, never existed in America, where government was set up to protect religion from the state rather than the other way around. The American state does not subsidize religious groups, does not establish one sect above others as most European states have done and many still do, and certainly has no need for a chief rabbi. But vestiges of the old pre-Napoleonic system exist anyway, not because American government insists on it formally—to the contrary—but because Jewish Americans of European descent, somewhere down in their tribal collective memory of Diaspora, insist on it informally. Some American Jews, or Jewish Americans more accurately, still like to think of and organize themselves as a corporate body. They desire to collectively represent Jews as an *ethnicity* within the American cultural and political melting pot, however, not Jews as a *religious* group and certainly not as the separate, formerly self-governing, autonomous *people* Jews have for millennia understood themselves to be. In short, they aspire to be *shtadlan*, or liaisons, despite the fact that there is no *poritz*, or baron.

The main mass-membership advocacy organizations of American Jewry—B'nai B'rith and its Anti-Defamation League (ADL), the American Jewish Congress, the American Jewish Committee, the Council of Jewish Federations and Welfare Funds, the National Conference of Jewish Federations, and the Conference of Presidents of Major Jewish Organizations (a kind of steering group for the major organizations), to mention only a few—are not religious organizations but ethnic ones. It is not necessary to have any Jewish religious affiliation to be a member in good standing in these organizations, and their leaderships are composed mainly of people who are not religious or Jewishly learned Jews. They are, in effect, the high priests of the second of the two religions of American Jews.

There is some Orthodox participation in most of these groups, even sometimes in leadership circles. But Orthodox Jews still affiliate with one another mainly through their synagogues and schools. Their self-definition is still essentially pre-Napoleonic: they see themselves as members of the Jewish people and have no need for ethnic organizations to express their Jewishness. Non-halachic Jewish Americans may or may not need these organizations either, but many seem to want them anyway. What have they claimed to be the purpose of such organizations?

We need not go into foundational texts and statements of purpose on the question of origins, for the answer is simple enough: organizations like B'nai B'rith and the American Jewish Committee were created to lobby for particular Jewish interests—in the latter case, for example, against a trade agreement with Russia in 1905 because of Russian anti-Semitism. The American-Jewish Joint Distribution Committee came into being to aid Jewish war refugees after World War I. The United Jewish Appeal came into existence in 1938 to help Jews trapped in Nazi Europe.

In time, these and most other Jewish organizations became explicitly or implicitly Zionist, and thereafter existed to one degree or another to support, first, a Jewish home in Palestine, and then, after 1948, the security and prosperity of the State of Israel. The American Jewish Appeal pivoted after World War II into the premier agency for collecting financial help for Israel. In other words, all these organizations have depended, and still depend, on the validity of their serving parochial Jewish ethnic interests that are simultaneously distinct from broader American interests but not related directly to religion.

The reasons that major Jewish American organizations exist today are several, and the distinctions among them are important to keep straight. Some, like the American-Jewish Joint Distribution Committee, Friends of Hadassah, and the Hebrew Immigration and Aid Society (usually called by its acronym HIAS), exist to do good works. They are more or less conventional charities, and it is not unreasonable for Jews to want to focus on maximizing Jewish philanthropy, and to target assets where the donors wish them most to go. Such service groups embody the rabbinic principle that all Jews are responsible for each other, wherever they may be. They therefore qualify as American Jewish organizations.

American Jewish service groups differ, however, from Jewish American advocacy organizations like the ADL that focus energy on political issues such as separation of church and state and a host of foreign policy issues. The reasons why these groups still exist today have nothing to do with principles that ben-Zakkai or traditional Jews from ages past would readily recognize, though, as suggested above, that was not always the case. American Jews used to feel they needed special help to attain the first-class citizenship that was legally their due, and rightly so. When B'nai B'rith and later the ADL and other organizations came into existence, there was plenty of anti-Semitism in America and good reason to lobby against it, and plenty of observant Jews supported them. That is no longer the case, but the ADL does not agree. In 1992, for example, the ADL claimed, on the basis of what it called a nationwide survey, that nearly forty million Americans—one in five adults—had expressed strong anti-Semitic views.[1]

This was and remains nonsense. Such distortions turn ADL leaders and their organizational associates into generals in an army with no more wars left to fight. But they try to find and fight them anyway. Without anti-Semitism, these organizations have no compelling reason for being, and they end up creating a circular dynamic as a result of needing to find anti-Semitism to justify their own existence. Having helped make the Holocaust and then Israel into icons of Jewish American identity, anti-Semitism and Israel-as-vulnerable have been necessary truths of organizational existence. But precisely these "truths" have exacerbated the assimilation problem, the major threat to American Jewry, by creating a form of faux Judaism that, for entirely understandable reasons, does not appeal to young people in search of spiritual guidance. This, however, cannot be admitted—and it isn't. Hence the bizarre claim, already previewed in chapter 6, raised by ADL national director Abraham Foxman in his 2003 book *Never Again?*, that high rates of Jewish assimilation are caused by anti-Semitic discrimination!

Of course, no organization, Jewish or otherwise, wants to close up shop even if its *raison d'être* has disappeared. That is as true of the World Bank as it is of the ADL. So even though what the ADL was originally set up to do no longer requires doing, the ADL does anyway, fundraising for what has been recently an annual $50 million budget through what can only be described as anti-Semitism scaremongering. As an organization, it is an anti-Semite-fighting hammer, and so it sees, or chooses to see, only anti-Semitic nails. A particularly vivid example occurred just a few years ago, concerning none other than Harry Truman.

It came to light in 2003 that Harry S. Truman's diary contained what Mr. Foxman referred to as "anti-Semitic canards." Foxman opined in a statement that "sadly, President Truman was a man of his times, and much less a man because of it."[2] A few days later Foxman published a short essay in the *Forward* in which he accused Truman of "attributing classic stereotypes about Jews."[3] He quoted Truman's diary as follows: "The Jews, I find, are very, very selfish. When they have power, physical financial or political neither Hitler nor Stalin has anything on them for cruelty or mistreatment of the underdog." Citing his childhood as a Holocaust survivor and displaced person, who believed in 1950 that Harry Truman had personally made it possible for him to come to America, Foxman wrote: "It personally saddens me to learn that he too was flawed."

No one can or should defend President Truman's comparison of the Jews with Hitler, or even with Stalin. Everyone has bad days that loose their demons, and Harry Truman must have had such a day on July 21, 1947, to have penned such a diary entry. But it did not take until 2003 for anyone to learn that Truman had made disparaging remarks about Jews. One example, from Truman's memoirs published in 1955, concerns the president's resentment in the autumn of 1947 of what he calls some "extreme Zionist leaders":

> Not only were there pressure movements around the United Nations unlike anything that had been seen there before, but that the White House, too, was subjected to a constant barrage. I do not think I ever had as much pressure and propaganda aimed at the White House as I had in this instance. The persistence of a few of the extreme Zionist leaders—actuated by a political motive and engaging in political threats—disturbed and annoyed me.[4]

The president also noted in a letter to Eleanor Roosevelt, "I regret this situation very much because my sympathy has always been on their side."[5]

In other words, Truman sympathized with the Jews, with Zionism, and with what would become Israel, but some then neo-professional Jews managed to irritate him all the same. It is possible to push a friendship so far as to jeopardize it, and Foxman's July 18, 2003, column seems an example.

Was Truman really guilty of espousing anti-Semitic remarks, or was he just letting off some dank steam? Let's look at the whole diary entry for July 21, 1947:

> Had ten minutes conversation with Henry Morgenthau about Jewish ship in Palistine [sic]. Told him I would talk to Gen[eral] Marshall about it. He'd no business, whatever to call me. The Jews have no sense of proportion nor do they have any judgement on world affairs.
>
> Henry brought a thousand Jews to New York on a supposedly temporary basis and they stayed. When the country went backward—and Republican in the election of 1946, this incident loomed large on the D[isplaced] P[ersons] program.
>
> The Jews, I find are very, very selfish. They care not how many Estonians, Latvians, Finns, Poles, Yugoslavs or Greeks get murdered or mistreated as D[isplaced] P[ersons] as long as the Jews get special treatment. Yet when they have power, physical, financial or

political neither Hitler nor Stalin has anything on them for cruelty or mistreatment to the under dog. Put an underdog on top and it makes no difference whether his name is Russian, Jewish, Negro, Management, Labor, Mormon, Baptist he goes haywire. I've found very, very few who remember their past condition when prosperity comes.[6]

Is Truman irritated at Morgenthau? Yes, in part because something he did, Truman believes, had negative political consequences for him and the Democratic Party. Did Truman not understand the dire plight of the ship Morgenthau must have been talking about, given the date: the Haganah ship *Exodus*? Probably not. Was Morgenthau right to try to get the president's attention despite the risk of irking him? Probably he was.

Let's look carefully, however, at the key passages. Is Truman really making a statement about Jews, or a statement about what power seems to do to all people? Some of both: he first says that Jews have no sense of proportion or judgment on world affairs. Might that actually have been true under the circumstances in July 1947? What sentient adult Jew at the time did not feel at least a little unbalanced, with the blood and ashes of European Jewry not yet settled and a war brewing in Palestine? But Truman is mainly talking not about what sets Jews *apart* from others—a key aspect of the definition of anti-Semitism—but rather what makes them the *same* as all others. Truman is asserting that, in this respect anyway—in what happens to the downtrodden when they suddenly find themselves at the top of the heap—Jews are just like everybody else. Truman made what amounts on balance to a non-Jewcentric remark, and Foxman saw the reverse—he saw anti-Semitism—and, unlike Truman, said so publicly.

In recent years, all the major secular Jewish American organizations have been increasingly skittish about the skyrocketing rates of assimilation, but they are not particularly well suited to doing much about it. One wonders if some have heaved private sighs of relief over the supposed rekindling of anti-Semitism—because that, at least, is a problem they know something about. The basic idea, rarely if ever spoken out loud, is that just as anti-Semitism supposedly created Israel through the cauldron of the Holocaust, it prevents Jews in America from assimilating away their own individual identities and collective future. Thus, in part one suspects, the neverending search for anti-Semitism.

Sometimes this search turns up actual anti-Semitism. But sometimes it becomes tragicomic. One example concerns the late Marge Schott, a nutcase who once owned the Cincinnati Reds baseball team.

In the spring of 1996 Schott shot off her mouth in an ESPN interview to the tune that Hitler started out okay "but then went too far." All the secular Jewish American advocacy organizations latched onto this as though it were money in the bank. Soon following Schott's addled remark came a limp apology offered to Rabbi Marvin Hier of the Simon Wiesenthal Center. Hier proclaimed Schott's apology not good enough. He had become a connoisseur of apologies, having recently been busy extracting one from a weepy Marlon Brando for some anti-Semitic raving he had let loose on the *Larry King Show*. Charles Krauthammer captured the essence of this farce and saw its larger context:

> Marge Schott is a rich ignoramus of zero consequence. Only an idiot celebrity culture—a culture in which Barbra Streisand lectures on politics at Harvard, in which the first issue of John Kennedy Jr.'s magazine features Madonna on "If I Were President," in which Jessica Lange plays a farmer in a film and then testifies before a House committee on farm legislation—would care what these people think. . . . Punish Schott on Hitler? The real scandal here is that what can only be called comic anti-Semitism arouses enormous indignation when the real thing evokes general cowardice.[7]

Here Krauthammer was referring to the genuine anti-Semitism of Louis Farrakhan. What Krauthammer forgot, however, was to follow the money; there was a practical point to Rabbi Hier's shenanigans. It's called fund-raising.

There are other reasons that secular Jewish American organizations exist: one is simply that a lot of Jews like to hang out with other Jews. That's a characteristic of all clans, and it is perfectly natural. What traditional religious Jews got from synagogue life—a sense of community, of connectedness—professional Jews can get from their organizations, which substitute for the religious culture of their parents and grandparents. It is a kind of neo-clannishness.

Some argue that neo-clannishness at least creates a platform for bonding among Jews that slows the pace of assimilation and intermarriage. Maybe, maybe not; it no doubt depends on the particulars of a given situation. What is not in doubt is that neo-clannishness is a substitute culture with a specific tone arising from the major historical events of the past few generations. The upward mobility of American Jews occurred at a time when traditional religiosity was often deemed old-fashioned, superstitious, and worse. Many first-generation American Jews were so eager to get ahead, and so poorly educated Jewishly, that they strove mightily to assimilate, casting aside anything that might block their way. They called this being modern. What it really was flowed from fear of ostracism and a perfectly natural desire not to be poor and marginal. What drew some first-generation and more second-generation Jews back toward Judaism, or something that substituted for it, was the one-two punch of the Holocaust and the Six Day War of 1967—but, oddly enough, in reverse order.

It is hard for younger people to imagine today, but for about twenty years after the end of World War II and the liberation of the Nazi concentration camps, there was little talk of the Holocaust among Jews living in the United States. Jews, of course, knew what had happened. But they did not use it as a focus for their fund-raising efforts. They did not make movies or write books or go on talk shows to discuss and analyze it. The wounds were so deep and so fresh that they mostly evoked inward turmoil and outward silence. The reborn State of Israel seemed to many a miracle, but a fragile miracle. Some American Jews held back from full and open support for Israel out of fear that the Arabs would destroy the country and kill the people, a second heartbreak just too much to take so soon after the first. When the black drama of May 1967 erupted—a time when many American Jews, ignorantly but understandably, feared that they might witness the annihilation of Israel before their very eyes—but then gave way to victory and vindication, something held deep in the psyches of American Jews surged forth. As Rabbi Neusner aptly described it, echoing Irving Howe's aforementioned observation, a Judaism of Holocaust and Redemption was born.

This Judaism was an ideology more than a form of religion, for no faith in God was or is necessary to it. Neusner was right, and he saw before most others the real message of the Holocaust Museum. As he put it, Holocaust memorials bore the message that gentiles cannot be trusted and that the State of Israel, armed, dangerous to its enemies, and victorious in battle, was the last best hope for Jewish survival—the Israel Defense Forces, not the Torah or Jewish education, the Jewish state, not Jewish faith and memory. In other words,

explained Neusner, vast numbers of Jews wanted to return to the
fold after the epiphany of June 1967, but most did not want, or know
how, to return to Judaism; they returned to "the ethnic fold, not
the ancient faith."[8] In this they took a path similar to that of many
German-speaking Jews in the nineteenth and early twentieth centuries, embracing Jewishness as a pariah culture of which to be proud
within a general culture, but rejecting Judaism as a faith.[9]

Of course this was a great boon, an unprecedented opportunity for
the Jewish American advocacy professionals, and they did not miss it.
They unwittingly helped to transform the State of Israel into a substitute for God. Even for many religious American Jews Zionism in effect
displaced Judaism as a belief system. Before 1967, many American
Jewish leaders felt that only other Jews could be counted on to advocate
for Israeli interests, and there was arguably a need to do so when most
of these groups were formed, not least AIPAC—the America-Israel
Public Affairs Committee—which came into existence in 1951. Israel
was then a small and poor country; it needed help, and the American
Jewish community, the wealthiest such community on the planet, rendered considerable service. For many years thereafter, professional
Jews devoted to the State of Israel were convinced that American Jewry
was more important to Israel than Israel was to American Jewry. This
was a parochial Jewish American form of Jewcentricity if there ever was
one, a special manifestation of stereoscopic exceptionalism magnified
by the events surrounding the 1967 war.

This proved quite an irony, however. Just as Israel became more
important to American Jews as a symbol of their identity, the objective importance of Jewish American help for Israel declined. Israel
today is far more important to American Jewry than American
Jewry is to Israel. Hence the shock to the system of secular Jewish
Americans working on behalf of Israel when, twenty years after the
Six Day War, prominent Israelis told them to keep their money at
home and to use it instead to educate their own children against the
ravages of assimilation.

It fell to Hirsh Goodman, then editor of the *Jerusalem Report*,
to explain to Jewish American pro-Israel philanthropists how pal-
try their UJA contributions were in the context of Israel's thriving
economy. When Americans buy Israeli bonds, he explained, they
cost Israel in bureaucratic expenses more than the investment is
worth. Goodman quoted a senior official of the Israeli Treasury
Ministry, "If these people really love Israel, they should know
that probably the last thing they should do is buy Israeli bonds."[10]

When Goodman tried to suggest that secular "ethnic" Jewish American organizations raise money instead for Jewish education, here is what one professional functionary told him: "Do you really think we could raise a dime for Jewish education? . . . Go tell Haim Shmerl that you want a pledge for Jewish continuity and you'll see the money go to the local golf course. We need Israel, even if Israel does not need us."

Israelis also told Jewish Americans and their secular organizations around the same time to butt out of Israeli politics. The leaders of these organizations had become supporters of whatever any Israeli government wanted, so when the Likud came to power for the first time in Israel's history in May 1977, AIPAC and other organizations learned quickly to switch from the Labor Party way of seeing the world to the Likud way. This turned out to be easy for several reasons.

First, the Likud's more visceral anti-goyish attitudes fit well with the Jewish American Diaspora's more insecure and hence combative mentality. It also fit because American Jews interested in world affairs had become more conservative and hawkish as the result of the vicissitudes of the Cold War, particularly the Soviet "refusenik" issue. And Likud politicians were not socialists as most Labor politicians still were, something that had made some American Jewish donors, who had made their fortunes in a capitalist haven, privately uneasy.

The real suborning of American Jewish organizations into parochial Israeli political battles started during the Israeli "rotation" government of the 1984–1988 period, and it was Shimon Peres who first explicitly asked for American Jewish support for his Labor Party side of the arrangement. That only led to the Likud following suit, and the professional Jewish organizations had little trouble getting used to Yitzhak Shamir as Israel's leader. When Israelis then returned a Labor prime minister to power in 1994, many Jewish Americans and their secular organizations were caught flat-footed. Most had become so enamored of Likud views that some actually opposed publicly the views of a sitting Israeli prime minister—in this case, Yitzhak Rabin.

Israelis were appalled by this, especially of course those who had voted for Labor. Aqiva Eldar, a columnist for *Haaretz*, put it this way in the midst of one of several flaps, this one concerning the status of Jerusalem:

[C]ollecting the signatures of 82 congressmen for the sake of Jerusalem would seem to be a heart-warming achievement for Israel and its friends in America. In fact it was a cheeky action on the part of Jewish functionaries, an unprecedented deed in relations between the sovereign State of Israel and the Jewry of the diaspora, perhaps even between any sovereign state and an ethnic minority that bears no responsibility for the consequences of its deeds and misdeeds. . . . Never before has a group of Jews so insolently exploited its political clout to thwart a diplomatic compromise reached by Israeli and U.S. Government leaders.[11]

If anti-Semitism and pro-Zionism were losing some of their luster as vehicles for organizational survival, there was always the Holocaust.[12] One can track the process by which the major secular Jewish American organizations shifted from trying to raise money the old-fashioned way to new efforts to integrate the marketing of the Holocaust. The ADL devised major ad campaigns and programs. For example, an advertisement in the December 1, 1996, *New York Times* celebrated the ADL's creation of a new magazine: *DIMENSIONS: A Journal of Holocaust Studies*.

As it happened, the Holocaust restitution issue arose at around the same time, after a major break in the decades-old search for Jewish property stolen and hidden, largely in Swiss banks, by the Nazis and their sympathizers in German-occupied Europe. There followed an organizational feeding frenzy in which the secular Jewish organizations saw a new angle to mobilize membership and raise money. Again, Krauthammer caught the essence:

> The pursuit of billions in Holocaust guilt money has gone from the unseemly to the disgraceful. What began as an attempt to locate actual confiscated Swiss bank accounts of individual Holocaust victims has turned into a treasure hunt for hungry tort lawyers and major Jewish organizations. . . . The only thing certain to come out of this grotesque scramble for money is a revival of Shylockian stereotypes. . . . Blood money for the Holocaust? . . . It should be beneath the dignity of the Jewish people to accept it, let alone seek it.[13]

It was worse than beneath the dignity of the American Jewish community to do this: it was also counterproductive. This American Holocaust-and-Redemption crypto-ideological form of Judaism could not keep Jewish Americans Jewish in any meaningful way, any more than self-proclaimed secular Central European Jewishness-without-Judaism did in an earlier time. As we have already suggested, the flourishing of Holocaust-and-Redemption "Judaism" has coincided with high and rising rates of assimilation and intermarriage, which have only accelerated since Neusner issued his warning a generation ago. Now two full generations of Jewish Americans have explained to their children why it mattered to be Jewish almost entirely without recourse to religion or faith. They told their children, in effect, that it was all about hatred, mass murder, and survival against the odds.

Another cousinly e-mail recently illustrated the point: called "Why I love being Jewish," this five-page stream-of-consciousness drivel drones on about how we Jews, who were led like sheep to the slaughter sixty-eight years ago, now have a country and an army, have won wars, have a high-tech economy and great doctors, have made the desert bloom, and along the way overcame Pharaoh, the Greeks, the Romans, the Spanish Inquisition, pogroms in Russia, Hitler, Saddam Hussein, and so on and so forth—and not one single word about faith, about God, about education, about compassion, or about piety. What healthy child would want to associate with a "religion" of unrelieved doom and gloom, of war and muscle flexing?

And to depend on the State of Israel, on a secular and naturally fallible government, for a spiritual anchor has been disastrous. "How have the children responded to this Judaism consisting only of memory" about recent history, and not of Torah, asked Neusner? "They have chosen not to live in the State of Israel and they have, more than any other previous generation of Jews anywhere, chosen freely not to raise another generation of Jews."[14] Indeed, a 2006 survey sponsored by the Andrea and Charles Bronfman Foundation found that only 48 percent of young Jews (defined as thirty-five or younger) in North America would regard the destruction of Israel as a personal tragedy, compared to 77 percent for those in older age cohorts.

Note, again, that Holocaust-and-Redemption faux Judaism is the precise reverse of rabbinic Judaism in its essence. It holds that for the Holocaust to have meaning, it must produce a political event: the rise of the State of Israel. This is the opposite of the way the rabbis interpreted political events: a political event could have meaning only if it was translated into a religious experience. The rabbis bet that spiritual strength would ultimately outlast the political variety. Rapidly assimilating Jewish Americans, so overwhelmingly fixed on the political, seem to be doing their best to prove them correct.

• • •

But if modern Jewish Americans either do not or cannot believe in God anymore, is there really anything wrong with the life of a secular Jew and the secular organizations that go with it? Alan Dershowitz, the notable lawyer and sometime Jewish activist, has argued that Jews in America need to develop a vibrant secular Jewish culture, which, he claims, can stanch the alarming rates of assimilation and intermarriage.[15] He wants Jews to show more chutzpah, more demonstrable assertiveness.

It is in one sense a matter of taste, perhaps, but yes, there is something uncomfortable if not exactly wrong with this. The reason at its essence is that the substitution of Holocaust-and-Redemption Judaism for the real thing, whether asserted with more chutzpah or not, induces Jews to misdefine their own identity. The only thing that makes Jewish peoplehood work, the force that created it in the first place and distinguishes it from a mere ethnicity, is Judaism. If we remove Judaism from the equation, and with it the commitment to Jewish education, the concept of peoplehood, sustained by a commitment to memory embedded in religious education and practice, dissolves into the ether.

Many halachic Jews believe, too, that the adoption by professional Jews of views at odds with Jewish law helps legitimize views on issues like abortion, gay marriage, and church-state relations that ought not to be legitimate. Case in point: the active advocacy of the ADL on the issue of gay rights, which lends a "Jewish" legitimation to the advocacy. Another case in point, this one about silent prayer in public schools. In 1996, the ADL criticized the U.S. Navy for its willingness to sponsor a Promise Keepers rally in Norfolk, Virginia. In response to the ADL demand, the Navy officially dissociated itself from the Promise Keepers. This appalled many Orthodox Jews, who worried that this would come across as anti-Christian bigotry. Most Orthodox Jews oppose removing all signs of religion, including pointedly Christian religion, from the public square. They do this not only because they fear a resentment-fueled backlash against American Jewry, but because they genuinely believe that Christians acting like good Christians reinforces the values and virtues that make American the tolerant and hospitable country that it is. How, they ask, can professional Jews claim on the one hand that there are no contradictions between being Jewish and being American, and on the other argue for the exclusion from the public sphere of what has made America American?

At the same time, contend their critics—including their Jewish critics—some of these organizations have marshaled an un-American effort to censor not only prayer but also speech when it comes to Israel and other writings critical of Jews, holding out the right to label anything they find disagreeable or even inconvenient as anti-Semitic.[16] That sort of thing can *create* anti-Semitism. So is this done deliberately as part of a master plan to stanch assimilation? That would at least be part of a coherent strategy, hence the possibility has to be discounted.

One gets a hint of just how conflicted the inner life of some professional Jewish Americans may be by juxtaposing what they seem to want with why that is a problem for the community's well-being. As Irving Kristol put it nearly a generation ago,

> A plain and simple truth is that so long as Christians are willing and eager to marry Jews, and Jews to marry (secular) Christians, inter-marriage will proceed apace. But another truth, not so plain and not so simple, is that while Jews are distressed by this situation, they are also flattered and reassured by it. One gets the impression that what many Jewish leaders want, ideally, is for Jews to remain Jewish, and to decline to marry the Christians who woo them—but *not* for Christians to be so Christian as to shy away from intermarriage with Jews. It is an impossible dream, reflecting the paradoxical situation in which American Jews find themselves today.[17]

Kristol described this situation as paradoxical. Another way to see it is as incoherent.

There is at least one other reason why secular Jewish American advocacy organizations continue to exist. It's the proverbial eight-hundred-pound gorilla sitting on the flowerpot that no one wants to acknowledge. It's about power, or rather, the giddy, unexpected feeling of power that the leaders of groups like the ADL, AIPAC, and others feel.

Over the past forty or so years, the clout of organized American Jewry has risen meteorically. Professional Jews have been able to tap into large sums of money, talented executives, and growing and dedicated staffs to influence a vast array of public policy issues. They have grown fast, AIPAC being an excellent example. In the early 1950s it was a three-person office operating on a shoestring budget;

twenty-five years later it had a staff of around 150 and a multimillion-dollar budget. Not only have Jewish American organizations amassed clout on matters relating to Israel, but Jewish organizational muscle has been flexed in the face of the Soviet Union and Communist Romania, on immigration and asylum policy, on trade policy, and on human-rights issues involving Haiti, Rwanda, and, more recently, Darfur. Jewish "professional" political clout, augmented by a larger-than-proportional number of Jewish senators and representatives, has also influenced many domestic issues.

Jews and non-Jews alike tend to perceive this development in Jewcentric mirror images. As J. J. Goldberg and others have observed, the Jewish leaders who run these organizations probably have trouble believing their good fortune, that Jews have become so influential so fast in the most powerful country on earth. This is an entirely understandable sensation, since it is so recent and contrasts so starkly with the dire, helpless condition of European Jewry in recent times. Many Jewish American professionals are convinced that this is unprecedented, but of course it is not: Jewish communities and individual representatives of those communities have often exercised outsized power, from Spain to the rest of Europe to the various empires of Islam.

Even more amazing, the elite of American professional Jewry are sure that many non-Jews, Americans and others, exaggerate wildly how much influence they actually have. These professional Jews, many of whom—particularly the older set—remain insecure about Jewish social status and influence, sense that they are playing a kind of smoke-and-mirrors game. Non-Jews, taking a page from the *Protocols*, so exaggerate Jewish clout that they engage in anticipatory deference to Jews when they sense Jewish engagement on various issues. Even the Congressional Black Caucus, when it used to prepare its counterbudget proposals in the 1980s and 1990s, never suggested removing aid from Israel because they did not want to bring down on their head charges that they were anti-Semitic. When others do what you want without your even having to ask them in so many words, this is real power.

Professional Jews in America have understood this from the start. Nahum Goldman, the greatest pioneer of Jewish organizational empire building, was "a master illusionist," said one Jewish leader some years ago. "All the organizations he created—the World Jewish Congress, the Conference of Presidents—were designed to reinforce the myth of a powerful, mysterious body called world Jewry."[18] Abe Foxman knows it, too.

The non-Jewish world to a large extent believes in the myth of the *Protocols of the Elders of Zion*, and to some extent we in the Jewish community have not disabused them. . . . I know every time I meet a world leader who comes to see me, he's not coming to me because I'm Abe Foxman, the national director of the ADL. I know he's coming because he has been told, or someone sold him the concept, that the Jewish community is very strong and powerful. You know it because when you finish the conversation, they want to know what you can do for them in the media, what you can do for them in the Congress, and so on.[19]

Power tends to make people swagger, unexpected power all the more so, and a private feeling of perhaps unearned power perhaps most of all. And in the strange Jewish bubble of Manhattan Island, where all the major Jewish organizations except AIPAC are head-quartered, this swagger builds upon itself in strange ways. It has somehow turned brashness, or chutzpah, into a positive character trait, something that is most un-Jewish, whatever Alan Dershowitz may think, and something that has considerable counterproductive potential.

Professional Jews do have power, more than most Jews suppose but less than many non-Jews assume. This whole structure of influence and perception, however, is fundamentally unstable. Many foreigners who come to Washington hoping that American Jews will help them influence the U.S. government in their favor are basically playacting a psychodramatic monologue in their own heads. First they exaggerate Jewish power. Then they beseech it, asking it to help them in ways well beyond the Jews' power to do. Then they become wary of Jewish power, and some begin to fear it. And what is feared is very often resented in due course, even sometimes hated. This renders the myth of Jewish power a ride on a tiger in the longer run. At a certain private level, knowledge of that reinforces the insecurities that many professional Jews often bring to the table in the first place.

American Jewish professionals are thus, in a way, trapped in their own pretenses. They cannot give up trying to be powerful, or the whole smoke-and-mirrors edifice of their influence would vanish into thin air. Nor do they wish *not* to have power. But their way of going about maintaining their power can provoke resentment among non-Jews, and it also increasingly alienates many Israelis and most Israeli governments over the past few decades. Professional Jewish leaders

thus often find themselves trapped in a monologue of their own making, too. They depend on and feed off of Jewcentricity in two ways:
They need anti-Semitism in order to maintain their base of influence
among Jewish Americans, and their power projection into the gentile world depends on gentile exaggeration of Jewish influence. But
since both needs are based on exaggerations, those who ply them risk
encouraging the evils they postulate. Holocaust-and-Redemption
ideology is not a barrier to assimilation but a path for its transmission. The obsession with anti-Semitism generates more of it than
it vanquishes. At the very height of their secular power, therefore,
America's professional Jews have become questionable allies of the
Jewish community in America they claim to represent.

10

Self-Hating Jews

By speaking, by thinking, we undertake to clarify things, and that
forces us to exacerbate them, dislocate them, schematize them.
Every concept is in itself an exaggeration.

—José Ortega y Gasset

By "self-hating Jews" I mean those who identify themselves as
Jews but who take sharply adversarial positions on virtually
all matters of concern to the Jewish community. They are in
a significant way the precise opposites of professional Jews. Yet these
two manifestations of Jewish Jewcentricity actually evince as many
underlying similarities as they do superficial differences. They both
manifest sociologically novel types of Jews: Jews for whom the question of faith that has always been at the center of Jewish civilization,
and definitive of Jewish peoplehood, has become either marginal
or nonexistent. In short, a professional Jew is one for whom Jewish
ideology and race—the residue of Jewish civilization without the faith
we now call Judaism—are taken positively; a "self-hating" Jew is one
for whom they are taken negatively.

The term "self-hating Jew" points to a special case of Jewcentricity
in that it amounts to a category defined by both compound and
circular exaggeration: some Jews obsess negatively about their own
Jewishness, and other Jews obsess about and exaggerate the extent
to which this in fact happens. Genuine self-hating Jews would not be

such a big deal if other Jews did not exaggerate their number, nature, and significance, and if anti-Semites did not latch on to them as tools of selective representation.

The phrase "self-hating Jew" is too often used as a kind of half brick, not as useful as a whole brick, perhaps, but able to be thrown about twice as far. The phrase is frequently employed as a preemptory slur aimed at anyone who disagrees with the hurler about matters Jewish and Zionist. It often marks an illicit attempt to seize the higher moral ground in the form of a lazy gesture of name-calling that takes the place of an effort to understand. Many ultra-Orthodox Jews are quick to pin the "self-hating" label on any Jew whose standards of observance are less rigorous than their own. The circular result is that alienated Jews—or Jews who are merely uncomfortable with current mainstream Jewish narratives—who are called self-hating by other Jews, become more alienated still. This is inside, Jewish-on-Jewish Jewcentricity of a particularly unfortunate sort.

That said, self-hating Jews do exist. The definition is exactly the same as that stated and discussed above: it is the definition of anti-Semitism itself, the only difference being that the bigot happens to be a Jew. This obviously implies a kind of compound neurosis: if anti-Semitism is itself a kind of sickness, then a Jewish anti-Semite has got to be very neurotic indeed. But just as not all anti-Jewish remarks, acts, and views are anti-Semitic, so not all anti-Jewish remarks, acts, and views held by Jews evince self-hatred. There is a wide range of views about almost everything in the Jewish world, but even a very wide disparity of opinion does not mean that a fundamentally irrational process has to be at work in each and every disagreement. This is why in order to use the term "self-hating" to any good purpose, and to see when it is used for not good purposes, one needs to be scrupulous about defining it. Unfortunately, those Jews who use the label "self-hating" most often are frequently the least scrupulous about what they really mean by it.

We know Jewish self-hatred exists because we see examples from the annals of Jewish history. Or at least we think we do. It is difficult to distinguish among three related but still different phenomena: self-hatred, renegadism, and the behavior of a parvenu. The self-hater is neurotic, at best, in the many variations neurosis can take. The Jewish renegade can also be self-hating, but is not necessarily so; either way, his behavior toward Jews is active and public, while genuine self-hatred usually takes quietist forms. The parvenu seeks to ingratiate himself with select circles of non-Jews, and thinks that anti-Jewish gestures and behavior will help in that. This, too, can involve self-hatred, but it need not—it can be merely selfish and venal. Separating any one of these three kinds of behavior from the other two is not always easy.

Yet, certainly, self-hating Jewish renegades have occasionally wreaked great damage on Jews. In the past most such renegades were formal apostates who publicly renounced Judaism for some other faith, an act rendered nearly superfluous with the advent of secular modernity. The self-hatred label may still apply to historical cases, however, for converts from the Jewish religion almost universally acknowledged their birth into the Jewish people and accepted that there were inescapable implications of being thus born. Let just a few brief examples set the stage for a more contemporary discussion.

Two of the most colorful Jewish troublemakers of all time were Jason and Menelaus; in effect, they caused Hanukkah.

After Alexander the Great's death, his empire split into pieces, and the pieces made war against one another. The Jews within the realm were split, too, in a different but already familiar way, taking different sides and adopting opposing views about Hellenistic culture and Jewish religion. At one point, a Seleucid ruler (Antiochus III) decided on a Hellenization campaign as a precursor to attacking the Ptolemies, and with them the Romans, in Egypt. The Hellenization campaign went well, except in Judea. The Jews balked at putting statues of the king in their Temple, arguing that their taxes and army service were proof enough of their imperial loyalty. Antiochus III relented, but his son and successor, Antiochus Epiphanes (Antiochus IV), who inherited the Seleucid throne in 176 BCE, decided to press the issue. Among the divided Jews, the Jewish aristocrats of the day (Sadducaic in persuasion, for practical purposes), speaking Greek and liking Greek manners if not necessarily Greek religion, wanted to help Antiochus Epiphanes for reasons of their own. Having the emperor behind them, they reasoned, would help them best their Jewish adversaries (Pharisaic in persuasion, for practical purposes), less cosmopolitan, more culturally conservative stiff-necked types who did not like Hellenism at all—any of it. So when it came time for the new emperor to appoint a high priest, something traditionally done at the suggestion of the Jews themselves, the pro-Hellenist faction contrived through bribery to get one of their own appointed: Jason.

Jason's qualifications to be high priest were modest and his Hellenistic ambitions were fairly modest, too. He wanted to turn Jerusalem into an official Greek polis. Soon, however, another priest, named Menelaus, who avidly hated the religion of his forefathers, bought the office out from under Jason, and to raise the money to do so he plundered Temple gold. Most urban Jews had not objected actively to what Jason did; many objected strenuously to what Menelaus did, however, and they revolted when he turned out to enforce Greek culture in ways that the king probably never intended or anticipated.

The spat among the Jews that this caused irritated the Seleucid king, who believed he had more important problems with which to deal. So, with Menelaus's eager help and advice, he tried to put a stop to it by outlawing the Sabbath and the rite of circumcision and by inviting pagan rites into the Temple. Naked boys ran all over the courtyard in athletic activities and one can only imagine what else. Greek statues obscured the view of the Holy of Holies. When these outrages sparked greater opposition, Antiochus invaded Jerusalem, slaughtering many people. A new revolt now broke out in the countryside, however, and to nearly everyone's surprise, the anti-Hellenistic Jews, led by a family called the Maccabees, won. In 165 BCE they rededicated the Temple; they then continued the war until they had restored national independence, and, in around 140 BCE, they instituted the Hasmonean dynasty.

A few hundred years later, ben-Zakkai and his fellow rabbis decided, with the Bar Kochba catastrophe in mind, not to include the two Books of Maccabees in the canon of the Hebrew Bible—too much fighting, too much zealotry. Instead, they focused on the legend, dating from earlier times, about a small amount of consecrated olive oil burning improbably, miraculously even, for eight days, and on the candle-lighting traditions that had arisen when the Hasmonean dynasty turned out to be corrupt and altogether unpleasant. As for the horrible Jason and the even more horrible Menelaus, well, the less said about them the better: so the rabbis said basically nothing in the Talmud—at least nothing explicit. This is why most Jews celebrating Hanukkah today have never heard of them, and think the whole business was started by an anti-Jewish Selucid king. Not at all; Antiochus Epiphanies was not Jewcentric, and if the Jews had not insinuated their internal disputes into his busy life he probably would not have given them a second thought.

One might think the Jews would have learned from this not to play imperial politics using their own religious and personal disputes as a football, but they didn't. Just as the Jews got caught up in Greek imperial intrigues, they got caught up even worse in Roman ones, when a truly loathsome self-hating character named Antipater made Roman rule more embedded and vicious. (He was poisoned in 43 BCE by his own family members at a lascivious feast with his concubines and was succeeded by one of the plotters, his son Herod. Ah, but that is another story.)

It was an anonymous apostate Jew in Norwich, England, who in 1144 started the whole blood-libel disaster—the accusation that Jews kill Christian children to use their blood to bake matzohs for Passover. Another self-hating apostate made it even worse a century later. A self-hating apostate Jew named Nicholas Donin first caused the Talmud to be burned, in mid-thirteenth-century France. There were several such apostates in Spain, too; one of them, Evner de Burgos, who converted to Christianity in 1321, helped create the conditions for the anti-Jewish riots of 1391. But the prize, if not for troublemaking then for historical impact, belongs to one Johann Joseph Pfefferkorn.

Pfefferkorn, a Jewish butcher in sixteenth-century Cologne, was, apparently, caught selling nonkosher meat as kosher. He was ordered punished by the Jewish court, but, to escape his fate, he decided to convert. Criticized sharply, Pfefferkorn then wrote a series of inflammatory pamphlets claiming that the Talmud slandered Christianity, whereupon the local authorities gave Pfefferkorn the job of removing from the Talmud all such alleged language. The Jews appealed to the emperor, who appointed the redoubtable Johann von Reuchlin, a Catholic, to defend the Jews.[1]

After a long, drawn-out battle that involved even Martin Luther and Erasmus, Reuchlin, aided by the after-hours coaching of several rabbis, prevailed in 1516. This in turn brought about one of the most astonishing arguments of that era, between a group of Catholic clergy who sought to brand Reuchlin a heretic and those, whom we now call humanists, who defended him. In this dispute Pfefferkorn joined the reactionary clerics as an aid and publicist. The affair, which spread to envelop nearly all of Europe, had a major influence on Luther, who the very next year nailed his famous papers to the church door in Wittenberg. The behavior of the Church fathers against his friend Reuchlin in the Pfefferkorn affair was apparently the last straw for Luther. Thus, a seminal event of the Reformation, an event, it may be appreciated, not without a significant bearing on subsequent Jewish history, may have been catalyzed by the shenanigans of a renegade

Jew. The moral of the story, perhaps, is not to look too closely at the business practices of kosher butchers.

Spectacular as some of these episodes were, they were on the whole rare. And contrary to the views of the playwright David Mamet in *The Wicked Son*, Jewish self-hatred is relatively rare today, as well.[2] But that raises the question: what sorts of rare behaviors do qualify as Jewish self-hatred, as Jewish anti-Semitism? Are Philip Roth and Woody Allen self-hating Jews just because they mock or embody derogatory stereotypes of Jews? Many Jews think so, and some say so. What is the indictment, and does it stick? Is it accurate, or is it an example of compound Jew-on-Jew Jewcentricity?

Despite his disastrous error of emphasizing Jewish race over peoplehood, Mamet does manage to put this particular question into some useful perspective. He describes the immigrant generation of Ashkenazi Jews in America as a heroic one, coming to the New World with virtually no material possessions, working their fingers to the bone for their children, and managing in a single generation to sire doctors, lawyers, scholars, scientists, and all the rest. And what thanks has "the world of our fathers" received from assimilated, alienated second- and third-generation Jewish Americans? They have gotten *Goodbye, Columbus* and any number of Woody Allen characters, including, of course, his own, that demean and lampoon this very achievement. Mamet goes too far as usual, but his dagger nevertheless strikes bone:

> The savaging of the Ashkenazi immigrants, in the novels of their children in the 1950s and '60s, bore fruit (inter alia) in the nebbish stage personalities of various post–Borscht Belt comedians, a Jewish gloss on a generally accepted form of entertainment—racial indictment.[3]

Mamet likens the process of the non-Yiddish-accented Jew turning on his forebears to white people having invented "darky" vaudeville and television programs like *Amos 'n Andy*. The parallel doesn't really work, but Mamet's subsequent observation does:

> Can one imagine African-Americans, the descendants of slaves, mocking their forebears' trials, and the fears and strategies both for accommodation and for self-respect, forged over two hundred years of inescapable bondage? Must that trauma not be respected?

So is it not a form of self-hatred for Jews to mock their poor, struggling immigrant forebears?

It can be, when combined with other signs of self-hatred, but it needn't be. Roth, Allen, and others—even Mel Brooks, who, after all, has put *payis* on El Al airplanes in his movies—deserve the freedom to work out their identities and discomforts through their art. Besides, a lot of what they and others have done casts a low light not on the immigrant generation and its ways, but rather on what their children and children's children have done with their sacrifices. A good deal of the mocking is self-mockery. That can be pathological, but it can also be a form of therapy, maybe, in these cases, run a little too much in public. Laughing at oneself is not necessarily a bad thing; it can be an exercise in humility—a paramount Jewish value.

There is also nothing self-hating about someone who wants to believe in God and has probably tried to do so, but just can't—and prefers to joke about the lingering consequences instead of crying over them. That is a reasonable way to interpret much of what Roth has done and most of what Allen has done with Jewish themes. They have not raised the American Jewish experience to the level of fine art, as did Isaac Bashevis Singer, Saul Bellow, Bernard Malamud, or, in Canada, Mordecai Richler. But the fact that their works are less sophisticated or lowbrow does not make them anti-Semitic. Indiscretion, insensitivity, and even bad judgment are not tantamount to self-hatred.

Literary figures aside, what about someone who is proud to be a nonpracticing Jew because he believes that all religions are chauvinistic and cause wars? What about the Jew who is invited to a Bar or Bat Mitzvah service where some non-Jews are also invited, and shows more obvious discomfort with the prospect of donning a skullcap than a non-Jew? What about a Jew in a mixed marriage who becomes angry if the non-Jewish spouse or a child expresses curiosity about an aspect of Judaism, Jewish philosophy, or Jewish history? What about the Jew who attends a family seder but invariably causes a scene by denouncing the ritual at the ritual? What about an alienated Jew who is proud of how many years it has been since he or she has set foot in a synagogue or said a prayer, but who does transcendental meditation? What if this Jew decries the irrationality of the Jewish religion and the rituals associated with it—and would never think of seeking out a rabbi to discuss a problem—but, as Mamet put it, thinks nothing of hiring a "life coach," or nothing of enacting rituals with a psychotherapist?

Well, if *all* religions are blamed for wars, if religious rituals and objects from *all* religions cause discomfort, if a family member's curiosity about *all* religious civilizations evokes anger, then no, this is not self-hating behavior. But if only Jewish issues evoke these behaviors, then yes, you are seeing Jewish self-hatred before your very eyes.

At the source of all self-hating behavior, Jewish and otherwise, is a palette of fear. The main hue in this palette is clear: This group into which I have been born is hated, tormented, despised. I do not want to be hated, tormented, and despised, but since I cannot escape my birth identity, I will not only dissociate myself from the group's views, I will affirm the narrative of those who hate us. In this way I can appease and propitiate them, and they will not harm me. Thus is fear father to cowardice, which in turn is father to self-abasement and self-hatred.

Jewish self-hatred, in other words, demonstrates the successful intimidation of Jews to the point that they affirm accusations of their own blameworthiness.[4] In some cases the self-hating Jew may think such behavior will actually protect him and his family. In others, the self-hating Jew may simply be trying to "get it over with," trying to relieve the horrible uncertainty of being hated and fated to be harmed. In still others, he may be suffering some intense guilt for one thing or another, and try to relieve the anguish by arguing to himself that he is not to blame because, after all, Jews are evil—offloading personal responsibility, in other words, onto a collective scapegoat for which he is not responsible.

A secondary hue goes like this: "I am brilliant and special just as my mother told me; but 'these people' will not recognize my brilliance or accept me as a leader. I will spite them by joining with those who hate us, and the leaders who have rejected me will suffer." Indeed, some people are contrarians by nature, or by accidents of childrearing. They differentiate themselves by artificially putting distance between them and the rest of the community. Contrarianism is common in adolescents, but some maintain contrarian personalities into full adulthood. If they happen to be Jewish, assimilated, and brilliant, they can fit the description of a self-hating Jew by this route, which, of course, contrarians that they are, they will in turn vociferously and necessarily deny.

A related hue can be summed up as "It's hard to be a Jew. The demands are great; the standards are high; my family's expectations are unceasing. I fear I will disappoint those who love me, so I will denounce the premise. I won't have to fear failure if I don't try. If my parents don't love me unconditionally, I don't want their love. Their expectations are hateful because they make me afraid."

Still another hue: "I covet my freedom not to submit to any external standard. If I join the group, I may become dependent on others for my happiness. They will then have power over me, so I will hold their power at bay by insulting what they hold most dear." For this person, to engage at all with "the Jews" when they are acting as Jews risks surrendering all. Any possible engagement, even just touching a yarmulke, touches off anxiety, even panic.

I do not claim to have mastered the extraordinary lengths to which the mind of a child or a young adult can go in order to cope with the baroque psychological peculiarities inherent in family life. I do know, however, that for any person to choose an identification built around what he or she has rejected rather than what he or she has embraced is not a rational choice. It is simply not true that an alienated Jew cannot leave the fold, renounce Judaism and Jewish peoplehood, convert to some other religion, and have done with it. It has happened for centuries, and it is easier today than ever. Self-hating Jews, however, do not take the exit ramp. Their anger and self-loathing, whatever its source, can have no outlet unless they remain in proximity to other Jews. Literal apostasy can have all sorts of causes, some of them rational. Self-hatred by its very nature is irrational, no less than groundless hatred directed outward is irrational.

So there really is Jewish self-hatred. It is a mental pathology, just like anti-Semitism as manifested in non-Jews. But these days the term "self-hating Jew" is rarely invoked in cases of real pathology. Because so many Jews in the modern era have themselves redefined Jewish identity in political terms, much of the self-hating debate has migrated in that direction, along with the ongoing issue of anti-Semitism. Just as not every criticism of Israel and Zionism offered up by a non-Jew is anti-Semitism in anti-Zionist drag, so not every *Jewish* criticism of Israel and Zionism is either.

Some Jewish anti-Israel invective is merely hot-under-the-collar criticism. Some people hold views on nationalism and the use of force that predispose them to loathe all Israeli governments over the past sixty years. Some Jewish American contrarians of the Left hate the U.S. government, and only because of the "special" relationship between the United States and Israel do they hate Israel by association. If Israel were a radical anti-American state, such people might applaud it, so this is not *Jewish* self-hatred, but American self-hatred once removed.

There is also, of course, a long-standing Orthodox Jewish form of anti-Zionism, and there are those who respect Orthodoxy and disparage the Holocaust-and-Redemption fakery that has usurped it, but who for one reason or another do not lead an Orthodox life. None of these are examples of Jewish self-hatred. But when nonreligious Jews single out Israel for its supposedly "criminal" behavior, when that behavior is in fact indistinguishable from German or Chinese or Russian or Serbian or even some American behavior over the years, that exemplifies selectivity at the least. And if a Jewish critic persists, at high emotion, linking most or all the ills of the Middle East and American foreign policy to Israel's supposed criminal misdeeds, then one has conspiratorial Jewish anti-Semitism lurking in the would-be protective shadow of mere anti-Zionism.

Are there any such people? Yes, but it is not always clear who they are. What is one to make, for example, of a Jewish couple who, upon naming their first son, write that they were moved by the idea of calling him "a Jew without the right of return" so that he could explore his Jewish identity without confusing it with a form of nationalism?[5] That's not self-hatred; just a matter of opinion about politics, and perhaps a bit of parvenu, show-off contrarianism.

Other examples are less ambiguous, many obscure but some not.[6] Is Noam Chomsky, whose mother was a Hebrew school teacher in Philadelphia, a self-hating Jew? Many Jews think so, and some point to what seems to them to have been some unusual family dynamics. But others point out that his accusations about Israeli "criminality" are not special; he thinks the United States is a criminal nation, too. This is also a man who was at one time an enthusiastic supporter of Pol Pot and the Khmer Rouge—anyone who is objectively anti–United States is a friend of his—so why anyone trusts his judgment on anything outside of his academic linguistics specialty is a mystery to me.

What about Richard Falk? Falk is a former law professor at Princeton who has likened Israeli behavior in the occupied territories to that of Nazis, has defended this statement from challenge, and has warned of Israeli intentions of genocide against Palestinians.[7] Many Jews believe he is self-hating. He might be at some sunken and unreachable level, but Falk seems not to care particularly about Jews one way or the other. He is a pacifist, has for decades been hostile to all U.S. government foreign policy strategies, and has not obsessed particularly about Israel until recently. His most recent obsession, rather, has been to doubt that 9/11 was the work of foreigners; he actually takes seriously the argument that the U.S. government itself may have staged the attacks. Others, however, have made use of Falk's nominal Jewishness for their own purposes; certainly anti-Israel forces at the United Nations have done so, maneuvering to appoint him to a special human rights rapporteur position for Palestine.

Norman Finkelstein, the son of Holocaust survivors, takes a roughly similar view of Israel, but unlike Chomsky and Falk, Finkelstein makes a living from talking about Jewish issues and comes close to denying the Holocaust. In his book *The Holocaust Industry: Reflections on the Exploitation of Jewish Suffering*, he wrote that Jews exaggerate and falsify the Holocaust in order to "justify criminal policies of the Israeli state and U.S. support for these policies." As he sees it,

> The Zionists indeed learnt well from the Nazis. So well that it seems that their morally repugnant treatment of the Palestinians, and their attempts to destroy Palestinian society within Israel and the occupied territories, reveals them as basically Nazis with beards and black hats.[8]

Finkelstein probably admired the T-shirt some anti-Semites in the Netherlands created last year, which showed Anne Frank in a red and white kaffiyeh. He is the exact opposite of a professional Jew, being in effect 180 degrees away from anything Abraham Foxman or Alan Dershowitz thinks, writes, and says. That does not make Foxman and Dershowitz right, but it does make Finkelstein a self-hating Jew.

There are also non-American examples of Jewish self-hatred, mostly posing in the costume of anti-Zionism and mostly in Europe. Many American Reform Jews were anti-Zionist in the period before World War II and for a while even after, having founded the American Council on Judaism for that purpose. Their fear, for these Jews who had defined the peoplehood out of their Jewishness, was that they would be accused of dual loyalty. The same is true for some Jewish intellectuals in Europe, except that the community they care about is far smaller— the left-wing, postmodernist academic-intellectual sanctum they see as their real home, and which they will do virtually anything to remain a part of.

This has been going on for years, but the craving of such Jews for acceptance into their desired ideological circles intensified after 9/11 when the undertone of European mutterings over Islamist terrorism quickly turned to blame Israel (read: the Jews) for all these problems. The number of Jews in Europe (and some American Jews who study Europe as a specialty) who have gone out of their way to publicly dissociate themselves from and denounce Israel is impressive.

These include Adam Shatz, a senior editor at the *London Review of Books* and the main reason the famous Mearsheimer-Walt essay, "The Israel Lobby," was invited into those pages; Brian Klug, an Oxford University philosopher who has turned his interest in and expertise on anti-Semitism upside down; and several others.[9]

These and other anti-Zionist Jews have been hailed in much of Europe as brave and honorable "dissident" Jews, the "authentic" voice of Judaism. They enable European anti-Semites to argue that they do not hate Jews, only Zionists. So Israel might be, as Daniel Bernard, the French ambassador to Great Britain put it in 2001, "that shitty country that threatens world peace," but Jews are not necessarily shitty people. These Jewish "dissidents" become European celebrities in the blink of a media eye. To give just one example, the May 8, 2008, issue of the French magazine *Le Nouvelle Observateur* features Avraham Burg (a post-Zionist Israeli of whom more in chapter 14) and Régis Debray talking up the "reinvention of Israel" as a non-Jewish, binational state, as though this were a practial mainstream idea that could actually be put into practice.

The artifice of dividing "authentic" Jewish dissidents from other Jews is nothing new either, particularly in Europe. When Jews were rootless, stateless, beleaguered, and in distress, they "proved" the Church's curse on them. When they stood up and reestablished themselves on their own terms, they posed a theological problem. The contemporary European leftist enthronement of anti-Zionist "dissident" Jews represents exactly the same phenomenon in secular form: Jews who define and pursue their own interests pose an ideological problem. And there has been, of course, a long intermediate history of the same phenomenon between medieval times and the present day. For a long time now some anti-traditional and anti-religious Jews have advocated that Jews dissent as Jews rather than as apostates from Judaism. For a long time, too, European anti-Semites have used these contrarian Jews by way of selective representation as an excuse for anti-Semitism, to wit: "I don't hate Jews, just Jews who insist on being 'too Jewish.'"

The European and American Left's self-interested adulation of Jewish "dissidents" is anti-Semitic not only because of its selective representation, but also because of its manifestation of double standards. "If someone quoted a black intellectual to support the theory behind slavery and apartheid," Emanuele Ottolenghi has pointed out, "or a woman to extol the benefits of infibulation [female genital mutilation], very few people would fall into the trap."[10] So why do leftists fall when Jews make what amount to anti-Jewish statements? Obviously, because they *wish* to do so; they are actively searching for a legitimizing pretext. So whether these critics are really Jewish anti-Semites or are merely trying to ingratiate themselves with their non-Jewish colleagues—as Hannah Arendt once famously defined Jewish parvenus—their favorable reception clearly shines a light on the nature of anti-Semitism on the Left in Europe, the United States, and elsewhere. It is still there.

Does it matter, though? Since it's such a minority view, largely sequestered in the academic world, one could easily conclude that it doesn't; but we should not rush to that particular judgment. If good ideas matter, so too can bad ones. Remember that while the master-race lunacy of the Nazis spewed from the mouths of madmen, these madmen came to rule some sixty million Germans, the vast majority of whom were not mad. This happened because the world had been partially anesthetized by the pseudoscientific writings of racists during the previous century, so that when mass murder was perpetrated in the name of racist insanity, the rest of the world barely uttered a word until it was too late.

Nationalism imperceptibly turned into racism then; today the anti-Jewish venom posing as anti-Zionism (again, not that *all* anti-Zionism is anti-Semitism) is reenacting this same sequence as a form of postnationalism turned into racism. The sorts of things that get said at Durban United Nations conferences on racism in the twenty-first century are directly analogous to the anti-Semitic anesthesia of the twentieth. They are also analogous to the set-piece religious disputations of medieval times, the important difference being that in medieval times the Jews at least had the right to defend themselves. If it ever comes to the point where Israel suffers massive casualties from an attack by weapons of mass destruction—not all that far-fetched a possibility—most of the world will, predictably, again say barely a word about it, until it is too late.

Other than to illustrate a general argument as I have done here, there is not much point busying oneself with whether this or that particular Jew is self-hating, a renegade, or a parvenu. Since self-hatred qualifies as a clinical condition, the only way to really diagnose a case is to be a qualified professional who can observe an individual in more or less controlled conditions. This is almost impossible to do, so it follows that making specific accusations of self-hatred ought to be at least as scarce as making accusations of anti-Semitism. Let us see what happens, however, when the strictness of these conditions is ignored.

Are the noted scholar and critic George Steiner and the financier and philanthropist George Soros self-hating Jews because they reject the idea of Jewish nationalism and hence the legitimacy of a Jewish state? If one believes that the destruction of Israel is tantamount to the final destruction of world Jewry—that there can be no future for Jews and Judaism if what is, in effect, the Third Commonwealth is destroyed, if one fuses politics and civilization as a whole—then sure, Steiner and Soros are self-hating. But in the nineteenth century, and for centuries before that, few pious Jews believed that Jewish nationalism was necessary for Jewish survival. The founder of modern Orthodoxy, Shimshon Rafael Hirsch, was anti-Zionist. So were many Hasidic sects, and many, like the Satmar, still are. And no one who understands traditional Jewish theology can claim that such thinkers are out of line with rabbinic Judaism, which traditionally has opposed forcing the end and fighting for the restitution of the Jews to the Land of Israel. How could such a position possibly be construed as self-hating?

What accusations of Jewish self-hatred based on political disagreements tell us is that Jewish identity itself no longer has a common core. When post-Emancipation and especially post-Holocaust Jewry transmuted the traditional formula of Jewish peoplehood into the new formula of political Zionism, the Jewish world split. True political Zionists are nationalists who negate the Diaspora, in other words, who want to end the Diaspora with the ingathering of Jews to Israel, and who argue that the Diaspora had no positive purpose in Jewish history. Jews who are not Zionists, however strongly they may feel about the necessity of the State of Israel as a "night shelter" for Jews in trouble, do not negate the Diaspora. We now have Jews in the first camp calling Jews in the second self-hating.

This is ironic in the sense that those who now claim to be the most Jewish of Jews as nationalists make arguments about the nature of the Diaspora that contradict mainstream rabbinic ones no less than anti-nationalist Reform Jews did two centuries ago. So before coming to Steiner and Soros, a short lesson on the now fractured Jewish understanding of anti-Semitism is necessary to clarify the key point in advance.

To the rabbinic way of thinking, anti-Semitism is evil, but evil is real. It has no specific root social cause; it is part of the cosmic drama God has created for reasons of His own, all bound up in the biblical message from the book of Numbers that Jews are "a people who live alone" and are "not to be reckoned among the nations." Orthodox Jews have traditionally seen anti-Semitism enigmatically, through the story of the Book of Esther, the Passover Haggadah, and even more basically through the perplexing commandment to "blot out the memory of Amalek." The commandment is enigmatic because it is accompanied by the adjuration "do not forget" to do it, the problematic logic being that if Jews ever succeeded in blotting out the memory of Amalek, there would be nothing left to remember.

Reflective in-the-tradition Jews have often seen anti-Semitism as a kind of cosmic necessity as well as an evil: the chosen Jewish mission was bound to sire its antithesis in order to create the tension necessary to propel that mission forward. This is one way Jews have interpreted the Book of Jonah, which is read publicly in its entirety on the afternoon of Yom Kippur. Jews are obliged, whether they like it or not, to stand as a reproach to non-Jews who are misbehaving as human beings, yet the Jews reap only calumny from failure and disappointment from success. This explains the otherwise indecipherable humor in Tevye's remark in *Fiddler on the Roof* that it's nice to be chosen, but please, God, why not choose some other people for a change?

Pious traditional Jews also shunned nationalism in its various changing shapes as a form of idolatry, and some affirmed the Diaspora in a positive as well as in a negative way. The negative way of affirmation we already know from the theology embedded in the siddur: Diaspora is necessary to cleanse Jews of their collective sins; it is roughly analogous to the biblical generation of the wilderness after the Exodus from Egypt, who had to wander forty years in the desert for their progeny, untainted by life in slavery, to be worthy of possessing the land. Positive affirmation of the Diaspora, on the other hand, involves both a theological and a philosophical attitude. Of course Jews have to wander, suffer, and be an example of nobility-in-difference to demonstrate to the world the holy traits of toleration and compassion; that is God's plan. But Jews gain though this experience, as well: exposure to historical variety and challenge accelerates the moral education of the Jews. The more Jews wander, the rabbis sometimes supposed, the wiser Jews become, and the better able they become to perform their appointed mission in the world.

This traditional view of the cosmic purposes of anti-Semitism, which had been almost universally held among Jews before modern times, gathered competition with the onset of modernity. Some secular Zionists of the nineteenth and early twentieth centuries, and most Reform Jews too, used to believe, usually without coming right out and saying it, that anti-Semites and Orthodox rabbis caused each other. Stop the religious chauvinism inherent in the idea of chosenness, and stop the ritual obligations that make Jews appear clannish in the eyes of non-Jews, and the anti-Semites will go away for lack of anything to misunderstand and complain about.

Jewish socialists believed, additionally, that the origins of anti-Semitism were economic, so that, along with jettisoning the rabbis, Jews needed to normalize their social situation by supporting anticapitalist revolution. If Jews were not forced by the capitalist system into occupational niches that made them be, or appear to be, exploitive of and parasitic upon the masses, the idea went, the anti-Semites would disappear, again, for lack of anything to complain about. Socialist Zionists advocated both courses, but believed that normalizing the Jewish social situation could not take place wherever Jews remained minorities in anti-Semitic lands: hence the need for a new, socially progressive Jewish society in *Eretz Yisrael* and, probably, a state of their own.

What these and other root analyses of anti-Semitism have had in common is the presumption that it's up to the Jews to do something about anti-Semitism. And why not? Is it logical that masses of people would become bigots for no reason? Doesn't it follow that it is really all about *us*, even if it is only our history having gone haywire, having caused *them*? Zionism was seen by its early adherents as the only way to get rid of anti-Semitism—by negating the Diaspora in which it was inherent.

As we have already seen, in-the-tradition Jews have never subscribed to the argument that Jews themselves somehow caused anti-Semitism. It therefore followed that neither Zionism nor anything else Jews could do would get rid of it. When our times turned so explicitly and massively political, when we all started "living in a political world," as Dylan put it, the Jewish attitude toward anti-Semitism and related phenomena split into not just two but four parts: secular Zionists who believed they could solve anti-Semitism through social revolution; religious Zionists who believed they could solve anti-Semitism by hastening the advent of the messiah; religious non- or anti-Zionists who affirmed the traditional view of anti-Semitism as part of God's plan for the Jewish people; and secular non- or anti-Zionists who, without necessarily knowing it, secularized the traditional view—that anti-Semitism exists but is neither caused by nor subject to eradication by anything Jews may do—by translating it from theology into philosophy. These secular non- or anti-Zionist Jews asserted that Zionism could not eradicate anti-Semitism, and so in effect they affirmed the Diaspora despite the anti-Semitism that went with it.

The affirmation of the Diaspora as a secular philosophical act suggests that being nowhere in terms of a conventional territorial existence means Jews are everywhere; and that were Jews again to be "somewhere," Jews might end up being nowhere. In other words, the positive affirmation of the Diaspora presupposes an irony: Were the Jews to normalize themselves and be like all the nations, they would in effect choose to be unchosen. They would replay in modern secular political terms the situation in Samuel I, chapter 8, where Samuel warns the people against their request for a king. This is what the great German Jewish mathematician Erich Kähler meant when he wrote:

> [T]he Jews did not survive the entire history of the world to end up with national power politics like any other. With its 3,000-year tradition and the inner structure developed from it this Jewry simply cannot be equated with other nations. It cannot be encompassed in the mold of a modern nation if its most precious heritage is not to be abandoned. Judaism is neither a mere nationality nor a mere faith or religious ritual. . . . It is different by virtue of a unique combination of atavistic rootedness with ideational, universally human substance. . . . a combination of extreme intensity with extreme breadth of aim.[11]

Clearly, Orthodoxy and Zionism were not compatible at the theological or the philosophical level at the beginning of modern Zionism. Rabbi Hirsch did not exemplify an exception but the rule. Indeed, it is the compatibility of Orthodoxy and Zionism that is novel, starting in the early twentieth century with the minority religious Zionism movement called Mizrahi and later canonized, so to speak, by the innovative Rabbi Avraham Yitzhak Kook, the Chief Rabbi of Palestine, in the interwar period. No even half-educated Jew would imagine calling Rabbi Hirsch a self-hating Jew. Why, then, George Steiner, whose positions arise from the same intellectual tradition, only expressed in secular form like that of Kähler and, for that matter, his colleague Albert Einstein?[12]

Steiner has gone out of his way to reject political Zionism and affirm the Diaspora, and he is not religiously observant. He has thrown into the faces of other Jews their own derivative political personalities by trying to force them to acknowledge that had it not been for Hitler, there would be no Israel.

Steiner is perhaps not very polite, but is he really self-hating? He was born in France in 1929 to Austrian Jewish parents. His father was a nervous man who always worried about the anti-Semites just outside the window. His mother was a brilliant linguist, who put young George through a regimen of homeschooling so draconian it might have driven anyone mad. He could read four languages, including Homeric Greek, by the time he was seven or eight years old. He was born with a with-ered right arm, but his mother forced him to write with it anyway. When he was eventually sent off to school, it was to a Jewish school.

Steiner and his parents left France in 1940 just weeks before the Nazis arrived, and he later learned that he was the only one of his classmates to survive the war. He then spent much of the 1950s and 1960s lecturing in Europe and America and writing about the Holocaust before it was popular in elite non-Jewish circles to con-sider it an event worthy of scholarly attention. American audiences and colleagues then, including those at Princeton, scolded Steiner for paying so much attention to it in his work.

Steiner has never agreed with Zionism and he affirms the Diaspora, but he has never lived under any illusions about the trade-offs involved. In a London talk on February 11, 2008, for example, Steiner shocked his audience—especially those who had come to hear him attack Israeli government policies—by saying that Israel has a right to defend itself by any means necessary, up to and including tor-ture. For that, unfortunately, in his view, is the logic that inheres in the nationalist path recent Jewish history has taken. Six years earlier he told another London audience something along the lines of what his nervous father probably once said to him in Paris, and along the lines of what traditional Orthodox Jews took for granted for centuries:

> Wherever Jews live they remain vulnerable to a hatred that never dies. So keep your bags packed and make sure your children learn foreign languages, to equip yourselves for permanent displacement.[13]

At the time, Jonathan Sacks tried to refute Steiner. Now, Rabbi Sacks's own view seems closer to Steiner's, at least in this regard, than to his own of a half dozen years ago, as British anti-Semitism and anti-Zionism have grown apace. With all this in mind, what Jew thinks he has the right to label George Steiner "self-hating"?

What about the other George—George Soros? As is well known, Soros was born in Hungary in 1930 to a wealthy family. His father was a prominent lawyer. When the Nazis occupied Budapest in 1944, Soros's father decided to split his family up. He bought them forged papers and bribed a government official to take fourteen-year-old George in and swear that he was his Christian godson.

On December 20, 1998, Soros spoke to Steve Kroft of *60 Minutes* about what happened next. As the show aired, vintage footage appeared of Jews walking in line in 1944 Budapest, and Kroft said: "These are pictures from 1944 of what happened to George Soros's friends and neighbors." The photos continued, of women and men with bags over their shoulders walking; then a photo of a crowd by a train, then the train leaving the station, and so on. Kroft went on to describe Soros watching as other Jews were sent to their deaths. Asked if he felt guilty, or was plagued by the memory, Soros replied:

> Well, of course I could be on the other side or I could be the one from whom the thing is being taken away. But there was no sense that I shouldn't be there, because that was—well, actually, in a funny way, it's just like in markets—that if I weren't there—of course, I wasn't doing it, but somebody else would—would, would be taking it away anyhow. And it was the—whether I was there or not, I was only a spectator, the property was being taken away. So the—I had no role in taking away that property. So I had no sense of guilt.

This is a strange, dissociated comment, to be sure. Soros depersonalizes an intensely personal experience by theoretical reference to market behavior. One would not be far wrong, probably, in seeing some sort of neurosis, long petrified by years of denial, lurking behind such a peculiar remark. But in this Soros is hardly unique among Holocaust survivors. Many, as noted, simply stopped being Jews at all, like George Allen's mother and Madeleine Albright's father. Soros, however, does not deny being a Jew, but for whatever reasons, neurotic or not, he has no particular interest in Judaism or in Israel. He is a financier by trade and has become active in liberal politics in the United States. He has funded a host of activities, including the Central European University and the Open Society Institutes. But he has never, as far as anyone knows, given any money to a Jewish charity. Even the synagogue in Budapest, where many Hungarian Jews were temporarily imprisoned and some died in 1944, was restored not with Soros's help, but mainly with donations from Bernard Schwartz (Tony Curtis, that is, as you may remember from chapter 7).

Soros fancies himself a citizen of the world, and in this he is not unlike many secular Central European Jews going back several decades. Like Steiner, he seemed to have inherited the patrician, antinationalist attitudes of the Hapsburg elite mind-set. As a result,

however, Soros has become a target of harsh criticism. Martin
Peretz seems to have taken a special dislike to him even before the
60 Minutes interview, but he is not alone.[14] Soros has been widely
accused of being self-hating. Is he?

Again, like him or not (I don't), agree with him or not about
politics (I don't), George Soros is not a self-hating Jew. He may be
morally insensitive, selfish, and arrogant. He may also be simply
incapable of coming to terms with what happened in his youth. But
let any who would call him self-hating try to relive what it must have
been like to be a fourteen-year-old Jewish boy in Nazi Budapest,
separated from his parents and looking on as his friends and
neighbors were being processed for mass murder. Until you are sure
you know what such an experience might have done to you, think
what you like; but please be so kind as to keep your mouth shut and
your ink in the well.

As I have suggested, professional Jews and self-hating Jews have much
in common: they both remain Jews without the necessary reference
to the faith and mission at the heart of Jewish civilization. In a way,
too, they need one another. Professional Jews in America need anti-
Semitism as a part of their raison d'être, and self-hating Jews help to
provide and justify it in non-Jews. The counterproductive behavior
of some professional Jews, on the other hand, gives self-hating Jews
something all too easy to loathe. Both are Jewcentric—the professional Jew because he thinks Jews are special even without the spiritual heritage that makes them so, and the self-hating Jew because, like
all anti-Semites, he thinks Jews are inherently and consequentially
noxious. Both are mistaken. Jews without Judaism are not special,
and Jews with Judaism are not noxious, inherently, consequentially, or
otherwise.

Alas, this does not exhaust the spectrum of Jewcentric behavior.
There is plenty more of it concerning, and in, the Middle East. So
pack your bags—we're off to part three of this book.

PART THREE

Jewcentricity
in
the Middle East

11

The Anti-Israel Lobby

'Tis a rule of manners to avoid exaggeration.

— Ralph Waldo Emerson

One would like to think that superstition, prejudice, bigotry, and other forms of irrationality are giving way to a more enlightened global society. One would like to think that the Whig interpretation of history, based on the belief that material and moral progress are not only real but tend to move forward in lock-step, is now reaching global scale through the rationalizing impetus of science-based economic growth and development. Whole theories of contemporary international relations are based on that supposition, just as whole theories are based on the seemingly contrary view that cultural cleavages in the world are likely to reemerge in reaction against the identity-smashing, homogenizing tendencies of global economic integration.

These may turn out not to be opposite tendencies so much as alternating ones, dancing in a dialectic of outward pulses toward rationality and one-world consciousness, and inward retrench-ments toward insularity and particularity. Evidence for the growth of both rationality *and* irrationality may be found within the complex forces of globalization. It depends on where, how, and at what one looks.

Which tendency will prove the more dominant we do not know, and cannot know, for the matter is subject to human agency yet unexercised. But we do know that both the historical and the American manifestations of Jewcentricity now meet back in the place where it all began—in the Middle East—and there are no signs that Jewcentricity in all four of its basic forms is shrinking. We start part three on American shores by analyzing the revealing Jewcentric extravaganza of the "Israel Lobby" affair, then look at the role of the Arab-Israeli conflict in the region and the world, at the Jewcentricity of contemporary Muslim societies, and finally at the curious phenomenon of post-Zionism in Israel.

So peculiar is Jewish history and so outsized are some Jewish achievements and tragedies that, to any objective observer, efforts at exaggeration should be superfluous. But, as we have seen, exaggeration occurs anyway. Maybe there simply aren't any objective observers, or maybe they have better things to do. In any event, there is no better illustration of this general phenomenon in the context of Jewcentricity than the debate, such as it has been, over "the Israel lobby," an ambiguous term describing the organized Jewish American community.

In recent years, this debate has revolved around the writings of John Mearsheimer and Stephen Walt, notably a paper and then a book they wrote called *The Israel Lobby*. The authors argue in essence that U.S. foreign policy has been distorted, particularly in the Middle East but really on a global scale, by the exertions of Jews in the United States who have managed to bend the American national interest to that of Israel. The authors believe that the Israel Lobby— they always use a capital L for that word—has made U.S. foreign policy too interventionist, notably in causing the Iraq war, and that U.S. support for Israel is a main source of Islamist terrorism directed against the United States.

This argument did not start out as a book. An essay by the authors appeared in the *London Review of Books* of March 23, 2006, and almost simultaneously as a somewhat longer Harvard Working Paper, after the magazine that originally commissioned the essay, the *Atlantic*, rejected it. The article and the working paper having created quite a stir, the authors parlayed the ruckus into the book, published by Farrar, Straus, and Giroux in 2007, for which the two reportedly received an advance of $750,000 to split between them. The book became a nonfiction best seller (as did a rebuttal to it quickly cobbled together and signed by none other than Abraham Foxman).[1]

Throughout the second half of 2006 and 2007, there was a great deal of political heavy breathing over *The Israel Lobby* among both its supporters and its detractors. As with most such affairs, however, its half-life proved fairly brief. Before the middle of 2008, the hubbub had pretty much faded away, with the actual affairs of states having been affected not one whit—despite the authors' efforts to keep the buzz buzzing, the better to sell more books and promote their views. What was somewhat surprising about all this, however, was the impression on the part of many that the views expressed in the book represented something new under the sun. They did not.

More than fifty years ago, a European-born analyst of world affairs commented that "Americans, as people go, have but a short history—and little to forget."[2] He might have added that, even so, they manage all the same to forget what little there is. The Mearsheimer-Walt attack on the supposedly disproportionate, over-weening influence of "the Israel Lobby" on U.S. foreign policy was merely the latest in a long line of contentions all with the same theme, their manifestations differing only on account of the real-world context in which they were set.

As we have already seen, as far as President Truman was concerned, there was an Israel lobby hectoring him since even before the State of Israel was proclaimed in May 1948. In 1957, long before the American Israel Public Affairs Committee (AIPAC) became the public relations juggernaut of renown that it is today, Secretary of State John Foster Dulles told California senator William Knowland, then the Republican minority leader, that

> I am aware how impossible it is in this country to carry out a foreign policy not approved by the Jews. Marshall and Forrestal found that out. I am going to try to have one. This does not mean that I am anti-Jewish, but I believe in what George Washington said in his Farewell Address that an emotional attachment should not interfere. . . . We cannot have our policies made in Jerusalem.[3]

Coming just weeks after U.S. policy had forced Israel to withdraw from the Sinai after the 1956 Suez War, a matter over which the pro-Israel lobby was completely powerless, it is not at all clear what Dulles was talking about. If any lobby played a major role in that presidential decision, it was the oil lobby, not the Israel lobby.

The question of the Israel lobby and its supposed influence has come up repeatedly over the years since Suez. Noteworthy episodes clustered around the mistaken Israeli attack on the USS *Liberty* during the June 1967 War, an episode that has become the source of almost limitless anti-Israel conspiracy theories. The same accusation arose again surrounding successful efforts in the 1980s to unseat politicians deemed unfriendly to Israel, like Senator Charles Percy and Congressman Paul Findley. (Findley wrote a terrible book about it, which only confirmed all the reasons why he did not belong in the U.S. Congress.) Other books making similar arguments followed: Noam Chomsky's *The Fateful Triangle* (1983), Stephen Green's *Taking Sides* (1984), Edward Tivnan's *The Lobby* (1987), and, above all, the *The Passionate Attachment* (1992) by George Ball, a widely respected former high-level State Department official. Arkansas senator J. William Fulbright liked to quip that the Congress of the United States was "Israeli-occupied territory." Zbigniew Brzezinski, national security advisor to President Jimmy Carter, has made similar kinds of comments for years, though usually in less colorful ways.[4]

All along, too, for decade after decade, organizations like the American Educational Trust have taken up the cause of the Israel-Lobby-as-danger-to-America. They have published newsletters like the *Washington Report on Middle Eastern Affairs*, put out magazines like *Middle Eastern Policy*, and sent speakers around on crusades to denounce Israel and its supporters. The organizations of the sectarian Left as well, in particular those that cluster around ANSWER (Act Now to Stop War and End Racism), have made roughly similar arguments for years. At every anti-Iraq-war rally held since March 2003, anti-Israel, pro-Palestinian groups, posters, speakers, and the like have been ubiquitous in indicting the Israel lobby as part of some sinister plot to destroy life, truth, goodness, and the (real) American way. Here right-wing and left-wing fringes merge in their anti-Zionist, and sometimes anti-Semitic, impulses.

We saw it all again in the summer of 2008 when Ron Suskind claimed that the CIA had forged a letter aiming to connect al-Qaeda and Iraqi intelligence, only to have a right-wing antiwar nut named Philip Giraldi argue in the *American Conservative* that, no, it wasn't a CIA forgery but one from Douglas Feith's Office of Special Plans when Feith served as Undersecretary of Defense for Policy. Giraldi claimed that Feith, a Jew, did it all for Israel, whereupon a host of far-left blogs, like thinkprogress.org, picked it up approvingly.

So the claim made by Mearsheimer, Walt, and their supporters that their argument was a new one because, as they asserted, all previous attempts at criticizing the Israel lobby had been throttled by the nefarious tentacles of the lobby itself was and remains manifest nonsense. The anti-Israel lobby is at least as old as any supposed Israel lobby. But it was an effective tactical line for Mearsheimer and Walt to take, because it was aimed to cast in advance any criticism of their argument as part and parcel of a witch hunt. They did, in other words, exactly what they accuse the lobby of doing: preempting criticism by labeling it as disingenuous. This resembles the tendency of anti-Semites to postulate Jewish conspiracies that are, in fact, mirror images of their own conspiratorial delusions.

It is not necessary to recapitulate the entirety of the Israel lobby debate in order to examine its essential Jewcentric elements. The most economical approach is to ask the most inflammatory question first, and then carefully unpack the answer: is Mearsheimer and Walt's work anti-Semitic in effect, and if so, does that make Mearsheimer and Walt anti-Semites? The answer is not so simple.

Mearsheimer and Walt's work is very Jewcentric. It exaggerates both the power and the homogeneity of the Israel lobby—or the Jewish lobby, if we are to be frank about what is being discussed here. Sure, evangelical Christians also support Israel and sometimes lobby on its behalf, and this was not an insignificant issue in an administration like that of George W. Bush that garnered so much support from evangelicals. But this isn't what Mearsheimer and Walt really care about—they care about the influence of the Jews, and they exaggerate it in a negative fashion.

So doesn't that make their work anti-Semitic? Eliot Cohen thought so, and he said as much in the April 5, 2006, *Washington Post*:

> If by anti-Semitism one means obsessive and irrationally hostile beliefs about Jews; if one accuses them of disloyalty, subversion or treachery, of having occult powers and of participating in secret combinations that manipulate institutions and governments; if one systematically selects everything unfair, ugly or wrong about Jews as individuals or a group and equally systematically suppresses any exculpatory information—why, yes, this paper [the essay by Mearsheimer and Walt] is anti-Semitic.

I wish it were that clear. Mearsheimer and Walt are obsessive, no question about it, but the source of their obsession is not the Jews. It is their insistence that the foreign policy of the United States is and has been fundamentally wrongheaded for many years. Mearsheimer and Walt are what is called in the international relations trade "off-shore balancers," a major subcategory within a school of thought called realism. They believe that U.S. policy is too interventionist, too activist, too entangled in foreign alliances and obligations. They believe, further, that the Middle East is the source of the harmful hyperactivism of U.S. foreign policy. And they believe that the only rational explanation for why so many seemingly intelligent high U.S. officials would take a view different from their own is that there must be some irrational source distorting the whole picture: a domestic ethnic lobby.

They are mistaken: successive U.S. administrations, Democratic and Republican, rightly or wrongly, have simply taken a view of U.S. strategy and its requirements different from those of the offshore-balancer school. But since Mearsheimer and Walt cannot accept that anyone could disagree with them on the merits of the argument, they have had to resort to some other explanation. This is vanity and hubris, yes; but it is not necessarily anti-Semitism.

What about Cohen's accusation that Mearsheimer and Walt characterize the Jews as disloyal, conspiratorial, and even possessed of occult powers? Disloyalty is implied, although in the book the authors explicitly try to protect themselves against such claims. Conspiracies? Not exactly, but Mearsheimer and Walt do conflate many different organizations and many different views on issues into one monolithic "Lobby," and their use of the capital "L" is therefore not incidental here, not just a literary gimmick. Occult? Not really.

Eliot Cohen is not the only one who has raised questions about anti-Semitism in the Mearsheimer-Walt mental universe. One of the most pungent of the many critiques of the book is that of Jeffrey Goldberg in the October 8, 2007, issue of the *New Republic*. Goldberg dwelled on the book's shoddy research and fundamental illogic, of which more in a moment, but he paused to point out a troubling case of double standards, a cardinal element of the core definition of anti-Semitism. The authors, Goldberg wrote, attribute "some" anti-Semitism in Europe to provocation by "Israel's behavior toward the Palestinians," although they admit that "some of it is straightforwardly racist." He then proceeds:

> This is a bizarre and foul passage, its foulness easily clarified by a simple act of substitution. Imagine Farrar, Straus and Giroux publishing the following sentence: "We would not deny that there is some racial prejudice among whites, some of it provoked by the misbehavior

of African-Americans, and some of it straightforwardly racist." Mearsheimer and Walt are the sort of scholars who think that, if you wish to understand racism study blacks, and if you wish to understand anti-Semitism study Jews. They are chillingly unaware that such views are complicit with the prejudice they claim to abhor.

There is one other loose end still to deal with in this regard, one that for some reason neither Goldberg nor most other critics picked up on. In the *London Review of Books* essay, Mearsheimer and Walt claim that Israeli citizenship rests "on the principle of blood kinship." As we have seen, this misrepresentation is a staple of modern racialist anti-Semitism and all of the anti-Zionist covers for it, including the "Zionism is racism" canard of the United Nations General Assembly. And it is flatly false. To repeat: one cannot convert to become a German or a Japanese or a Kurd. Those nationalisms and many others *are* based on a principle of blood kinship. But anyone who has converted to Judaism according to Jewish law can claim citizenship under Israel's "right of return," and many have done so. It has *nothing to do with blood.* Since error of several sorts pervades the Mearsheimer-Walt essay and book, I assume this statement was born not from anti-Semitism but from ignorance. I hope I am not proved wrong.

What about systematic bias in the book's portrayal of Israel and the Arab-Israeli conflict? Doesn't that suggest anti-Semitism? Not necessarily, but it does raise an interesting problem in logic. The claim that American Jews have an overweening influence on U.S. Middle East and foreign policy is separate from the issue of Israeli policies or the Arab-Israeli conflict. Suppose, just for the sake of clarifying the point, that Mearsheimer and Walt loved Israel and thought it was in the right in its policies with regard to its neighbors. That would say nothing about an American domestic lobby that had, in their view, too much influence over U.S. decision-making processes. Since the question of influence is at the heart of their thesis, their one-sided demonization of Israel does raise troubling questions. What is the point of it, if not to express a visceral dislike for Israel, if not also for Jews?

There is, however, a more likely explanation than anti-Semitism for why Mearsheimer and Walt belabor their anti-Israel narrative: they are trying to show not only that the Jewish lobby in the United

States is too influential, but also that its influence harms U.S. interests in the Middle East and in the world. To the extent they can show that Israeli policies are anathema in the region and beyond, it helps them to make the case that supporting Israel and associating with it harms U.S. interests. With this aim in mind, the failure of Mearsheimer and Walt to present a balanced picture of the Arab-Israeli conflict is understandable.

Their failure to make their critique credible to experts, how-ever, even to those not particularly well disposed toward Israel, has another source. Like many other Israel lobby critics before them, Mearsheimer and Walt are not themselves Middle East experts. Before their Israel lobby essay and book, neither had written much on the region and anything at all for scholarly, expert audiences. They have never claimed to be regional experts, and rightly so, for neither seems to have studied, let alone mastered, any Middle Eastern language. The many factual errors they make illustrate their lack of familiarity with the basic literature on the subject. So it stands to reason that if their intent is to dramatize how harmful U.S. support for Israel is to U.S. national security interests, then their account of the conflict will come out sufficiently unleavened by any deep knowledge of the region to explain its lack of credibility with scholars.

One-sided analyses based on political bias are hardly unique. But serious scholars are supposed to respect certain standards of logic and rules of evidence, and tenured faculty at prestigious institutions are presumed to be among those professionals. Yet the illogic of the main argument Mearsheimer and Walt make is astounding. The Israel lobby argument over the years has depended, as noted, on context. In this case, the context was outsized, formed as it was by 9/11, the Iraq war, and all the miseries associated with both. Mearsheimer and Walt have argued, as the acid test of their thesis, that it was the Israel lobby, in cahoots with neoconservative conspirators in the Bush administra-tion, that brought about the Iraq war. They have also argued more broadly that "the U.S. has a terrorism problem in good part because it is so closely allied with Israel." In the context of 9/11, the Iraq war was, they claim, all about protecting Israel, all about Israeli interests, not U.S. ones, and they argue, as have others, that going to war in Iraq has made the threats the United States faces worse.

Of course, Mearsheimer and Walt opposed the war, as virtu-ally all "offshore balancers" would. But trying to pin the blame for it on Israel and its American supporters is a stretch well beyond credulity. As former presidential speechwriter Michael Gerson put it, Mearsheimer and Walt's "naïve belief that 'the U.S. has a terrorism problem in good part because it is aligned so closely with Israel' [is] the equivalent of arguing that Britain had a Nazi problem in the 1930s because it was so closely allied with Czechoslovakia."[5]

The best, and most entertaining, criticism of Mearsheimer and Walt on their Iraq war argument, however, was that by Harvey Sicherman, a former aide to three secretaries of state and a Middle East expert in his own right. Mearsheimer and Walt, wrote Sicherman, "depict Israel and the Lobby as desperate to get the United States into war against Saddam" for several years before September 11, 2001, but concede that the lobby failed to persuade both Presidents Clinton and Bush to do so. They also, by the way, fail to distinguish those Jews who wanted to overthrow the Baath regime in Iraq for reasons that had little if anything to do with Israel from those who put Israel first in their concerns. Then Sicherman quotes Mearsheimer and Walt from the *London Review* essay as follows: "They [the Israel lobbyists] needed help to achieve their aim. That help arrived with 9/11. Specifically, the events of that day led Bush and Cheney to reverse course and become strong proponents of a preventative war." Sicherman then goes straight for the jugular:

> So you see, the war was "due in large part to the Lobby's influence" except that the influence failed until 9/11 to change the President's mind, that is, his concept of what the national interest required. Elementary logic demands this conclusion: the Iraq war should be put on Osama bin Laden's account, not AIPAC's or Israel's. The authors, however, seem so anxious to make their case for the Lobby's baleful influence that they have unmade it themselves. A blunder of this kind would flunk a freshman.[6]

A book whose argument undermines its own thesis is bad enough, but that's not the only flaw of *The Israel Lobby*. Another contradiction lurks, too. As I have said, Mearsheimer and Walt are motivated in the main by strong views on U.S. foreign policy strategy, not necessarily a negative view of Jews. What is odd about their approach, however, is that, as academic realists, they are obliged to believe that domestic politics has no major bearing on the behavior of states in the international system. Academic realists hold that the balances of power as distributed among states, and the happenstance of geography and topography, are sufficient to explain the behavior of states. In a 2001 book entitled *The Tragedy of Great Power Politics*, for example, Mearsheimer wrote at length about what he called "the stopping power of water," and he did not ascribe this power to the Jews. It is a contradiction of realist dogma for Mearsheimer and Walt to attribute the behavior of a great power like the United States to a domestic political factor.

Actually, they were right the first time. Domestic politics does affect U.S. foreign policy, of course, to some extent. Ethnic lobbies are among the many interest groups hoping to have a say in the nation's foreign policy agenda. This is true not only of the Jewish lobby on behalf of Israel, but also of the Armenian lobby, the Greek lobby, the Polish lobby, the Irish lobby on Ulster, the anti-Castro Cuban lobby, and several others besides. So at least one of the basic tenets of academic realism is not true—or not true anymore, as ethnic lobbies have become more numerous, sophisticated, and influential.

On the other hand, ethnic lobbies tend to affect U.S. foreign policy only at the margins. The efficacy of such groups over most of the past forty or fifty years has been through the power of mass-membership organizations writing letters to and otherwise lobbying members of Congress. The Israel lobby too, through AIPAC and other groups, has wielded most of its influence over the legislative branch, not the executive branch. What does this mean in practice?

It means, to keep the focus on the Jewish lobby, Israel, and the Middle East, that U.S. military and economic aid levels to Israel are to some degree influenced by the lobby, since Congress has to authorize the budget for such aid. It means that all manner of resolutions that Congress may pass, nonbinding resolutions for the most part, or resolutions subject to "national security" exceptions that allow the president to set aside their provisions at will, can be influenced by the lobby. These might be about whether the U.S. embassy in Israel should be in Jerusalem rather than in Tel Aviv, or about loan guarantees for the settlement of Soviet Jewish immigrants, or about major arms sales to Arab countries. But when it comes to critical decisions about war and peace, about sensitive diplomacy, negotiations, and mediation, Congress has little leverage over the executive branch. The president, along with the national security advisor, the secretaries of state and defense, and a selected few others, makes the key decisions without regard to any lobby, and, indeed, most of the time without much regard to Congress either.

That is what the record shows without significant exception. Thus, Richard Nixon decided to resupply Israel during the midst of the October 1973 War because of strategic concerns vis-à-vis the Soviet Union. It had nothing to do with lobbies, and it had nothing to do with politics: Jews did not, and never would, vote in large numbers for Richard Nixon.

We can go back even to 1948 for another example. Those who insist on claiming that Harry Truman recognized Israel in May 1948 to secure the Jewish vote in the November election, a very common claim, generally fail to appreciate the fact that Truman was not a political dunce. His Republican opponent in 1948 was Thomas Dewey, the governor of New York State. Truman did not expect to win New York, Jewish vote or no Jewish vote in the only state in which it might have made a difference, and he didn't. He won the presidency anyway, but that's not the point. The point is that Truman's decision was based on both moral and strategic considerations, not on lobbies or politics one way or the other. Truman acted as the American Christian Zionist and pro-democracy Western statesman he was: In 1953, then former president Truman visited the Jewish Theological Seminary in New York City with his old friend Eddie Jacobson. During their conversation with Rabbi Louis Finkelstein and the historian Alexander Marx, Jacobson said: "This is the man who helped create the State of Israel"; but Truman interjected, "What do you mean 'helped' create? I am Cyrus; I am Cyrus!"[7]

Or take the case of President George H. W. Bush after the first Gulf War. After that war the United States, led by Secretary of State James Baker, arranged the Madrid Conference. This was a very important undertaking, and it is not too much to say that it led to notable advantages for Israel. It helped to break down Israel's international isolation; the fact that photos of the Israeli prime minister sitting in the same plenary session with Arab statesmen and kaffiyeh-bedecked princes were beamed all over the Muslim world was of enormous and enduring significance. In the complex negotiations over the nature of Palestinian representation to Madrid, the Israeli government of Yitzhak Shamir laid down ten strict conditions, and President Bush and Secretary Baker acceded to each and every one of them. From an objective point of view, the Bush 41 administration was as pro-Israel as anyone could expect, and yet, because there was no sense of warmth between American Jewry and that Republican administration, Bush got little credit for his efforts. Baker got even less.

This lack of warmth resulted from, among other sources, the fact that a few months earlier, when the issue of U.S. loan guarantees for settling Soviet Jews in Israel came up, the administration had tried to leverage its support for those guarantees in such a way as to advance Arab-Israeli negotiation, by putting pressure against Israeli settlements policy. The "professional" Jewish lobby erupted with a vehemence that surprised nearly everyone who wasn't a member of it. When hordes of lobbyists descended on Washington, President Bush claimed on September 12, 1991, "I've heard today something like 1,000 lobbyists are on the Hill working the other side of the question. We have got one little lonely guy down here doing it." Around the same time, Baker, being even more the political animal than Bush 41—and that is saying a lot—famously quipped (in private of course), "Fuck the Jews, they didn't vote for us anyway."[8]

Meanwhile, Bush's national security advisor, General Brent Scowcroft, had never been particularly friendly toward Israel, so it was not surprising that he blamed Israel for the diplomatic impasse, which in turn made it hard for the administration to readily accommodate its requests for loan guarantees. Actually, the administration's position was reasonable given the constraints and varied interests weighing upon it. But pro-Israel partisans were simply unable to comprehend that, not being trained or experienced in how foreign policy and diplomacy actually work, and thus unable to understand, let alone credit, any view that did not align with their own. When Harry Truman complained in his day that the Jews lacked all sense of proportion in understanding world affairs, allowing their own worries to drive out consideration of all other interests, this is exactly what he meant. These are the kinds of loyalists who freely acknowledge that the partisans of any other ethno-national conflict are bound to distort objective truths while in the throes of emotional attachments, but insist that they are somehow immune from that danger.

Contrast the experience of the Bush 41 administration with that of the Reagan administration just a few years earlier. It was the Reagan administration that decided to open a formal dialogue with Yasir Arafat's Palestine Liberation Organization (PLO), an unprecedented affront to the organized Jewish lobby. And yet since Secretary of State George Shultz had established warm personal relationships with the professional Jewish lobbying organizations—he had once led a cheer at an AIPAC conference, saying, "PLO, Hell No!"—when the decision came down, the Israel lobby was nearly speechless.

What all of this goes to show is that when a president knows what he wants, whether it pleases Israel and its supporters or not, he does it. He does it because, as the steward of American national security and the commander-in-chief of the armed forces, he thinks it best for the country. He may be right or wrong in his judgments, but lobbies have never decisively influenced any major U.S. strategic judgment concerning the Middle East. Perhaps George Shultz himself said it best, in the preface to Abraham Foxman's rebuttal to Mearsheimer and Walt:

> We are a great nation, and our government officials invariably include brilliant, experienced, tough-minded people. Mostly, we make good decisions. But when we make a wrong decision—even one that is recommended by Israel and supported by American Jewish groups—it is our decision, and one for which we alone are responsible. We are not babes in the woods, easily convinced to support Israel's or any other state's agenda. We act in our own interests.

Mearsheimer and Walt could have asked Shultz and dozens of other veterans of the U.S. government's policymaking trenches to describe for them how the process really works and how much influence the Israel lobby really has. Though they are both social science PhDs who rightly make their students do real research before commenting about some subject about which they have modest background, they did not hold themselves to this same standard. They interviewed no one, blithely commenting in their introduction that doing so would not have affected their argument. (How did they know that?) Having never served in government themselves, they thus managed to get the story quite wrong.

A proof for this is easy to make. If, as Mearsheimer and Walt argue, even against their own realist convictions, a domestic lobby is responsible for U.S. policy decisions at the highest level and with the greatest consequence—not least the U.S. war in Iraq—and if their own argument is as new and revelatory as they claim it is, then it follows that their book should have had a major impact on how U.S. foreign policy is made and what its basic tenets are. Yet no such thing has happened. The Bush administration did not throw up its hands in surrender after the Mearsheimer-Walt book was published, and shift its policy on cue. None of the Democratic or Republican primary contenders in the run-up to the 2008 presidential election mentioned the Mearsheimer-Walt book or said anything remotely endorsing their case against the Israel lobby. In short, the book and the fracas over it have had no discernable influence on U.S. policy, and the book is not likely to have any influence on policy decisions in the Obama administration. If this doesn't demonstrate that U.S. policy at the strategic level is in fact not determined by domestic political factors, then nothing can.[9]

Are we finished, then, with this unpleasant topic? Not quite. The negative Jewcentricity of Mearsheimer and Walt is matched at least to some degree by manifestations of positive Jewcentricity. As intimated toward the end of chapter 9, the successes of many professional Jewish advocacy organizations seem to have gone to their heads. Just as Truman complained in 1947 about some extreme Zionist leaders being pushy, arrogant, abrupt, ill-mannered, and without a sense of proportion, one could make the same argument about the tone of discourse in the 1991–1992 loan guarantees blowup and in the 2006–2007 Mearsheimer-Walt debate—although in the latter case Jewish professionals had no reason to complain about the behavior of the White House, or any other part of the U.S. government, for that matter.

Without questioning the right of Jews, or any other group of U.S. citizens, to organize and lobby for their interests, Jewish lobbying has become so proficient, so well financed, so unvarnished, and so persistent as to have generated a certain amount of ambient resentment. Not even the political animals who get elected to Congress like to be pushed around, and to put it generously, Jewish lobbying tactics are not always subtle. There is something almost the equivalent to nouveau riche behavior in the way some Jewish organizations lobby for what they want. Instead of "Look, I can afford to pay five thousand dollars for a lamp I don't even like," it's "Look, I can contribute five thousand dollars to this guy's congressional race and in effect exercise a veto over what he says about Syria." Do this sort of thing too often and it will generate resentment regardless of the beauty of the lamp or the merits of the argument about Syria.

It is true that Washington is a rough-and-tumble place, and that too much subtlety or care in expression will often not be effective. Nonetheless, standard-issue professional Jewish lobbying techniques probably created a natural audience-in-waiting for John Mearsheimer and Stephen Walt. Insofar as their case drew sympathy from bureaucratic insiders, it was not because of the flawed logic of their argument about the causes of the Iraq war. It was because they provided a vehicle for the venting of accumulated resentment. Of course, genuine anti-Semites loved *The Israel Lobby*, and said so. What is more troubling is that many people who are not obviously or necessarily anti-Semitic, some in the U.S. military, some in the intelligence community, some in other parts of the U.S. bureaucracy, some on Senate and House staffs, sympathized with Mearsheimer and Walt not because of the logic of their arguments, but because of the targets of their arguments. Let the wise take note.

As I argued at the outset, the four forms of Jewcentricity across our two-by-two matrix need and feed one another. For example, if professional Jews did not so assiduously market the Holocaust, it would be harder for people like Norman Finkelstein to make over-the-top arguments about the exploitation of Jewish suffering and have any objective observer credit them. The whole complex of issues involved in the ongoing Israel lobby affair, too, exemplifies that dynamic. We can expect to see examples of it from time to time long into the future. An example right out of central casting involved the March 2009 choice of Director of National Intelligence Dennis Blair to make Chas Freeman director of the National Intelligence Council.

As soon as Freeman's appointment was leaked, a hail of criticism fell upon Chas Freeman's head. Some of it concerned comments he had made about China and the Tiananmen Square incident of nearly twenty years ago. These are the comments that ultimately sank his nomination, thanks no little to the wrath of House Speaker Nancy Pelosi. But Freeman, a former U.S. ambassador to Saudi Arabia, has also made comments critical of Israeli government positions over many years. His criticisms have often been acerbic—for that is how Ambassador Freeman expresses himself about nearly everything—but not extreme. He has never said in public or written that Israel is illegitimate, that it is not a democracy, that Zionism is racism, or that terrorism directed against Israel and Jews is anything other than odious and unacceptable. He has sharply criticized Israeli settlements and occupation policies, but so have lots of Israeli Jews.

Nevertheless, while AIPAC took no formal position on Freeman's nomination, a smear campaign against him mounted by American Jewish partisans of Israel sprinted into high gear from a standing start. Some of this criticism linked into insinuations that Freeman had acted as an unregistered agent for foreign governments—Saudi Arabia and China were mentioned—which is illegal. But no evidence was produced that this was so. Some criticisms of Freeman sought, in a manner typical of extreme partisan polemic, to collapse any differences between Freeman's criticisms of Israel and those of a more extreme sort. Much of this was tactical, in the sense that the polemicists knew what they were doing and did it anyway. But some of it was sincere in the sense that hyper-partisans are often incapable of distinguishing types or gradations of criticism. They devise what is for all practical purposes a Jewcentric conspiracy theory that is the equal and opposition equivalent to the Israel Lobby's Jewcentric conspiracy theory—that there is a monolithic conspiracy to destroy Israel, and that all critics, no matter how mild or well-intentioned they seem, are part of this conspiracy.

As unfortunate as this was, Freeman's reaction to the attacks against him was just as unfortunate. Here, at some length, is what Freeman wrote in a Salon.com post as he headed for the door, remarks that could have been lifted with little effort from the Mearsheimer-Walt book itself:

> The libels on me and their easily traceable email trails show conclusively that there is a powerful lobby determined to prevent any view other than its own from being aired, still less to factor in American understanding of trends and events in the Middle East. The tactics of the Israel Lobby plumb the depths of dishonor and indecency and include character assassination, selective misquotation, the willful distortion of the record, the fabrication of falsehoods, and an utter disregard for the truth. The aim of this Lobby is control of the policy process through the exercise of a veto over the appointment of people who dispute the wisdom of its views, the substitution of political correctness for analysis, and the exclusion of any and all options for decision by Americans and our government other than those that it favors.
>
> There is a special irony in having been accused of improper regard for the opinions of foreign governments and societies by a group so clearly intent on enforcing adherence to the policies of a foreign government—in this case, the government of Israel. I believe that the inability of the American public to discuss, or the government to consider, any option for US policies in the Middle East opposed by the ruling faction in Israeli politics has allowed that faction to adopt and sustain policies that ultimately threaten the existence of the State of Israel. It is not permitted for anyone in the

United States to say so. This is not just a tragedy for Israelis and their neighbors in the Middle East; it is doing widening damage to the national security of the United States.

Of course, much of this is nonsense. As the editorialists of the *Washington Post*—not known to be a card-carrying member of the Israel Lobby—pointed out on March 12, Freeman's charges

> will certainly be news to Israel's "ruling faction," which in the past few years alone has seen the U.S. government promote a Palestinian election that it opposed; refuse it weapons it might have used for an attack on Iran's nuclear facilities; and adopt a policy of direct negotiations with a regime that denies the Holocaust and that promises to wipe Israel off the map. Two Israeli governments have been forced from office since the early 1990s after open clashes with Washington over matters such as settlement construction in the occupied territories.
>
> What's striking about the charges by Mr. Freeman and like-minded conspiracy theorists is their blatant disregard for such established facts. Mr. Freeman darkly claims that "it is not permitted for anyone in the United States" to describe Israel's nefarious influence. But several of his allies have made themselves famous (and advanced their careers) by making such charges. . . . Crackpot tirades such as his have always had an eager audience here and around the world. The real question is why an administration that says it aims to depoliticize U.S. intelligence estimates would have chosen such a man to oversee them.

It was all so sad. One may disagree with Chas Freeman on the Middle East; I know him and I have often disagreed with him. But a collision of conspiracy theories was no way to end the career of a sincere and effective public servant, a Foreign Service Officer who sometimes went out of his way to do what he thought needed to be done. One has the unfortunate feeling that we've not seen this kind of Jewcentric collision for the last time.

12

The (Non)-Centrality of the Arab-Israeli Conflict

All news is an exaggeration of life.

—DANIEL SCHORR

One of the many problems with Mearsheimer and Walt's *The Israel Lobby* is that it places Israel and its supporters at the very epicenter of U.S. foreign policy. It is Israelcentric, which in today's political world comes to fewer than six degrees of separation from being Jewcentric. So, as usual, Israel and the Jews have an outsized image, beyond any objective measure of their importance.

In this the Jews implicate the entire Middle East by association: the Middle East itself, important as it is to U.S. global interests, is not as important as is widely assumed.[1] Yes, radical Islam is centered there, and yes, a lot of oil and gas is there, too. But there is a disagreement about how serious a security threat to the United States radical Islam really is, and about the extent to which the Middle East as a whole is really the main source of it—after all, Mohammed Atta, one of the key planners and leaders of the 9/11 hijackers, plotted his deeds in Hamburg, not in Hama or the Hejaz.

This is not the place to detail all of these debates; suffice it to say that the terrorist threat to the United States has been and remains in my view real but exaggerated, and that one factor underlying this exaggeration is that too many people believe, rather Jewcentrically, that U.S. support for Israel is indeed the main source of the terrorist danger; it isn't.[2]

The truth about the connections between Israel, oil, and terrorism is vastly more complex than that. For example, the threat to the United States does not emanate from the region as a whole, only from a few discrete parts of it—Saudi Arabia, parts of Yemen, some social spheres in Egypt, the Pakistani-Afghan border province of Waziristan, Pakistan proper, and Muslims who are caught between cultures, living in the cities and towns of Western Europe. Palestinians, generally perceived as the most direct victims of Israel and Israeli policies, have been relatively rare among radical Muslims involved in anti-U.S. violence, something that would not be true if the Palestinian issue were really the main source of anti-American Muslim violence. Radical Muslims in Palestine and in most Middle Eastern countries constitute minorities that may or may not cause trouble locally, but have demonstrated little ability or inclination to harm the United States.

As to oil, most economists who specialize in energy markets argue that oil-producing states will sell their resources more or less regardless of politics, and history supports the point. Many Americans still think the 1973–1974 Arab oil embargo was a response to political issues surrounding the Middle East war of that year, and that it was successful. Both assumptions are wrong. The embargo was endorsed and directed in part by the shah of Iran—obviously not an Arab, and the leader of a country that had quite good relations with Israel at the time—for purposes of organizing OPEC's power to raise the price. And the embargo was not successful. The exporting countries had no control over where their oil went once it left their shores, thanks to the control the major oil companies had and still largely have over transportation, refining, and marketing. There was no significant shortfall of supply in the United States. The main reason for the gas lines at U.S. service stations back then, and again in 1979 after the Iranian revolution, was panicked consumer behavior fed by a sensationalist media, all augmented grandly by an incompetent federal energy policy bureaucracy.

It is true that oil revenues, particularly in the Saudi case, do sometimes trickle down to sinister figures engaged in planning terror attacks. But that hardly makes the Middle East a place of great economic dynamism, scientific and cultural creativity, or even substantial demographic significance. The Middle East is important to U.S. foreign policy as a form of mini-max game, which is to say that it could serve as the staging ground for some low-probability but high-impact events—for example, terrorists' acquisition of a nuclear bomb made or stored in the region. But it is East and South Asia and, still, the Atlantic world that will compose the center of the action in international politics in coming decades. Even sub-Saharan Africa and Latin America may prove more consequential than the Arab world in the global scope of things.

Even if this assessment is wrong and the Middle East proves to be the central stage of global affairs over the next several decades, it still does not follow that Israel is central to the dynamics of the region. Israel is not the main provocateur of Islamic radicalism. That source lies in Western pressures more generally that put the corporate identity of traditional societies at risk. Western powers colonized much of the Arab world (and the larger Muslim world) in the nineteenth and twentieth centuries, and in doing so pluralized their cultures anew. Western power and the subsequent introduction of Western technology, literature, political ideas, and cultural artifacts undermined the traditional authority structures of what were still largely tribal and traditional societies from Morocco all the way to Indonesia. These pressures have only increased over time, despite the post–World War II independence of nearly all Arab and Muslim-majority countries, with the advent of international media and globalization, and the fact that these independent countries' governments have generally been unable to develop their economies and societies and bring them up to advanced modern standards. All of this has had little or nothing to do with Israel, or the Jews.

Moreover, Israel has little or nothing to do with the price and supply of Middle Eastern oil. Yes, of course, political conflict can affect risk perceptions, but the conflicts that have had major impacts on the oil market in the past few decades have been the 1980–1988 Iran-Iraq War, the 1990 Iraqi invasion of Kuwait and the subsequent war to liberate Kuwait, and the Iraq war launched in 2003. None of these involved Israel as a major player or factor.

And the reason Middle Eastern governments are or are not friendly to the United States rarely has to do mainly with Israel or peace-process issues, but rather with a whole host of other historical and contemporary matters. The U.S. relationship with Saudi Arabia, for example, involves a basic trade: Saudi oil made available to the world market at convenient prices in return for U.S. protection for the oil and, of course, the regime. The same goes, more or less, for the U.S. relationships with Kuwait, Bahrain, Qatar, and the United Arab Emirates. The U.S. relationship with Morocco and Tunisia has had more to do over the years with protecting those pro-Western countries from more radical, pro-Soviet regimes in Algeria and Libya. The U.S. relationship with Lebanon, too, has had more to do with protecting Lebanon from threats to its sovereignty and integrity coming from Syria and, some years ago, from Egypt. Even for the countries that border Israel—Egypt, Jordan, Syria, and Lebanon—U.S. relations with them only partly have to do with Israel. For countries farther away from Israel, such as Sudan and Oman, for example, U.S. relations with them engage Israel-related issues only at the rhetorical margins, for the most part.

Imagine, if you can, that one day Israelis decided to pack their bags and move away, giving the country to the Palestinians with a check for sixty years' rent. Would the Arabs suddenly stop competing among themselves, and would America and the Arab world suddenly fall in love with each other? In a sense, Israel is to America and the Middle East what the Iraq war has been to Republicans and Democrats in recent years: as volatile a matter as it has been, the two sides aren't going to stop going at each other once it goes away.

But those of a Jewcentric persuasion, whether negatively disposed or otherwise, do not see things this way. They take for granted that anti-Americanism in the Middle East is mainly a function of U.S. support for Israel. Here is Jimmy Carter's view, for example:

> There is no doubt: The heart and mind of every Muslim is affected by whether or not the Israel-Palestine issue is dealt with fairly. Even among the populations of our former close friends in the region, Egypt and Jordan, less than 5 percent look favorably on the United States today. That's not because we invaded Iraq; they hated Saddam. It is because we don't do anything about the Palestinian plight.

When pressed for evidence on the point, Carter simply insisted: "I don't think it's about a linkage policy, but a linkage fact. . . . Without doubt, the path to peace in the Middle East goes through Jerusalem." Likewise Zbigniew Brzezinski: "The Israeli-Palestinian conflict is the single most combustible and galvanizing issue in the Arab world."[3] Brent Scowcroft agrees with this; so may James L. Jones, President Obama's national security advisor, and, from the evidence of the 2008 campaign and his first interview as president, given to Al-Arabiya on January 26, 2009, so may Barack Obama himself.

Of course the Palestinian problem does play *some* role in Middle Eastern anti-Americanism. It does so in some places more than others, however—in Jordan, for example, with its very large Palestinian population, where the "street" is far more anti-American than the government. However, in Iran, whose government is as anti-American and as anti-Israel as can be, its people are not anti-American at all; quite the contrary. There is an important lesson here, and it is that the bitterest anti-Americanism, which one finds in places like Saudi Arabia and Egypt, stems not from U.S. support for Israel but from U.S. support for the Saudi and Egyptian regimes, among others, which are so deeply unpopular. As Leslie Gelb put it, "America's central strategic problem in the region . . . is that we need our corrupt, inept and unpopular Arab allies because the likely alternative to them is far worse," even though this need produces more anti-Americanism than anything having to do with U.S. support for Israel.[4]

As Tip O'Neill once famously said, all politics is local, and that is surely the case in the Middle East. Most people care most about their immediate circumstances, and they care about matters farther afield only insofar as they have some special reason to do so, or the luxury of time and energy to think about them. The less educated they are, too, the more they tend to be locally and parochially focused, and less likely to understand the connections between remote events and their own circumstances. In that regard, it is important to remember that fairly large numbers of Middle Easterners are still functionally illiterate and have few ways to get reliable information about far-flung events. Insofar as most Arabs and Muslims get what we may charitably call actual news about other places, including Palestine, they get it from television, notably from the new group of Arab satellite TV networks. Most of these outlets are government-owned, and all, to one degree or another, heavily propagandize certain views. Al Jazeera, Al Arabiya, Al-Manar, and other networks have invested heavily in demonizing Israel and the Jews: many are major outlets for regional anti-Semitism.

Thanks to the existence of such outlets, some Palestinian leaders for some years now have created what some have dubbed Paliwood—the capability to stage events detrimental to Israel for the sake of television cameras. The September 2000 killing of twelve-year-old Mohammed al-Dura in Gaza may well have been one such event. The boy died during a confrontation between Israeli soldiers and Palestinian demonstrators, and there is reason to believe that his death was *not* the result of Israeli gunfire. The supposed Israeli rocketing of ambulances in Lebanon in August 2006 is another, which certainly fooled Reuters. The Palestinian Authority supposedly held a midnight meeting, complete with candles, to show how hard-working it is, and it fooled *Time* magazine; it later came to light that the meeting had been held around noon.

Not only are some Arab television and radio stations regularly complicit in Paliwood productions, but some European stations play along. Some know they are being manipulated but do not object, because they either sympathize with the Palestinians, are simply credulous, or do not want to risk having their access denied or their lives threatened. The result is that lots of modestly educated people in the region, who are primed to dislike Jews anyway for reasons of religious education and ambient regional folklore, are whipped up by the emotional power of pictures and literally never hear any other side to the story. The use of fakery in television images is simply a recent extension of the fact that autocratic governments in the Middle East have made an art of deflecting discontent with their own lack of achievement onto others, and the most popular others to be fingered in mostly government-controlled presses over the past half century have been Israel and the United States.

Uneducated people are, of course, not necessarily stupid people, and Arabs as a group certainly are not stupid, however much or little schooling they have had. They usually know when others are trying to deceive and manipulate them. There is plenty of latent and active anti-Jewish sentiment in Arab and Muslim countries (which we describe in the next chapter), and so there is plenty of anti-Israel sentiment, as well. But this sentiment translates into background noise to most people most of the time, except when pollsters ask about it, and, for reasons of self-protection and public etiquette, it comes out. But most adults in Arab countries know that the inequality, the injustice, and the corruption in their societies are not caused by Israel. They know that their societies' failure to generate strong and widely distributed economic growth is not because of Israel, despite the efforts of military regimes to insist on the need to allocate a large portion of national resources to the army because of the alleged threat of Israeli expansionism. They know perfectly well that the absence of free elections or a free press or real labor unions is not because of Israel.

Moreover, what Arab intellectuals engaged in conversation with gullible Western diplomats and journalists will say to assuage their sense of honor or to advance a case is one thing; what they know and believe in private is often something else. When some Westerners take the public comments of Arabs in discussion with Westerners at face value, without bothering to make themselves aware of the circumstances that provide context for those comments, they are the ones who can reasonably be said to be stupid.

Whatever the reasons and however mistaken it may be, the view that the Arab-Israeli conflict is the be-all and end-all of virtually every problem in the Middle East, and beyond, is ubiquitous. There is no doubt, of course, that the resolution of the conflict would have a benign impact on the region. A settlement would to some unknown and probably unknowable degree reduce pressures for radical and terrorist recruitment and mobilization, for example. U.S. diplomatic efforts to fashion a settlement, whether they succeed or not, also give some Arab governments more elbow room in their own diplomatic maneuvering, which benefits the United States when that maneuvering runs parallel to our own—say, for example, in opposing Iranian regional pretentions. Such efforts might also moderate anti-Americanism in the Middle East, but that is not obvious; nor is the real impact of anti-Americanism on what leaders in that part of the world actually do obvious either. It is a lot less than many Westerners seem to think.

Nonetheless, the idea that an Arab-Israeli settlement would have a major positive impact in the war on terror, that it would somehow decisively affect energy issues, that it would have a major beneficial effect on the future, say, of Egypt, Saudi Arabia, and Morocco—all of greater consequence in global political and economic terms than Palestine—is a fantasy. What is so striking about this mantra is that, with few exceptions, this assertion is never followed up with an actual argument. It is merely stated, and then the writer or speaker, acknowledging a tacit salute, moves on.

Examples are nearly endless. A typical official example from an Arab state, which could be replicated a thousand times over with ease, is that of Saudi foreign minister Saud al-Faisal, who said before the UN General Assembly on September 29, 2007, that "current circumstances in the Middle East are extremely dangerous. The Israeli occupation of Arab land continues to transform the whole region into multiple crisis zones accompanied by the dramatic suffering of Palestinians which is linked to the spread of despair and extremism. . . . No regional crisis has greater potential to affect other regional conflicts or world peace than this conflict."[5] The Arab-Israeli conflict more portentous than was the war in Iraq at that time? More threatening to Saudi interests than growing Iranian power and Shi'a ambition? The suffering of the Palestinians worse than that of the people of Darfur, of the Kurds over many decades? Faisal did not say.

One expects this self-serving line from Arab officials, who of course know that the world is more complicated than that. Others, however, appear to make such comments as wholly innocent believers. Former Italian prime minister Romano Prodi, for example, used to say repeatedly that the Arab-Israeli conflict is "the mother of all conflicts."[6] He has never explained why, partly because it seems that no Italian journalist ever asked him to. Tony Blair, when he was British prime minister and a confidant of George W. Bush, made this argument all the time, but reportedly did not get very far with it.[7] He referred often to the Palestinian-Israeli problem as the "crux" or the "core" of the region's ills.[8] After leaving office and being made, in effect, development minister-at-large for the peace process, he has made the same statements, but he has yet to muster an actual argument supporting them. The *Washington Post* columnist David Ignatius closed his January 17, 2007, offering with this advice: "In this volatile part of the world, there's just one area where I wish President Bush would take more risks—and that's in diplomatic efforts to resolve the Israeli-Palestinian dispute. If you want to strike a blow at Iran, Sunni insurgents, and Shiite death squads all at once, that's the way to do it."

Really? I wrote Ignatius an e-mail asking, in essence, "Why? What's the argument here?" His answer was brief: "credibility, diplomatic credibility." Well, for more than a year thereafter the Bush administration more or less took Ignatius's advice (and that of many others). Secretary of State Condoleezza Rice devoted a huge amount of time to this problem. The United States staged the Annapolis Summit to great expectations in November 2007 and followed up assiduously. To set up and then follow up Annapolis in 2007 and 2008, Secretary Rice made thirteen trips to the region, spending well over a month's worth of secretarial time there. From all this considerable investment was a blow struck against Iran? Is this what got the attention of Sunni insurgents in Iraq (Ignatius was against the surge)? Is this what reduced the violence meted out by Shi'a death squads in Baghdad and Basra? As Daniel Kurtzer, a former U.S. ambassador to Egypt and Israel, aptly put it, "If the United States brokered peace talks between Israel and the Palestinians, do you think a single Iraqi gunman would put down his weapon? Not a chance."[9]

Nonetheless, the "linkage" thesis, in which Israel and the Arab-Israeli conflict are seen as being at the center of the entire Middle East and beyond, has been a staple of some American commentary and analysis for years. This approach manifested itself in the Iraq Study Group Report of December 2006, cochaired by James Baker and Lee Hamilton. That report, which was mainly about the Iraq war and what to do about it, stated, among other things, in its executive summary:

> The United States cannot achieve its goals in the Middle East unless it deals directly with the Arab-Israeli conflict and regional instability. There must be a renewed and sustained commitment by the United States to a comprehensive Arab-Israeli peace on all fronts.[10]

This language was repeated in the body of the report, and many specific recommendations followed, most of which were either undefined, incoherent, or unachievable under then and still-current circumstances. Nowhere in the report was any causal analysis offered for why the United States "cannot achieve its goals in the Middle East unless it deals directly with the Arab-Israeli conflict."

The Iraq Study Group's penchant for linkage did not stop with the Palestinian-Israeli conflict. The report also contended that engaging Iran and Syria was a key to settling the Iraq war. Both countries, the report stated, had an interest in stabilizing Iraq. This was simply wrong, and, yet again, no actual support for this assertion was ever offered. Israel figured in this proposed approach, too, for the report argued that the best way to engage Syria was by promising that Israel would return the Golan Heights to it. This, it was argued, would split Syria off from its alliance with Iran and get it to stop aiding Hezbollah in Lebanon and Hamas in the Palestinian territories.

This might have worked then, and it may still work in the future; then again it might not. The Report gave no consideration whatsoever to the possibility that the ideological rationale the Iranian and Syrian governments give for their policy positions is not mere rhetorical bluster, but that they actually take these views seriously. This used to be called condescension. As Rob Satloff summed up the Iraq-war version of the linkage illusion: "The road to Baghdad does not pass through Tehran, Damascus, Jerusalem or Gaza—it is a cul-de-sac that begins and ends in Iraq."[11]

You don't have to be Jewish to fear Jewcentric efforts at linkage, by the way. Just as the Arab-Israel linkage argument to Iraq stirred the

Israeli government in December 2006 to rebut its logic and engage in some diplomatic spin of its own, so the Syria-Iran linkage argument got under the skin of the Saudi government. The Saudis were so worried that the Bush administration might take the Iraq Study Group Report's argument seriously, and thus play into the hands of two countries the Saudis see as enemies (one mortal, Iran, the other complicit, Syria), that they summoned Vice President Cheney to Riyadh to say it wasn't so.[12] He went; he said it wasn't so.

The real reasons why assertions about the centrality of the Arab-Israeli conflict to Islamist terrorism and all the other challenges faced by the region are never followed by an actual argument is that no plausible argument can be made. An Arab-Israeli settlement, all Western diplomats and politicians agree, will further legitimate, protect, and support a Jewish state in the land of Israel within *some* borders. Anyone who thinks that such a result will satisfy Muslim religious fanatics clearly does not understand their views. More likely, Islamist radicals would redouble their efforts to prevent any such settlement, and violence and terrorism would most likely rise, at least in the short term—"short" defined in that part of the world as, oh, say, twenty to fifty years. Opponents of such a settlement would attack any Arab, and any Muslim, who would dare put his seal to such an agreement, and they would attack any Western state whose good offices helped to mediate or otherwise bring it about.

This, however, has not stopped many seemingly intelligent people from arguing that if only the United States tried hard enough, it could settle the matter, if necessary by imposition. But it is not as though imposition is easy to impose, or wise in any case; and it is not as though U.S. diplomacy has not tried hard to solve the problem short of imposition. None tried harder than the George H. W. Bush administration and the two Clinton administrations, and they did not succeed.

The most fundamental reason for this failure comes down to a simple truth that pervades international history: while it takes two (or more) parties to resolve a conflict and bring peace, it takes only one to continue a conflict and to bring war. And as ought now to be plain to all but the most obtuse, the PLO of Yasir Arafat was unwilling to make peace on terms any Israeli government could accept. Also plain is that the Palestinian Authority today is not strong enough to make peace even if it wanted to—which it may, given that its own existence depends on Israeli armed force to protect it against its more popular Palestinian rivals.

There is, however, a less fanciful corollary to the belief in the centrality of Israel and the Arab-Israeli conflict to all that goes on in the Middle East. This corollary to the centrality claim is more subtle, coalescing in the insight that even if major progress toward a settlement is not now possible, the U.S. government should still go through the motions of trying. It should do so not because it revels in acts of diplomatic masochism, but because it maintains the value of American diplomatic equities with all parties against the day when progress might actually be possible, and trying may have value for other reasons, as well. It can, as already suggested, provide friendly Arab regimes with protection to cooperate with the United States and one another over Iran, and it can at least keep the situation from getting worse by retarding the rise of the least conciliatory wings of the respective sides. This view is what led several veterans of Arab-Israeli diplomacy to remark in the course of the Israel-Hezbollah summer 2006 miniwar that never before had an American administration allowed the appearance of perfect concurrence between U.S. and Israeli interests in a moment of crisis.

This was a criticism not so much of the substance of American policy as of its "optic"—how it looked. When a U.S. secretary of state flies to the Middle East and cannot find a single Arab capital to land in, that is bad. It suggests that U.S.-Israeli relations are too close for the good of both sides. This is what motivated Secretary of State Colin Powell in the first Bush term to spend time and attention on the optic: creating an enhanced perception of Arab-Israeli peace process diplomacy. Powell knew that the conflict was not ripe for major progress, but he understood the broader diplomatic utility of appearing to engage.

The optical argument is also why Secretary Rice suddenly developed such an interest in the Israeli-Palestinian peace process. She grasped the need to use peace-process theatrics in order to circle the regional wagons to deal more effectively with Iran. Perhaps she and others had hoped that the fear of Iran among the Sunni Arab states would be sufficient to motivate them to pressure the Palestinians to reach a reasonable settlement with Israel. If they thought that, the February 2007 Mecca Agreement, in which Saudi Arabia in essence defended Hamas against the Palestine Authority, should have disabused them of that hope.

It is worth pointing out that Jewcentricity has been present not only among those of the linkage persuasion, but also among some others of a different persuasion. Jewcentricity helps to explain some of what went on in U.S. diplomacy during the Bush 43 administrations. It certainly helps explain the administration's initial reluctance to exhaust itself with a major Palestinian-Israeli peace process effort.

The senior figures of the Bush administration were an unusually blunt group as politicians-cum-statesmen go. A good deal of what some abroad took to be arrogance was, at least by the light of administration figures themselves, merely unvarnished honesty. When it came to the Middle East, George W. Bush was never ashamed of his admiration for Israel, his pride in U.S. support for Israel, and his personal belief as a born-again Christian that Israel, as the state of the Jewish people, plays a unique role in history. Though some diplomats may have rued the administration's reluctance to concern itself with appearances, the president's approach was broadly popular, particularly among the growing legions of evangelical Protestants, a trend that, as we know from chapter 2, contributes for theological reasons to growing manifestations of Jewcentricity in the United States.[13]

President Bush understood, too, that many Muslim societies today harbor strong anti-Semitic impulses. Jewcentricity is a fact of Muslim life; why else would Osama bin Laden's infamous 1998 fatwa refer to "crusaders and Jews"—are crusaders not challenge enough? None of this implies that the Bush administration gave the Israeli government a completely free pass on everything it did, although at times that seemed to be the case, looking at it from the outside. It does mean, however, that President Bush found it unseemly to criticize Israel for show, for the sake of the diplomats' proverbial "optic," in the face of irrational hatred and such an unpromising political environment for peace.

If the Arab-Israeli conflict really isn't central to the many other problems of the Middle East, then why do so many people insist otherwise? Here, once again, we must ponder the psychological reach of Jewcentricity.

Some Western observers think that the conflict is central because Arabs and Muslims so often tell them it is. Most of these observers, it seems, do not readily appreciate how convenient the conflict is for deflecting discontent within Arab countries, where most people see recent history not, as Westerners do, through the lens of the Cold War, but through the lens of colonization and decolonization. To them, Israel appears Western, so it fits as well within the anticolonialist interpretive prisms it does within traditional Islamic images of the Jew as cowardly and sneaky.

Palestine is, moreover, one of few issues nearly all Muslims can agree on, so it becomes a natural rhetorical vanguard in any political conversation with Americans and other Westerners.[14] Not that many Arabs and Muslims do not feel deeply about the matter; they do, and they do increasingly so because of how the conflict is invariably portrayed on their television screens. They have devised their own narratives accordingly, just as protagonists in all existential conflicts often do. The centrality of Palestine has thus become a kind of social-psychological fact, and as such it is hardly trivial, because what people believe tends to have self-fulfilling and self-denying consequences. But a social-psychological fact is not the same as a strategic fact, which is what national leaders base decisions upon. Beliefs can be and often are mistaken, but strategic logic tends to be more resistant to the play of images. That is why, as already suggested, a U.S.-imposed solution to the Israel-Palestinian impasse, were it possible, would not have a major effect on the wider war on terror, would not make democratization and liberalization within Arab countries appreciably easier, would not affect world energy markets, and would not make the United States more popular in most Muslim countries so long as U.S. policy continued to support mostly unpopular regimes.

Another reason for the linkage delusion is that Europeans in the main, but some Americans too, improperly compare Europe and the Middle East. As Martin Kramer has pointed out, Europe was and is a single integrated regional system for the most part, as its wars and its peace conferences from the sixteenth to the twentieth centuries show. And in Europe first the Anglo-French and then the Franco-German relationships were in fact the core conflicts that radiated outward to affect every other European state. Looking at how Europeans, with American help after World War I and especially World War II, put these core conflicts to rest, and looking at the systemic effects of having done so, many observers have wrongly analogized the Arab-Israeli conflict to the entire Middle East as if it, too, were really a single, integrated system. It is not—a fact that should have been clear by the mid-1980s. The Egyptian-Israeli peace treaty of 1979 was a key to reducing, if not solving entirely, the dangers of the Arab-Israeli conflict. And yet in its wake other conflicts within the region—in the Gulf, and in many civil conflicts besides (Algeria, Sudan, Yemen)—got worse, not better. Somehow, those fixated by the Jewcentric axiom of the Arab-Israeli conflict's centrality to the region have managed not to notice this.

There are other reasons, too, for the excessive European focus on Israel and Palestine, many of them obvious once pointed out. One is that large and increasingly problematic Muslim populations in many European countries affect how politicians speak, and arguably think, about the Middle East. Yet as we saw in the May 2007 French presidential election, this can work both ways. French politicians tilted toward the Arab side in the Arab-Israeli conflict from 1967 onward, and over time the growing size and social volatility of France's Muslim population played into and reinforced that tilt. But it gradually dawned on many Frenchmen that the benefits French leaders sought through this tilt never arrived, and that in domestic terms the policy was probably counterproductive. So a world long accustomed to French anti-Israel rhetoric was astonished in the spring of 2007 to find the two front-runners to succeed Jacques Chirac as president, Nicolas Sarkozy and Ségolène Royal, each falling over the other to appear more pro-Israel. Not only that, but, as some recent polls suggest, many Frenchmen have been so annoyed by expressions of anti-Semitism among Muslim radicals in France that they have become more pro-Israel.

Another reason for the high profile of the Israeli-Arab conflict is that Western journalists tend to cluster in Israel rather more than in, say, Amman, Riyadh, or Khartoum. This is because Israeli culture, including its nightlife, is more open and convivial to Westerners— and where the journalists and their cameramen are, that's where the news is. Additionally, to the naked eye, most Israelis appear to live and think like Westerners, and it is natural that Westerners would take a greater interest in people who remind them of themselves than in people who don't.

Then there is the venerable age of the Arab-Israeli conflict, nearly sixty years old and still going strong, so that obsessing over it is, for many, a habit, and for some academics and journalists a career. Because the conflict is so old, and because Israelis seem thoroughly Western to the eye of most journalists, many have come to the view that they actually understand the Arab-Israel conflict—even without having studied its dynamics or its history. Few will venture to claim that they understand Sunni-Shi'a divisions, or the history of Arab-Persian enmities, or the rise of Kurdish nationalism. These are esoteric issues to most Western observers, and so evoke a natural humility. But this humility rarely applies to the Arab-Israeli conflict, notwithstanding the fact that it should.

Then there is guilt, especially of the European postcolonial sort. A lot of Europeans, including British Europeans, believe that somehow they are responsible for having caused the Arab-Israeli problem in the first place, so it is natural that they would take a special interest in its solution. This argument, at least, has some validity if one happens to be British.

Another "human interest" reason may involve something more recondite. Educated Europeans know that their own histories are entwined with that of the Jews. Jews were for many centuries the most prominent "other" within most European cultures, and the enormous influence of Christianity over everything that Europe is owes at least half its origins to Judaism. So even in a largely post-Christian Europe (at least in its Western parts), Israel remains near the center of the European political worldview as a secularized vestige of an old religious obsession. It is a little like the phantom flashes that one sees after looking into a bright light; Europeans have seen such phantom images of Jews for so long that many still see them today, even where they aren't.

Finally, of course, there is old-fashioned European anti-Semitism. The Jewcentric delusion about the centrality of the Arab-Israeli conflict usually flows from plain ignorance annealed by wishful thinking. At other times it bears the unmistakable aroma of colonialist guilt in the form of a predisposition to blame one's own ignoble past for every problem in the non-Western present. But at least sometimes it gives off the even less pleasant stench of anti-Semitism—as if to say, "It's all the fault of the Jews; slap them down, and the Muslims will stop threatening us." It may be primitive, but that does not make it all that unpopular as an explanation for the threat of Islamist terrorism.

It is, on balance, an argument driven by fear. For many years, motivated by a well-intentioned liberal universalism (and also labor shortages), European governments allowed large numbers of Muslim immigrants, guest workers, and asylum seekers into their countries. Over the years, too, given variable demographic momenta, generous welfare benefits, and cultural barriers to the integration of these newcomers, unassimilated Muslim populations in many European countries came to be viewed as threats to national identity and social order. Politics in the Netherlands, Austria, France, Germany, Denmark, Sweden, Great Britain, and elsewhere have been increasingly roiled by this problem, and after 9/11 the problems at home seemed to fuse with an extremely frightening problem abroad. With the post-9/11 terror attacks in Spain and Britain, these fears metastasized among many, at least for a time, into near panic.

Now, what to do in Europe when fear turns to panic? At least a small number of people unearth an atavistic cultural instinct to blame the Jews. That is what happened during and just after the Black Death: the Jews were accused of poisoning the wells. Roughly the same thing has been happening, thankfully to a much lesser degree, since 9/11—only now "the Jews" and Judaism have become Israel and the Zionists. One saw this vividly exemplified in the anti-Israel demonstrations during the January 2009 Gaza war. Placards reading "Jews back to the ovens," "Kill the Jews," and other such noxious things were commonplace, although, it is true, most of those placards were made by Muslims living in Europe and not by typical Europeans. Of course the ADL jumped on this, doing an instant survey and proclaiming, yet again, the rise of anti-Semitism in Europe and in South America.[15] In this particular case, the ADL may have been correct.

Germany is, as always, a special case. More than any people on earth, Germans are afraid of their own strength and have made great efforts to enshroud the demons of their history in various forms of multilateralism. Many German intellectuals have turned the United Nations and other forms of multilateralism for its own sake into a kind of fetish. Some Germans unwittingly project these attitudes about multilateralism and the illegitimacy of using force on behalf of merely national interests onto others. They have real trouble understanding or sympathizing with any country, including Israel (and the United States), that uses force on behalf of its own interests, particularly when it does so apparently against majority UN sentiment. This is an uncomfortable place for Germans to be in, however, because the same historical factors that have led them to fetishize the UN, and to make a virtue of their own postnational selflessness and restraint, also mandate that they maintain an especially supportive stance toward Israel.

German political support for Israel is unconditional in principle, and sincere as far as it goes. German opposition to anti-Semitism, wherever it may arise, is unconditional in principle, too. The German people really did go through national agony after the Holocaust. They endured a process of psychological and spiritual contrition that never happened in, for example, Japan—although Japanese war crimes were less horrible than Germany's only in quantity, not quality.

No one should doubt the sincerity of German national repentance; it is thoroughly real. Not only that, German governments since Konrad Adenauer's have not just talked the talk; they have also walked the walk. Israeli military engineers and scientists have better professional relations with their German colleagues than with those of any other European country.

Yet the source of Germany's devotion to Israel's security has led to a major confusion. Many Germans believe that Israel's right to exist is based on what Germans did to Jews during World War II, that Jews are entitled to a part of Palestine not by right but by the sufferance of repenting Westerners. The fundamental problem with Germany's Israel policy is that it implies that had the Holocaust not happened, Israel would have no right to expect German support. Naturally, therefore, many Germans incline to accept at face value the Arab propaganda line that Palestinians should not pay the price for what Germans did to Jews on another continent in another time. This has resulted in a displacement of German guilt: At first Germans felt guilt toward the Jews; now they feel guilt toward the Arabs over the consequences, they think, of their guilt toward the Jews. The psychological consequence is that, according to recent polls, Germans were the least favorably disposed toward Israel of all countries in Europe with the single exception of Spain.

This tension has given rise to some strange phenomena. In essence, it has given rise to a German attitude toward the Middle East that insists that all it does it does in Israel's interests, and yet that attitude and the policy behaviors that often flow from it ultimately harm Israel's security. Thus, for example, the German Social Democratic Party, which controls the Foreign Ministry in the present Merkel government, sympathized with the argument that Israel's reactions to the steady rain of rockets into its territory from Gaza were "disproportionate," and that Israel's military operation in January 2009 to stop those attacks also was disproportionate. It argued that this kind of Israeli response is ultimately bad for Israel.

This is amazing. Rocket fire from Gaza into the town of Sderot in Israel was designed to deliberately kill civilians. Israeli responses were designed to quiet the source of the fire, but since those who fired the rockets deliberately did so from within apartment buildings, schools, and mosques, Israeli responses did sometimes injure and kill civilians. That is what Hamas, Islamic Jihad, and other radical groups in Gaza wanted to happen: headlines of "massacres" so that they could keep shooting rockets into Israel while Israelis felt restrained from responding. One reason for Israeli tactics in the January 2009 operation in Gaza was to disabuse Hamas once and for all that it could gain anything from such tactics. If German criticism would have had Israel respond "proportionately" to Hamas missile fire, it would have meant that Israel should have fired missiles deliberately, if randomly, at schools and kindergartens in Gaza. That is the literal logical endpoint of German criticism, but no one who made such criticisms would accept that logic.

More than that, no country in the world, not even Germany, would respond "proportionately" if some nonstate militia started rocketing their towns from across some border and killing German civilians. If a government could not get the state from whose territory the rockets were being fired to take responsibility for ending the threat, then it would have no choice but to silence the threat itself. Why do German intellectuals, journalists, and politicians expect Israel alone to act differently? And why do they, of all people, insist that the use of force must always be a last resort in any political confrontation among states, when that kind of thinking is exactly what allowed Hitler to cause the Second World War? Germans frequently talk like Neville Chamberlain at Munich, when they ought to realize that it was Winston Churchill who was right: the readiness to use force in an appropriate and judicious manner is not what causes wars; it is often what prevents them.

Nonetheless, the leftward side of the German policy debate is today utterly persuaded that Western countries should sit with Iran unconditionally, under UN auspices if possible, to try to persuade it not to build nuclear weapons. They oppose serious sanctions because they fear this will taint the atmosphere for negotiations. If negotiations fail and the Iranian state builds a nuclear arsenal anyway, they believe that Iran is doing this for defensive purposes, to protect itself from Israel and the United States; hence it follows that deterring the use of Iranian weapons will be easy. Most believe—and this is true of most West European opinion, not just German opinion—that all weapons of mass destruction are self-deterring, so there is no reason to risk war to prevent an Iranian arsenal from coming into being. A war under such circumstances would not only be immoral, since it is not a last resort, it would also serve only to create more resentment of the West and with it more terrorism. Germans who make these arguments always insist that they are in Israel's best interests.

One cannot help but wonder, however, if the real reason for this attitude is to keep Germany off the Iranian target list—appeasement, in other words, as in, once again, if we distance ourselves from Israel (read, "the Jews"), then our Islamist enemies will leave us alone.

One cannot help but wonder, too, whether some younger Germans who make these kinds of arguments do so in search of a little psychic relief. If so, one can hardly blame them. It is a burden, after all, to feel such intense guilt over crimes that took place before one was even born. It is a particular burden for a whole nation and a whole civilization to carry such guilt if one believes that Nazism was not an essential expression of German culture but a bizarre and tragic aberration from it. It is natural to resent being made to feel guilty, and to want to harm the source of that resentment—in this case, Israel and the Jews. In the especially Jewcentric case of Germany, then, we see a form of passive-aggressive behavior in which objectively anti-Israel policy recommendations and commentary are shrouded in the rhetoric of pro-Israel protestation. In the most extreme cases, this yearning for relief can take the form of projecting Nazi atrocities and attitudes onto Israelis and Jews—hence the popular political cartoon-ist's gimmick of conflating swastikas and Stars of David. Germans can stop feeling guilty about the Holocaust to the extent that they imagine Jewish behavior so heinous that the Jews no longer deserve German guilt. "With friends like these . . . ," Israelis say under their breath.

13

Muslim Jewcentricity

Never exaggerate your faults; your friends will attend to that.
— Bob Edwards

Muslim societies today are the site of the most virulent and widespread anti-Semitism on the planet. It is as bad as it was in Germany and in East-Central Europe in the 1930s and early 1940s, possibly even worse. Conspiracy theories about Jews and the Israeli Mossad are rife, partly because the population as a whole is poorly educated, partly because autocratic governments have no incentive to allow unbiased media reports, and partly because the region is experiencing a time of disorienting rapid change.

Not every Muslim believes outlandish tales of Jewish power, wealth, conspiracy, and intrigue, of course; but rather too many do, and that number includes relatively educated as well as not so well educated people. Most typical citizens of Cairo, Damascus, Rabat, and Amman still believe that the CIA and Israel were behind 9/11, not any Arabs. The Arabs, most believe, are not clever enough to pull off such a feat. They believe overwhelmingly that Jews knew about the attacks ahead of time and so stayed away from the World Trade Towers that day—a notion obviously disproved by the list of the dead. And this is why, in turn, very large numbers of people in the Muslim Middle East do not believe the United States is really fighting a war against terror, but is using the excuse of terrorism to fight a war against Islam and to seize the region's resources. As Michael Slackman put it, reporting from Cairo nearly seven years after the attacks on New York and Washington:

> Again and again people say they simply did not believe that a group of Arabs—like themselves—could possibly have waged such a successful operation against a superpower like the United States. But they also said that Washington's post-9/11 foreign policy proved that the United States and Israel were behind the attacks, especially with the invasion of Iraq. . . . Asked how Jews might have been notified to stay home, or how they kept it secret from their co-workers, people here wave off the questions because they clash with their bedrock conviction that Jews are behind many of their troubles and that Western Jews will go to any length to protect Israel.[1]

Indeed, for many it is clear that Israel and the Jews are really behind it all—all defined as everything significant—just as Israel and the Jews have invented the myth of the Holocaust as a device to gain advantage over gullible Westerners. According to a recent poll, even about 25 percent of the Arab citizens of the State of Israel deny the Holocaust ever happened.

Many Middle Easterners seem willing to entertain such theories about Jews for lack of any better way to explain the often dire and dicey circumstances in which they find themselves. Conspiracy theories about Jews, whether today in the Middle East, in the 1890s in Russia, or in the 1930s in Germany and East-Central Europe, are not always aimed at actually explaining events. Their function instead, most often, is to ward off feelings of uncertainty and fears of a precarious future. They serve as anxiety-control mechanisms. Their purpose, too, is to solidify social bonds, for in numbers there is a sense of security. The storyline that helps those bonds to form doesn't have to be literally accurate; it has only to resonate emotionally. It has to articulate what should be, and offer a reason why what should be is not. This is particularly important in societies where collective identity and responsibility are strong, and where the Western concept of individual political and intellectual agency remains weak.

Until quite recently by historical measure—say, about a century ago—Muslim anti-Semitism as such did not exist. I do not mean that anti-Jewish sentiment did not exist; it did, and it goes back all the way to the origins of Islam.[2] But, as we have been at pains to point out, these are two different things. Anti-Jewish sentiment inheres in the sacred narrative of Islam, both in the Quran and in the oral tradition written down both as Hadith, or sayings of the Prophet, and in the *sira* literature (writings concerning the biography of the Prophet). The reasons for this anti-Jewish sentiment are roughly similar to the reasons for it in Christianity: just as Judaism is the foundational plinth for Christianity, so it is for Islam, even more so than for Christianity.[3] And just as Christianity had to find some way to separate, distinguish, and distance itself from its foundation in order to justify its claims of superiority, so did Islam.

Anti-Semitism, on the other hand, defined as a form of mental disease that addles the mind with obsession, demonization, selective representation, and conspiracy theories—the kind of irrationality that drives sometimes large numbers of people to do unspeakably ugly things—is something else altogether. Within the far-flung history of Islam, dating from the death of Mohammed to the start of the past century, there were few examples of such behavior. Yes, Muslims sometimes acted fanatically, like the Almohads in twelfth-century Spain, but Christians and heathens suffered as much as, or more than, Jews from such episodes. Yes, an occasional Muslim leader lost his grip on reality—the Fatimid caliph al-Hakim in Egypt in the early eleventh century, for example—and undertook violent religious persecutions. But again, these were directed at everyone who dared disagree with al-Hakim, not just at Jews.

Indeed, insofar as Muslims mounted persecutions against other faiths, they tended to spare Jews and Christians as "people of the book"—in their view, legitimate monotheistic precursors of Islam. And on those occasions when they did not spare the peoples of the book, Muslim fanatics overwhelmingly targeted Christians for the simple reason that there soon came to be vastly more of them both within and without the domain of Islam. And unlike the Jews, Christians were organized politically and militarily in ways that threatened Dar al-Islam.

Recall, too, that anti-Semitism in Europe went through discrete historical phases. It began as religious prejudice, but was later entwined with the social role of Jews in premodern European societies. It then became enmeshed with the role Jews played in early capitalism, during the transition from feudal to early modern times. And it then merged with modern scientistic racism, producing the viral anti-Semitism of the nineteenth and twentieth centuries. But Islamic social and intellectual history differs from that of Europe.

Jews did play often similar social and economic roles within Islamic domains, but not exclusively so. Whereas by the sixth

century Jews were the only significant non-Christian social element within Europe, it was never true that Jews were the only significant non-Muslim element within the Islamic world. There were
always more Christians within Dar al-Islam than Jews, and there
were other peoples, as well. Moreover, the European transition from
feudalism to capitalism never took place in Muslim societies; Islamic
lands remained precapitalist in economic organization, if we mean
by capitalism the finance capital, surplus-value system described in
chapter 4. Most important of all, perhaps, the tradition of Western
science that was distorted in the nineteenth century into "scientific"
racism never emerged in Islamic lands.

Taken together, these factors explain at least in a brief, simple
way why the serial expulsions and mass murder Jews suffered in
Europe over the centuries did not occur, virtually without exception
and certainly with no major exception, in Islamic realms. This does
not mean, of course, that Jews enjoyed a kind of extended golden
age while living in the various climes and eras of Muslim history.
Nonetheless, again, the religious and social prejudice Jews suffered
within Dar al-Islam was nothing special: these were epochs in which
toleration was at best relative, so whatever Jews may have suffered,
others who were not a part of the ruling group of the time also suffered. This means that there was no Muslim anti-Semitism, strictly
defined, before about a century ago.

There is now. Contemporary Muslim anti-Semitism has been layered on top of centuries' worth of preexisting anti-Jewish sentiment,
and for that reason it has "taken" to a broad extent in Muslim societies. It has done so also because conspiracy theorizing constitutes the
political grammar, to so speak, of so much of the region, so that the
movement from old folklore to new pathology has proved easier than
it might otherwise have been. It has taken, too, unfortunately, because
some prestigious Muslim clerics who ought to know better have lent
their aid to this trend (of which more below).

Still, contemporary Muslim anti-Semitism is not Islamic in its
idiom or essence—it has been imported from Europe.[4] Only recently
has anti-Jewish hatred among Muslims been associated with modernity, urbanization, and pluralism. And only recently has the basic
inversion characteristic of genuine anti-Semitism taken place: once,
everything Jewish was evil because it was not Islamic, but Jews stood
in line with other evil non-Islamic peoples and religions; now, everything evil is "Jewish." In short, an extreme form of Jewcentricity has
appeared where once milder and mixed forms existed.

Note, too, that anti-Semitism in Muslim societies is for the most part an anti-Semitism without Jews—a very different circumstance from that which produced and sustained anti-Jewish sentiments of old in Europe. There are only a few, tiny Jewish communities left in the Arab countries—mainly in Morocco and Syria—and only about twelve thousand Jews in Iran, seventeen thousand in Turkey, and almost none in other Middle Eastern countries. In other words, Muslim anti-Semitism has skipped the economic and racist stages and gone straight to the political-ideological one—the current standard form of global anti-Semitism. And we all know about the zealotry of new converts: anti-Semitism today in the Muslim world is so virulent not because it is old, but because it is new.

Negative Jewcentricity is virtually everywhere in the Muslim world these days; it has become the default view of Jews, not the exceptional view. It is in the most prestigious seminaries, like Al-Azhar in Egypt, and Muslims who come to Al-Azhar to study have taken the anti-Semitic tracts they have been exposed to there back to Pakistan, Somalia, Indonesia, Bangladesh, Malaysia, and elsewhere. Now the Internet, the language of which is mainly English, spreads the same arguments to first- and second-generation Muslims in Europe and in the United States and Canada. In each place such tracts go, they are adapted to local conditions, adumbrated and interpreted, and passed along.

Anti-Semitism is now so pervasive in many Muslim societies that it frequently amounts to a card that has to be stamped in order to obtain political approval. Is Mahathir Mohammed, the former prime minister of Malaysia, an anti-Semite? From all appearances he certainly is, but perhaps the matter is not as it seems. Jomo K. Sundram, an economics professor at the University of Malaysia, explained that Mahathir has had to speak in anti-Semitic cadences precisely because his internal policies were on balance anticlerical:

> Anti-Semitism is the kind of thing you do to establish your ostensible Islamic credentials. Mahathir does this because his Islamic credentials are so weak, and because he spends so much time attacking the ulemma. He was saying, "In case you think I am anti-Muslim, here is some anti-Semitism."[5]

That really says it all: if anti-Semitism is a prerequisite for political acceptability in a place like Malaysia, one need not strain hard to imagine the situation closer to the Arab Muslim core.

But just in case one needs to strain, consider the remarks of Captain Sayyed Shahada, a member of the Egyptian Unique Mustache Association, who opined as follows on Egyptian television on July 11, 2008:

> I respect the mustache of this Hitler, because he humiliated the most despicable sect in the world. He subdued the people who subdued the whole world—him with his "11" mustache. . . . When I was little, my father, may he rest in peace, grew that kind of mustache, and so did all his classmates. They all had this "11" mustache. That was in the days of Hitler.

Everyday, ordinary, wild-eyed anti-Semitism in Egypt—an anti-Semitism without Jews—is pervasive, and it has been since before the Iraq war, before 9/11, before the administration of George W. Bush, before even the creation of the State of Israel.[6] If a guy whose hobby is growing designer facial hair can be so second-naturedly anti-Semitic, imagine what many if not most Egyptians who lack a sense of humor or a hobby probably think.

The difference between then and now, perhaps, is that governments sponsor anti-Semitism today, whereas before they generally did not. Thus, Egyptian, Syrian, and Palestinian television now regularly run "documentaries" based on Holocaust denial tracts, particularly during the holy month of Ramadan. The Iranian regime has sponsored entire Holocaust-denial international conventions. The majority of average citizens in most Muslim countries today, not just the Arab states near Israel, think that Israel is illegitimate, Zionism is racist, the Holocaust either never happened or has been vastly exaggerated, and that Arabs and Palestinians are pure victims of Israeli aggression, having themselves never contributed one whit to the conflict. This is now spread by official and semi-official media and taught in schools to an extent that was not the case in most parts of the Muslim world even twenty-five or thirty years ago.

Muslim anti-Semitism is mainly a European import, but its underlayer of anti-Jewish folklore gives it a vocabulary and a tone of its own. To convey how and why this is so, and how Jews have viewed Muslims, let us go back, one last time, to the Hebrew Bible.

As is widely understood, the nineteenth-century European philological term "Semite" is derived from the name Shem, one of the three sons of Noah (the other two being Ham and Japheth). As Jews have traditionally understood the biblical text, Shem was the father of the peoples of the Middle East, Japheth the father of the peoples of Europe, and Ham the father of the peoples of Africa. There are no "Arabs" as such in the Hebrew Bible, but lots of other peoples are mentioned. These are tribes, basically, understood to be descended mostly from Ishmael, and hence cousins of the Israelites. Some are typified as being quite vile—Amalekites, for example. Some bear their own inner creation story: Noah's drunken indiscretion after the Flood gets the Canaanites (Canaan is the son of Ham) cursed forever as slaves, and this one verse was later turned into a Christian justification for slavery. Lot's incest with his two daughters after the destruction of Sodom and Gomorrah leads to the creation of the Moabites and the Ammonites, respectively, and the biblical text implies that this disgusting origin more or less explains the depraved cultures of the peoples themselves centuries later. Edomites also run through biblical and postbiblical texts—especially in the Talmud—and they are descendants of Esau, Jacob's twin brother.

As to Ishmael himself, here a complexity that needs some parsing. As Abraham's firstborn son, Ishmael is the apple of Abraham's eye, even though he was born of Sarah's Egyptian handmaid Hagar. This is clear, for when Sarah wants to send Hagar and Ishmael away, it grieves Abraham, who relents only when God tells him to "listen to the voice of your wife." Indeed, when God promises Abraham a son to carry on his spiritual innovations, Abraham grows humble, asking only that "Ishmael may live before you." Ishmael, the Bible tells us, later attends Abraham's funeral along with his half-brother Isaac, and this is no small deal in biblical terms. So it seems obvious from the plain meaning of the biblical text that when God promises a huge chunk of what later came to be called the Levant to Abraham's descendants, Abraham understood the promise to apply to Ishmael as well as to Isaac.

Nonetheless, Ishmael does not get good press, so to speak, in rabbinic Judaism. That is partly because the rabbis often interpreted passages allegorically, sometimes using a biblical figure or episode to comment on something contemporary, in a kind of code. Esau became a symbol for Rome in the Talmud at a time when Roman persecutions were contemporary or near-contemporary affairs. This is not the place to trace the Talmudic image of Ishmael and his descendants: suffice it to say that, in spiritual terms, the line runs from Abraham to Isaac (not Ishmael) and from Isaac to Jacob (not Esau).

Everyone related to, but outside of, this line gets the equivalent of a premodern bum rap. They, after all, are not chosen.

The Bible's view of the Arabs is important because through the Hebrew Bible it also became the Western view of the Arabs. But how do Muslims see things? They see them through the Quran, of course; but it so happens that the Quran depends in a way on the Hebrew Bible's account as well. Many of the historical parts of the Quran are taken, but taken with differences, from the Hebrew Bible.

It is no great mystery how this happened. Mohammed himself lived among Jews and Christians for a time, in Syria as well as Arabia, and was clearly influenced by both. Muslim tradition affirms this: according to a Hadith, a story from the Islamic oral tradition, a relative of Mohammed's first wife, Khadija, named Waraqa ibn Nawfal, was a Christian convert who wrote out the Gospels in Arabic using Hebrew letters. More broadly, the Arabs excelled at oral tradition and poetry, and so gave rise to a kind of whistle-down-the-wind phenomenon wherein stories were told and handed down, changing here and there and being "domesticated" as they passed from mouth to mouth, generation to generation. For at least four centuries before Mohammed this was going on within Arabia, with respect to both Jewish and Christian legends, so that when this oral tradition was set to writing, it was fairly Jewcentric in character. When the Quran was first written down in the seventh century, these oral traditions got fixed in print.

This is not how a religious Muslim understands the origin of the Quran, of course. In-the-tradition Muslims believe that the Quran is the product of complete and perfect revelation, just as the Torah is for in-the-tradition Jews. This is what creates the problems. In the domestication process wherein the Arab oral tradition was transformed into a written one, the complicated recent history of Arabs and Jews came into play. Mohammed, rather like Martin Luther after him, thought the Jews would flock to his beliefs and his banner. He was dismayed when they didn't, and he turned on them. This is how the direction of Islamic prayer got shifted from Jerusalem to Mecca, but, more important, it is also how in due course the critical biblical story of the binding of Isaac got transformed in the foundation narrative of Islam.

As the Hebrew Bible tells it, and as the rabbis have always understood it, the binding of Isaac happened on Mount Moriah, the future Temple Mount in Jerusalem, and it is Isaac who inherits Abraham's covenant with God. In the Quran, and as Muslim adepts have always understood it, it is not Isaac but Ishmael who is bound (and of course saved), and the place is the Valley of Arafat, in Arabia, not Mount Moriah in the Land of Israel. (That is where, by the way, Yasir Rauf al-Qudwa al-Husseini, also known as Yasir Arafat, took the second part of his *nom de guerre*.) So in-the-tradition Arab Muslims and Jews agree that they are all Semites, they agree about Abraham's call, they even agree about Moses and the Exodus and more besides, much of which is related, in its own fashion, in the Quran. But Muslims argue that the Jews distorted the record, and that the Hebrew Bible's account of this critical event, the "binding" of Abraham's son, is a post-Mohammedan fabrication. The Muslims, especially in the Wahhabi Qurans in wide circulation courtesy of well-heeled Saudi evangelism, accuse the Jews of having inserted Isaac where Ishmael should be, and of having substituted Moriah for Arafat.[7]

Objectively, this is nonsense, for the canonical biblical text, here of the Torah itself, predates the birth of Mohammed by about a thousand years, and the precanonical storyline probably by many more years than that. It is rather Muslims who have the explaining to do when it comes to borrowed and distorted texts. Parts of the Quranic sura called *Yusuf* (Joseph), the twelfth sura for those keeping score, are taken largely verbatim from the Mishnah. That something from the second or third century CE (at the latest) found its way into the Quran, which was canonized in the seventh century CE, makes chronological sense. But a seventh- or post-seventh-century interpretation claiming precedence over a written account canonized around 450 BCE (that is, the Torah) makes no sense at all. This is impossible to credit logically, and so explains why Muslims had to claim that Jews and Christians had tampered post hoc with the holy word of God.[8]

For this reason—that the Jews had the audacity to distort the revealed word of God Himself—if not for others, in-the-tradition Muslims have, it is fair to say, a disparaging attitude toward Jews and Judaism, despite the dependence of the Quran on so much of the Jewish narrative. This negative attitude is no worse than Christian attitudes toward Jews. The Jews are cursed in the Islamic theological view no less than in the classical supercessionist Christian belief system. This becomes a little clearer if we understand basic Sunni Islamic eschatology, or end-of-days theology.

Most variants of Muslim theology look forward to an end of days when Islam will be universally triumphant, and in the lead-up to that condition there will be a series of convulsive events, including major wars. If this sounds like Armageddon in Arabic, and a little like the Protestant dispensationalist interpretation of things, that's because it is. Most in-the-tradition Muslims believe that Jesus will return and fight the anti-Christ or anti-Allah, called *dajjal* in Arabic. All the good Jews will become Muslims, and all the bad ones—most of them—will die. (Again: sound familiar?)

Now, there is a statement near the end of the Hadith that goes like this: "The Jews will hide behind the rock and tree, and the rock and tree will say: O servant of Allah, O Muslim, this is a Jew behind me, come and kill him!" There is both more and less than meets the eye here. There is less in the sense that this statement bears a context, that of the end of history, or of normal historical time. This is when the rocks and trees will miraculously take on voices, telling the good guys how to find and kill the Jews to hasten the destiny of history. In the hadithic mythology, there is even a particular tree the Jews will hide behind, a Jew-tree, so to speak. It is called the *gharqad* tree and is said to be large and thorny.

So killing Jews is not a religious obligation in the Islamic tradition, and the statement about the talking rocks and trees does not come from the Quran. It is a prophecy about the "end of days," and it carries what is for most Muslims the lesser authority of Hadith. Moreover, there are many offsetting verses in the Quran (and in Hadith) that *forbid* violence against non-Muslims, that set conditions as to when violence and war are permitted, and that bear special protection for other members of the Abrahamic tradition—Jews and Christians in particular.

Nonetheless, the in-the-tradition Muslim view of Jews and Judaism is that while Judaism is one of the two legitimate and even sacred forebears of Islam, the Jews (and the Christians) strayed from the true path of God, distorted God's word, and show traits of cunning, betrayal, and deception. This is hardly unusual: most religious adherents are chauvinistic about their faith, and demean other religions so that theirs may be exalted in comparison. This is an almost universal phenomenon; nothing to get excited about. Traditional Muslims do not need, and have never needed, the line about the trees and the rocks and the *gharqad* tree to have a low opinion of Jews. Besides, more than a thousand years of Muslim-Jewish cohabitation in the towns, villages, and cities of Dar al-Islam, in which Jewish communities, though "protected," found themselves in a defenseless and inferior social position, helped to solidify these images.

But Muslim fundamentalists have taken this and other verses from the Quran, the Hadith, and the *sira* literature out of context to create a virulent form of religion-based anti-Semitism, and it is important to keep the two straight. There is a difference between widespread anti-Jewish folklore among the masses and actual anti-Semitism, which is key to a small, politicized minority but which has recently spread outward to encompass significant parts of the populations of many Muslim-majority countries.

The political is again the key here. Salafi fundamentalists do not hate Jews because they believe differently; they hate Israel and Jews who support Israel because Israel represents the political incarnation of the "chosen" concept. This is directly at odds with their ambitions to resurrect the Caliphate, which they see as divinely chosen, as the political manifestation of Islam as the "seal of the prophets." Yet Muslim radicals have done exactly what they accuse Jews of doing in Israel: they have trivialized Islam by turning it into an ideology. Along with European anti-Semitism came European political ideas, both left- and right-wing socialism. They rage against idolatry, yet they themselves are the idolaters. They hate European colonialists and Jewish Zionists, yet they have unwittingly adopted so many of their underlying assumptions about the nexus between religion and politics that they have become like them.

It is also important to recognize that much fundamentalist distortion of Islamic tradition is apocalyptical in nature. Both Sunni and Shi'a fanatics nowadays believe the world is about to end, that the wars of Armageddon are upon us, that the redeemer, the Mahdi, is coming soon. This is obvious in the rantings of the Iranian president, Mahmoud Ahmadinejad, but it is also present in the Salafi cults and cells of mainly the Arab world as well. This accords with our earlier discussion of the way highly chaotic times often give rise to apocalyptic movements.[9] Thus, in the Muslim world today end-of-days delusions and anti-Semitism tend to converge.

It follows that one important preventative against fundamentalist Islam, and its contemporary anti-Semitism, is better and genuine Islamic education—and by education is meant not only religion, but also the wider fields of Islamic literature and history.

It would be a good thing, for example, if young Muslims were made aware that in the century or so after the death of Mohammed, the rancor of Islamic leaders against Christians and Jews who refused to convert to Islam virtually died out. It would be good if they knew that beyond Christians and Jews being treated as protected peoples, as *dhimmis*, early Islamic leaders did not treat Christians and Jews the same. Umayyad and early Abbasid caliphs affirmed the peoplehood as well as recognized the religious distinctiveness of the Jews. Indeed, the Jews were treated as a political entity: the Gaon or Exilarch—the leader of the Jewish community in Mesopotamia—held the symbolic rank of a head of state, and the heads of the then still-functioning Talmudic academies became eminences of Judaism, having a rank below but comparable to that of Islamic legal scholars.

This basic Islamic approach to the Jews continued for many centuries. Benjamin of Tudela, the Jewish "Marco Polo" of the twelfth century, provided a firsthand account of Jewish life in Abbasid Baghdad, and of how the Exilarch was treated in public:

> In Baghdad there are about 40,000 Jews and they dwell in security, prosperity and honor under the great Caliph. . . . And every fifth day when he goes to pay a visit to the great Caliph, horsemen—Gentiles as well as Jews—escort him and heralds proclaim in advance "Make way before our Lord, the son of David, as is due unto him," the Arabic words being *Amilu tarik la saidna bin Daoud*. He is mounted on a horse and is attired in robes of silk and embroidery with a large turban on his head, and from the turban is suspended a long white cloth adorned with a chain upon which the cipher of Mohammed is engraved. Then he appears before the Caliph and kisses his hand, and the Caliph stands and places him on a throne which Mohammed has ordered to be made in his honor, and all the Mohammedan princes who attend the court of the Caliph rise up before him. And the Head of the Captivity [the Exilarch] is seated on his throne opposite to the Caliph, in compliance with the command of Mohammed to give effect to what is written in the law—"The scepter shall not depart from Judah nor a law-giver from between his feet, until he come to Shiloh: and to him shall the gathering of the people be."[10]

It would be nice, too, if contemporary Muslims knew that Muslim leaders before the twelfth century—before the devastation wrought by the Mongols—tended to divide subject peoples into basically two groups: those who were interested in science and its practical applications and those who were not. In the former group Muslim leaders placed the Jews, as well as the Greeks and the Persians. In the latter they placed the Turks, the Chinese, and most Christians.

Similar traditions continued to exist when the Muslim scepter passed to the Turks, and there were times when the Ottoman Turks used Jews (as well as Armenians and others) as agents of commerce and as social buffers in newly acquired territories. In their European domains the Ottomans would take local Jews from within the empire and place them out on the new border, and take Jews from newly acquired lands and send them deep into long-held Ottoman territories to be acculturated. This area included Palestine. During much of the fifteenth and sixteenth centuries it was the policy of Ottoman caliphs to repopulate Palestine with Jews. That is, for example, how Joseph Caro, the Toledo-born author of the Shulchan Aruch, ended up in Safed.

And it would be nice if Muslims today knew that while the Crusades were actually happening, they were not an obsession for most Muslims. Nowadays the sinister image of the Crusades in the Muslim world is pervasive. This is natural, in a way, since the primary prism through which Muslims have viewed the world over the past century or so has been that of Western imperialism and how to escape its clutches. If Europeans are the problem, it (sort of) makes sense to project current frames of reference backward onto history in such a way that makes Europeans the problem in the eleventh and twelfth centuries, too.

The truth of the matter, however, is that when the Crusaders were tromping around Jerusalem and Acre, the real strategic action for Muslim rulers—the issues they were really worried about—was far, far away. For the most part, these were internal disputations; certainly before the nineteenth century, most Muslims killed in war were killed by other Muslims—and the same is true for European Christians.[11] Insofar as Muslims and Christians did clash during Crusader times, they did so with far more geopolitical significance in Spain, in Africa, in Malta, in Sicily, and further north in Europe, as is proved by a reading of the actual contemporaneous historical record in Arabic, Persian, and Turkish. Palestine at the time was a backwater, and Jerusalem a city of no consequence strategically; Arab historians of that day and for centuries later barely mention it. Rather, it was mainly a small handful of French Romanticist historians in the nineteenth century who, for reasons of their own, tried to make the history of imperial France central to that of the Muslim world. The Arabs, having no contemporary historiography of their own at the time, read the French and took them at their word.

Now this is rich, especially in light of the late Edward Said's theory that all Western scholarship on Muslim societies has been part of a deliberate Western imperialist scheme to undermine and conquer Islamic domains. Here Western scholarship introduced a distortion for ideological reasons, and it became embedded in Arab historiographical consciousness not because these French historians wanted to mislead the Arabs, but because the Arabs, considering the French and other Europeans advanced and powerful, simply assumed the French version to be accurate. One might say, therefore, that a foundation for Said's own bias was an episode that undermines that foundation.

The same basic dynamic explains much about contemporary Muslim Jewcentricity. Muslims, and Arabs especially, became obsessed with Crusaders because Christian imperialists got in their faces starting in the late eighteenth century. This was natural because Muslims, mainly under the Turks, and European Christians had been mortal geopolitical rivals for hundreds of years in the Eurasian heartland.[12] But in the twentieth century, and especially after 1948–1949, not only European imperialists but also Zionist Jews were in their faces, and thus the reinterpretation of history to find old Jewish, as well as European, origins of current troubles.

That the Muslims should have borrowed European techniques and narratives of anti-Semitism to do so is equally rich, and tragic. The Muslim tradition was far too capacious, tolerant, and experienced to have such insane images of Jews ready to hand; so they, like so much else, had to be imported from Europe. To take a specific and not inconsequential example, the Baath Party, which used to rule Iraq and still rules Syria, got its start in the 1930s partially modeled on Nazi methods, which were very popular in the Arab East. That is why, in turn, the ranting of former Syrian defense minister Mustafa Tlas, who wrote a book in the 1980s resuscitating the 1840 Damascus blood libel, was probably to be expected.

One might say, therefore, that a partly delusional Eurocentricity among Muslims was ransacked to produce an equally delusional Jewcentricity. This reminds us of a prescient warning, attributed to the philosopher George Williams: Be cautious when you choose your enemy, for you will grow more like him. Some Muslims chose Europe as an enemy, and became like Europeans at the very least in the sense of internalizing their anti-Semitism.

It is thanks largely to European influences that contemporary Muslim anti-Semitism is more widespread than are the narrow ranks of true fundamentalist fanatics. As we have already noted, religion-based anti-Jewish stereotypes are deeply rooted in traditional Islam, just as practical tolerance for Jews and Jewish communities is rooted in many places. The creation of modern Jewish nationalism, Zionism, the success of the Zionist movement in building the sovereign State of Israel, and the broad aftermath of the June 1967 Middle East War, however, have re-woven these religion-based stereotypes and anti-Jewish biases into the very fabric of contemporary Muslim cultures. The fact, too, that every significant Jewish community in the Arab world has all but disappeared since 1948 has deprived younger generations of Muslims of the experience of actually seeing, interacting with, and knowing Jews, which is the best antidote to the bizarre stereotypes and caricatures held by Muslim anti-Semites. The result is that there is today a much more receptive audience for tradition-distorting fundamentalist anti-Semitism.

Part of the problem has to do with simple bad luck. The grand imam of the Al-Azhar mosque in Cairo, Sheikh Mohammed Sayyid al-Tantawi, has bought into Islamic anti-Jewish themes and expanded them. While Tantawi has been a moderate for the most part as grand imam on most political issues, in a seven-hundred-page book written in the 1970s and reissued in 1986, he revealed himself to be a dyed-in-the-wool Jew-hater. He has repeated in Friday sermons, for example, the common claim among Muslim anti-Semites, based on three Quranic verses, that Jews are the enemies of humanity and are literally descended from pigs and apes.[13] To bind the enormous influence of Al-Azhar, by far the most prestigious and influential institution in the Sunni Muslim world, to anti-Jewish bigotry has done enormous harm. In the long run, what is taught at Al-Azhar is far more important than the ignorant pseudo-fatwas of Osama bin Laden. It did not have to be this way. A wiser man than Sheikh Tantawi could have taken a different view and not raised an eyebrow about its Islamic legitimacy in so doing.

That would have made a difference, too. It is important to note that the fundamentalist view of Jews is not the traditional one. There is one thing about all sorts of fundamentalists—Muslim, Hindu, Christian, Jewish, whatever—that cannot be overlooked: they are glassy-eyed ignoramuses within their own traditions. They generally do not have serious, let alone seminary-based, religious educations. They are generally not students of religion at all, but often of engineering or business; excepting those educated in the Saudi system, almost no Islamic fundamentalists have even remotely serious madrassa (seminary) backgrounds. They rarely appreciate the full moral logic of their own traditions, nor do they particularly care about them. Instead, charismatic Islamist fundamentalist preachers ransack the Islamic tradition for verses or fragments of verses that serve their political purposes. The masses, agitated by some real or imagined slight to their interests or pride, often don't know any better, and so all too often believe what they hear. That is why the authority of legitimate clerics is so important in keeping the vast majority of Muslims from falling for Salafi distortions, and why it is so tragic that the record of those clerics, so far, is not a very robust one.

This is ironic, because Muslim apologists are always going on about how tolerant Islam is compared to Judaism and Christianity. Some of these assertions can be silly and self-serving, but most are historically grounded and sincere. The silly argument is the one that says Islam recognizes and honors Judaism and Christianity as Abrahamic precursors of Islam, the "seal" of the Prophet, but that neither Judaism nor Christianity thus honors Islam in its texts and traditions. This is silly because Islam came after Judaism and Christianity, and the only way for Judaism and Christianity to "honor" Islam would be to revise its own sacred texts after the fact. Since Muslims accuse Jews and Christians of having doctored and altered the Bible—Old and New Testaments—anyway, they see no reason why it cannot be altered again to honor Islam. Jews and Christians obviously have different views of their respective scriptures. No group of rabbis, for example, would ever imagine that it had the authority to go back and edit the Talmud, let alone the Torah, to make room for the virtues of Islam.

As to the reality of Islamic tolerance for Jews over the centuries, this is unarguable. Given a hypothetical choice, no educated Jew would trade the Jewish experience within Islam for the one within Christendom. But it is easy to tolerate a protected Abrahamic minority, or any other kind for that matter, when that minority is both weak and often useful in one way or another. When a minority plays its part in bolstering the pride of the dominant group, it confirms the social cosmology of that dominant group; it works, it fits. It is another thing to show toleration when that minority has its own politically sovereign state in one's midst, is stronger, more modern, and wealthier than one's own states—as the State of Israel is in relation to all the Arab states. That has made all the difference.

So, unfortunately but not surprisingly, the charter of Hamas takes unto itself official religious anti-Semitism, and goes well beyond mere distorted tradition: it quotes the *Protocols of the Elders of Zion* as if it were a proof text. This should be an embarrassment to sensible Muslims today, of course, and to some it is. To many, however, it isn't.

Over the past few decades of intifada, the religious community oriented toward Hamas, which is an offshoot of the Muslim Brotherhood, has enumerated in detail all of the anti-Jewish verses in the Quran and the Hadith, and ignored the others. The statement about the rocks and the *gharqad* tree has been repeated endlessly, and to compete with Hamas-affiliated clergy, PLO-affiliated clergy have used it, too, on many occasions, including on PLO/Palestinian Authority radio and television. Indeed, in countless Friday sermons the clergy has piled interpretation upon interpretation. Take, for example, the symbolism of the thorny *gharqad* "Jew-tree" itself. Sometimes the tree stands for Zionism. Sometimes the tree is said to have been planted around all the Jewish settlements in the West Bank and Gaza, protecting them from the Muslims' wrath. Sometimes the tree is said literally to be planted outside the Jaffa Gate in Jerusalem to protect the Israeli occupation of the Old City and its Haram al-Sharaf, the Temple Mount. Sometimes the tree has been said to refer to Palestinian collaborators with Israel, and in recent years Hamas-affiliated preachers and policy hacks alike frequently identify the PLO itself as Israel's friend and collaborator for deigning to discuss peace.

What goes for Hamas also goes for Hezbollah in Lebanon, and for Iran's Shi'a clerics, as well. The anti-Semitic rants of Sheikh Hassan Nasrallah are legendary and legion. During the summer 2006 "small war" with Israel, when other Lebanese leaders such as the Druze chieftain Walid Jumblatt criticized Nasrallah for bringing destruction to Lebanon, Nasrallah could think of no greater insult for Jumblatt than to call him a Jew. Earlier, in 2002, Nasrallah had turned himself into a kind of Zionist, wishing that more Jews would come to Palestine so that "we won't have to chase them all over the world" in order to kill them, as Hezbollah did by attacking a Jewish community center in Buenos Aires on July 18, 1994, murdering eighty-six people.

The Saudis, however, have managed even to top that, in a way. On the anti-Iranian Saudi-owned Al-Arabiya network's Web site, an article appeared on February 27, 2009, claiming that Iranian president Ahmadinejad is of Jewish origin. The article, which was decorated by a picture of the Iranian president almost kissing an Orthodox-looking Jew, says that the writings of the son of the conservative Iranian cleric Ayatollah Khazali claim that Ahmadinejad's family changed their name to hide their Jewish roots, and that "power and wealth" today rests in the hands of "a generation of Jews in Iran."

Not to be outdone, Iranians have shown they can be just as bizarre. In early 2009 Iranian television aired a show the thrust of which was to suggest that the series of Harry Potter movies based on the J. K. Rowling books are the brainchild of a Ziono-Hollywood conspiracy. The whole thing, the Iranians experts onscreen claimed, takes its source from the witchcraft of ancient "Jewish rabbis in Egypt," whatever that is supposed to mean. It is representative, said the experts, of devil worship and "the evil essence of Zionism." Rational people who saw this show, "Harry Potter and the Ziono-Hollywoodist Conspiracy," or just the clips on YouTube (and by rational I include Iranians, Arabs, and others as well as Westerners) reacted mainly in laughter, so absurd was the premise and so ridiculous the argument. But this is not funny, for who knows how many Iranians actually have come to believe such blather?

It is not funny also because the show reflects a view, deeply embedded in the Iranian clerical leadership, that has major implications for U.S. and Western policy with regard to Iran's nuclear weapons aspirations. Many commentators in the United States and Europe do not worry very much about the advent of an Iranian bomb; their view is that such a capability can be deterred, as all use of nuclear weapons has been deterred for more than a half century. They contend that those who think otherwise are guilty of racism or condescension: To say that Iran would not be deterred, they claim, rests on an assumption that while Americans, Russians, Chinese, French, British, and others are rational, Iranians are not. This is the reddest of herrings. To fear an Iranian nuclear-weapons attack on Israel, one does not have to think that Iranians are irrational in general, only anti-Semitic in particular—and no one who studies the views of the Iranian mullahs can come to any other conclusion. But just shy of sixty-five years after the end of the Third Reich, some otherwise intelligent people cannot imagine any form of anti-Semitism being relevant to the behavior of contemporary states. This is hard to explain.

The plain fact, to repeat, is that an anti-Semitism that is a powerful combination of religious prejudice and racial-ethnic bigotry, further inflamed by anti-Western political themes, is rife throughout the Muslim world today. It expresses a raw and irrational hatred that compares well with the virulent anti-Semitism of pre–World War II Central and Eastern Europe, and with most West European fascism. Contemporary Muslim anti-Semitism has been bolstered by the relics of European anti-Semitism, and not only because of the ubiquitous text of the *Protocols of the Elders of Zion* in translation—available in any bookstore of significant size in the region, along with an Arabic translation of Henry Ford's *The Historical Jew: The World's Foremost Problem*. Also widely available in Arabic is the book that Ford influenced to the point of inciting plagiarism—Adolf Hitler's *Mein Kampf*. These are books, please remember, whose origins all lie in the West.

Most Europeans and Americans who become vaguely aware of such hatred, thanks to the unpleasant accident of being exposed to actual facts, tend to dismiss it as simply impossible, so incompatible is it with predominant reality in the twentieth and certainly the twenty-first centuries. Americans, in particular, optimistic Enlightenment universalists that they are, have a hard time wrapping their minds around the reality that such attitudes toward Jews could exist in such high places and at the same time be so popular on the lower rungs of the social ladder.

This failure becomes manifest from time to time. To take a trivial but revealing example, when the Chabad House in Mumbai became a target of terrorism in late November 2008, it struck both a *New York Times* and a *Wall Street Journal* reporter that this might have been accidental, since all the other targets were major centers. Here is how Abraham Cooper and Harold Brackman summarized much of the initial coverage:

> The *New York Times* theorized that Chabad House may have been an "accidental hostage scene." This speculation follows in the ignominious footsteps of the BBC, which initially chose to hide the Jewish character of the target by describing it as just "an office building," of Britain's Channel 4, which claimed that the terrorists showed "a wanton disregard for race or creed," and of *Al Jazeera*, which refused to show Chabad House as the site of the carnage. Some Western media outlets unsympathetically labeled victims there as "ultra-Orthodox" or "missionaries." Finally, the *Pakistan Times* explained it all. Mumbai was "a false flag operation" by Israel's Mossad agents disguised, apparently, as bearded rabbis and mothers nursing babies.[14]

How oblivious does a *New York Times* reporter have to be not to know that Islamist terrorists would indeed go out of their way to find and kill Jews?

Because Americans have trouble crediting the nature and scope of anti-Semitism in Muslim societies today, they are prone to misinterpret the anti-Israel rhetoric and intentions of many Muslims as being about the occupation of the West Bank, or about discrete Israeli actions in Lebanon or elsewhere. Of course some of it is precisely that, but most of it isn't. They assume that such opposition can be mollified, that Israel can take, or be forced by the United States and others to take, certain remedial actions that would cause Muslim anti-Israel fulminations and violence to go away. They assume that some kind of stable compromise is possible. This is, anyway, how most liberals and most lawyers tend to think—that there is always a deal out there somewhere, and that reasonable people can find it in due course if they try hard enough. They are such reasonable people that they cannot credit the existence of nonnegotiable unreasonableness in others.

Fortunately, not all Muslims are afflicted with fundamentalist attitudes, and not all are anti-Semitic in the clinical sense. Indeed, the vast majority in most countries probably still are not—their folkloric anti-Jewish sentiments have not yet mutated into actual anti-Semitism. Few of the leadership cadres in Muslim countries are thus afflicted either; only those in Iran, Saudi Arabia, and Sudan seem to fit today in that category. But all Muslim leaders have to reckon with such views within their own societies, and in many of them, even in Turkey and in places like Malaysia, where few if any Jews live, Jewcentric views are gaining adherents. The truth is that the only way U.S. policy toward the Middle East could ever please large numbers of people in places like Saudi Arabia, Pakistan, Egypt, Jordan, Syria, Iran, and elsewhere is by becoming as irrationally anti-Semitic as they are. This kind of Jewcentricity, one hopes, will never become a U.S. policy option.

14

Post-Zionism

All passions exaggerate; and they are passions only because they
exaggerate.

— NICOLAS CHAMFORT

There is a good deal of emotional fatigue today among Jews in
the United States, and some in Israel as well. Some secular
and generally left-wing Jews in the United States, Europe,
and Israel itself have come down with a case of Stockholm syndrome,
sympathizing with their would-be destroyers. I really do mean the
Stockholm syndrome, too: Israel has in a way been taken hostage by
the antipathy of much of the world. It has earned this antipathy by
sinning in an unforgivable way: it has succeeded, or at least appears
to have done so for the time being, and because that success makes
others uncomfortable, it makes some Jews feel guilty. That guilt is
then projected outward as a form of self-deprecation. This is the root
of a particular kind of fatigue, of Jewshaustion, called post-Zionism.

Post-Zionism is, or was, mainly a phenomenon of the middle to
late 1990s. "Was" because some claim that it was merely a fad that has
pretty much evaporated, having been spawned by the dazzling prospect of peace and normalization after the signing of the Oslo Accords
in September 1993, and subsequently buried with the eruption of
Palestinian violence, and the simultaneous Islamicization of Palestinian
nationalism. We'll see about that. In any event, post-Zionism came

into existence mainly in Israel and mainly in Hebrew, and almost exclusively in intellectual circles. It has since spread, however, into the Jewish Diaspora and to non-Jews, as well, and it has linked up with the older secular tradition of non- or anti-Zionism discussed in chapter 10.

Anything that involves Jews in philosophical and literary debates tends to get out of hand, and post-Zionism has done just that. Fed from several sources, it has developed several variants and many internal fissures, fertilized a good number of personal animosities (the pettier the more vicious, after all, is the motto of academia worldwide), and, at last count, generated hundreds if not thousands of articles, essays, symposia, and books. In some forms of post-Zionism the State of Israel as a Jewish state is illegitimate, but Jewish society in geographical Palestine and Jewish peoplehood are not. In other forms, all either are illegitimate or at least have no justifiable basis. In some versions, Zionism used to be fine as Israeli society and the State of Israel were being built up and made permanent—say between 1897 and the middle 1960s—but is now obsolete. There is even a form of post-Zionism developed by alienated members of Israel's *edot mizrahiyot*—Jews who came to Israel from Arab and other Middle Eastern countries—that Zionism was and remains a form of internal Ashkenazi Jewish imperialism.

But despite all the many streams feeding the idea and the several forms it has taken, all manifestations of post-Zionism have in common the conviction that Jewish nationalism, as given concrete political expression in the contemporary State of Israel, is in the main invalid, noxious, illegitimate, harmful, unjustifiable, or all of the above. That at least a few citizens of the State of Israel themselves express such views is bound to have some impact on Israel's relations with its non-Jewish citizens, with its neighbors, with the Jewish Diaspora, and with the hosts of that Diaspora, too.

As with several other subjects treated in this book, post-Zionism is the subject of a large, often tedious, and generally esoteric literature.[1] For our purposes, however, the main question is a simple one: how does the phenomenon of Israeli and Jewish post-Zionism relate to Jewcentricity? Is post-Zionism simply a form of Jewish self-hatred attuned to a political era? If, as some Orthodox Jews have claimed, Zionism is just another pseudovariety of Judaism—a secular messianic heresy whose messiah was Theodor Herzl—then is post-Zionism a form of reverse apostasy? What, if anything, do post-Zionist arguments have in common with those non-Orthodox and even wholly secular Jews, like George Steiner for example, who have been anti-Zionist from the start of the modern Zionist movement? How do non-Jews think about post-Zionism, and with what effects?

The first instinct of pro-Israel Jews in the Diaspora is to simply dismiss post-Zionism as a form of intellectual infantilism, to see it as a special form of Jewish self-hatred. No doubt many of those who espouse post-Zionism are guilty of narcissistic alienation. Many do come across as secular contrarians, pains in the ass of this particular time and place. All the same, their arguments are not so easily tossed aside.

For one thing, some tenets of post-Zionism qualify as versions of arguments Zionists themselves have been having with each other for more than a century. It has never been easy to reconcile secular nationalism with religion in Israel; for that very reason an argument erupted over what to name the state in 1948, and whether to mention God or Judaism in the declaration of the state (they were not mentioned). It has never been simple to reconcile the idea of a state for the Jewish people with full democratic rights for non-Jews either. In a sense, and whether they realize it or not, post-Zionists are engaged in a form of secular *pilpul*—the methodology of studying Talmud, which stretches and pushes the logic of political and moral concepts to their extremes. And it is not always self-evident, either, that these arguments are something other than "for the sake of heaven."

The debate over post-Zionism and anti-post-Zionism has everything to do with Jewcentricity. In a way, as we have intimated, in a political, ideological age, Zionism at first blush seems to be the transmutation of the idea of the Chosen People back into concrete social political history. Those Jews and non-Jews who reject the idea of Jewish chosenness as illusory, arrogant, or both are bound to reject any such transmutation. In other words, critics have picked up the Toynbeean notion that Jewish chosenness was an intolerable Jewcentric conceit from the start, but applied now not to Judaism or Jews but to Zionism and Israel.

But it's not so simple, for there is a paradox lying in wait here. If Zionism sought to normalize the social and political circumstances of the Jewish people, as it claimed it wished to do, the only way to go about it was abnormally. If it had never happened before, as it says in Exodus, that one people had been taken from the midst of another, it had also never happened that a people had survived nearly two millennia of exile and managed to reconstitute itself as a nation on its ancestral soil. So the only way to accurately describe the Zionist "normalization" quest was as an abnormal one, a quest suitable only for a people who in some way were, well, chosen. If this sounds a little crazy, note that Haim Weizmann himself once quipped that a person does not have to be crazy to be a Zionist, "but it helps."

If to succeed in normalizing Jewish history within world history was simultaneously to insist on Zionism's abnormality, it follows that what post-Zionists seek, in essence, is to normalize the still abnormal. They want to get rid of all notions of Jewish chosenness, usually with help from the antifoundationalism of postmodernism. Indeed, for the most part, post-Zionism is a particularist variety of postmodernism, and as such it is nothing new. The idea that the world is not bound by a first cause and the causal connections that emanate from it goes back at least to the philosophy of Epicurus in the fourth century BCE. It was Epicurus's insistence that God or the gods took no interest in and could exert no control over human life, and that what humans did had no necessary effect on future generations of humans, that led the rabbis to single out Epicurean philosophy as the most heinous of its time. That's where the Orthodox slur word *apikoros* for a person who rejects the foundational premises of Judaism comes from, after all.

New or old, it doesn't really matter, for there are, in practice, only a few finite and fragile ways to eliminate the idea of Jewish chosenness in its current political form without risking the destruction of Israeli society itself. Most Israeli post-Zionists do not want to go so far as that, or at least they think they don't, which leads them to a host of highly improbable scenarios in which Israeli society can be normal without being in any historically meaningful sense Jewish or chosen. Hence the basic problem with the whole enterprise.

But even if we reject post-Zionist ideas and their implications, we must admit that not all of them are superficial intellectually or trivial. They therefore deserve examination. Let us begin that process, as we have before, with matters of definition, without which we literally cannot know what we are talking about.

Zionists describe Zionism as the national liberation movement of the Jewish people, and that is true as far as it goes. But by way of real historical explanation it does not go very far, at least not in a straight line. In other national liberation movements, the people who make up the nation in question have been located in the territory to be liberated from colonialists or usurpers of various descriptions. In the case of Israel, most of the members of the nation, and most Zionists, were somewhere else for the first critical decades of the movement's existence. So the oppressors of the Jews—Russians, Germans, Poles, French, and so on—literally had nothing do to with geographical Palestine when it was part of the Ottoman Empire or when, after World War I, it became a British Mandate. At the time, too, no Zionist would have said that Arabs living in Palestine were their oppressors. The Arabs were conceived either as fellow working-class victims of imperialism or as a minority to be dealt with as minorities are generally dealt with by decent governments. Or, in a minority of cases, they were simply not thought about at all.

As complexities go, however, that is not the half of it. Clearly, Zionism aimed to establish at a minimum a "national home" for the Jewish people, those being the words used in the Balfour Declaration of November 1917. But from the start most Zionists aspired to gaining an independent state, to restoring Jewish political sovereignty, as well. Most, but not all. Even from the beginning, there were divisions within the Zionist movement over precisely this question. Herzl was so pessimistic about the possibility of Jewish acceptance in Europe as Jews, and so worried about the possibility of mass violence, that he was willing to consider a proposal to set up a Jewish state in British East Africa—euphemistically referred to as Uganda—instead of Palestine. Others agreed, and became known as territorialists. But it quickly became apparent that there was insufficient support for such a plan: only *Eretz Yisrael*, only the Land of Israel, would do.

Herzl was willing to consider other lands for the sake of urgency; others, however, were concerned about the practicality and morality of establishing a state in Palestine. As we have seen, the would-be prooftext of Zionist original sin—"For a people without a land, a land without a people"—was actually a Christian Zionist invention long before there even was a modern Zionist movement. If there were early Zionists who validated that phrase, however, they did not do so easily or for long. Asher Ginsberg, who wrote under the pen name of Ahad Ha'am, penned in 1891 a famous essay called "The Truth from Eretz Yisrael," alerting all the Zionists still waiting back in Europe that there were tens of thousands of Arabs living there. When Herzl's right-hand man, Max Nordau, informed Herzl of this very fact on the eve of his first visit to Palestine, Herzl's reply was, "But then we are doing an injustice." Israel Zangwill himself, the man who transmuted the "for a people without a land" phrase into the early Zionist lexicon, became a territorialist himself on this account.

Aside from the distinction between territorialists and those who were determined to establish a Jewish homeland in Palestine, there was a tripartite ideological division within Zionism as well. Herzl was a man of Mitteleuropa, of the Hapsburg Empire. His model of Jewish settlement in Palestine took its tone from the European colonial projects of the day, from the structure of the old East India Company, for example. His book *Der Judenstaat*, usually translated as *The Jewish State* but more accurately translated as *The Jew-State*, reads in places like a plan to establish a colonial project company like the ones then current in Mozambique or Rhodesia. Herzl had very practical reasons for writing this way, of course: he hoped to interest the heads of state of Europe and assorted wealthy courtiers in supporting the Jewish colonization of Palestine, and to get the Turks to agree as well, all in the name of the national and financial interests of the various parties. This was how people thought in the nineteenth century.

Herzl was vague about what sort of economy the Jewish state, once established, would have. He seems to have assumed that it would operate a lot like Vienna, his hometown—plutocratic capitalism, in other words, would hold sway. And like the progressives of his day, he was very much a developmentalist, a believer in the transformative power of modern technology. In Herzl's futuristic novel *Altneuland* ("The Old-New Land"), all sorts of technological marvels bedeck the Jewish state, and all its citizens, Jewish and Arab, live happily and contentedly together. There are no traditionally religious Jews with major roles in *Altneuland*, but there does seem to be at least the suggestion of invested foreign capital.

The Jews of Central and Western Europe were not enthusiastic about Herzl's vision. The modern and assimilated, mostly Reform, Jews among them worried about accusations of dual loyalty. If the Zionists said Jews were a people and not just a religious community, then what was to stop Frenchmen and Americans and Dutch and so forth from worrying that their own Jewish citizens would hold an allegiance to a foreign government? Indeed, the only member of the British war cabinet to argue against the issuance of the Balfour Declaration in 1917 was a Jew, Lord Ashley Montague. Many American Reform Jews had the same reaction and remained anti-Zionist up to and beyond the establishment of the State of Israel in May 1948.

These Diaspora Jews opposed Zionism on political grounds. But most Orthodox Jews opposed it also, as we have already seen, on theological grounds. Modern Orthodox Jews in Germany were nearly all anti-Zionist, and so were nearly all ultra-Orthodox Jews. They associated Zionism with Shabbtai Tzvi and other calamities, and identified it, too, with the disaster of Bar Kochba, of trying to "force the end." Yet some Orthodox Jews disagreed and became Zionists. The first progenitors of modern Zionism, decades before Herzl, were rabbis who devised a formula that said, in effect, God helps those who help themselves. By the time of the First Zionist Congress in 1897, therefore, there was a religious Zionist movement and organization—Mizrahi.

But neither "political" Zionists like Herzl nor the religious Zionists of the Mizrahi movement made up the majority, and the political center of gravity, of the movement. The majority was composed of Jews from Eastern Europe, largely from within the Czarist Empire, who were secular and socialist in orientation. Some were Marxists, a few even Communists. The last thing they wanted was to form a colonial company in Palestine to be funded by plutocrats. They believed in changing the political situation of the Jewish people by changing its social structure—by going to Palestine and establishing a new Jewish society based on socialist principles, by building the Jewish state with their own hands from the ground up. When Herzl died in 1904 at the age of forty-four, these "practical" Zionists took control of the movement. They maintained collegial relations with religious Zionists, although they considered their thinking reactionary or just plain weird. At the same time, they did not leave off entirely trying to play the great power game in the parlors of Europe. Ironically enough under the circumstances, the biggest breakthrough the movement achieved, the Balfour Declaration itself, was made possible by just such a liaison, conducted by the remarkable Haim Weizmann.

These divisions within Zionism were profound on the philosophical level. Herzl and those who believed as he did were in search mainly of a night shelter for European Jews, who he thought were on the verge of disaster. Religious Zionism soon developed a conception of the state to be, as Rabbi Avraham Yitzhak Kook described it, as "the beginning of the dawn of our redemption," in other words, of the coming of the messiah. Socialist Zionists acted for the most part in the prophetic tradition, only secularized. Some sought only the normalization of the Jewish situation, it is true, an ambition that carried no notion of being chosen or special. But many and probably most were quite Jewcentric, seeing socialism as Judaism modernized and globalized, and, as developmentalists themselves, they saw salvation in material as well as moral terms.

In other words, the first- and second-generation socialist Zionists still saw Israel, both as a people and as a would-be state, as a light unto the nations, as something special and different from other nationalisms—as something, in effect, chosen. The state-to-be would not serve merely as a night shelter for those who needed it, nor be merely a prop in some religious fantasy: it was to be the negation of the Diaspora, the final solution to anti-Semitism, the normalization of Jewish history after two thousand years and, above all, the vanguard of the Jewish prophetic tradition brought back to life in the political flesh. This is what has led sagacious non-Jewish observers of Zionism to see something odd about it as a form of nationalism. Said the late Conor Cruise O'Brien, for example, "The central mystery of Zionism, it seems to me, is the relation within it of religion and nationalism, with the suspicion, within the mystery, that religion and nationalism may ultimately be two words for the same thing."[2]

Of course, it is: what O'Brien saw but did not name is that before the nineteenth century, Jewish religion had never been abstracted and compartmentalized away from the history of Israel and the Jewish people, as post-Reformation Christianity was abstracted and compartmentalized away from European tribal identities. It was inevitable, therefore, that a movement that rejected root and branch what the European exile had done to Jews would end up reversing this compartmentalization, whether it meant to or not, whether it understood what it was doing or not. As a consequence, Jewish nationalism could never be purely secular even when advanced by those who thought of themselves as radically secular. In rejecting Europe, they rejected in effect the secularism invented there, too.

Given these different conceptions of what Zionism is and is supposed to achieve, how can post-Zionism be simply one thing? It turns out that it can't be, or at any rate it isn't.

Before describing post-Zionism in more detail, it is worth pointing out something close to obvious: Zionism, because it was in large part an idealistic enterprise, has always had a strong sense of moral

consciousness, this despite the inevitable compromises a real movement and a real state have to make in parlous circumstances. Zionists
have been unusually hard on themselves, which is not surprising, given
that the legacy of chosenness has led many Jews for a dozen centuries
to be fairly hard on themselves individually.

Other Jews and Zionists were not so hard on themselves, however,
at least not in that way. And here most Israelis on the Left would
group Revisionist Zionists, led originally by Vladimir Zeev Jabotinsky.
If post-Zionism is a form of left-wing extremism, it was preceded in
the 1970s and 1980s by much right-wing extremism in the form of
the "whole land of Israel" (*eretz yisrael shleyma*) movement. There
were some bona fide anti-Arab racists on the fringes of that movement, and it drove morally conscious Zionists to despair. This, they
said, is what Ahad Ha'am, Martin Buber, Judah Magnes, and others
warned against when they disparaged the demons of nationalism. So
it is important to recognize, for those who are unfamiliar with the
rhythms of Israeli society, that post-Zionism did not come entirely
out of nowhere, hatched solely in the university offices of charismatic
Jewish personalities. To some extent it was always latent in the moral
logic of a Jewcentric movement—Zionism.

There are still many Israelis and Diaspora Jewish pro-Zionists who
take the moral dimension of statehood seriously. The Israeli Supreme
Court has been their active conscience over many of the past thirty
or so years. Much of this moral sensibility expresses itself in Israeli
literature, too, through the writings of novelists and poets like Amos
Oz, David Grossman, Yehuda Amichai, and others, and it is altogether possible to take the moral dimension seriously and still remain
a committed Zionist like these and other writers. It is a struggle, but
then, that is what the word *Israel* means—he who struggles with God,
or, more philosophically if one likes, struggles with the idea of God.
Indeed, the large majority of Israelis who care what the state does
in a moral sense remain Zionists. Post-Zionists were always a small
minority, and they are smaller today than they were ten years ago. In
their diversity, they sometimes constitute a minority with a minority,
amounting to only a handful of people.

There are Jewish post-Zionists, first of all, who reject any notion
of Jewish chosenness, and so therefore oppose idealist socialist
definitions of Zionism as well as religious definitions of it. They are
or try to be anti-Jewcentric purists. There are those who ridicule the
idea of Israel as a shelter, and from two directions. Some argue that
anti-Semitism has virtually disappeared, so that Jews in the Diaspora

do not need such a shelter anymore. Some go so far as to argue that what anti-Semitism the Jewish Diaspora now faces is actually *caused* at least indirectly by the wrongheaded actions of a succession of Israeli governments. And there are those who argue, too, that in a world of proliferating weapons of mass destruction, Israel is the most dangerous place on earth for Jews to be. Some shelter.

The intellectual sources of post-Zionism in its various forms come from many directions. The bulk of anti-Zionism comes from anti-nationalist sentiment in general. As we have seen, Jews of Central European origin like George Steiner have long been of such a view. The more serious of these critics note the irony that just as the civilized world seems to be weaning itself away from chauvinistic and destructive ethnic nationalism, what do the Jews do? They plunk themselves down on a piece of land to catch the fading tailwind of the historical zeitgeist. The Jews, they tend to argue, have been a creative and largely successful transterritorial civilization; these critics affirm the Diaspora and see Israel as a place for, at most, a center of Jewish culture, but not a state based on what they see as ethnocentric criteria.

That was the view of Hannah Arendt and Albert Einstein (and it was close in some ways to that of Ahad Ha'am). They opposed political Zionism not because it wasn't achievable but because, in their view, it wasn't desirable. This mirrored the attitudes that Jewish liberals and internationalists took in the nineteenth century, and that most Reform Jews affirmed. Reform Judaism denounced the idea not just of Jewish nationalism but of Jewish nationality altogether, and some actually had fun doing so: Gabriel Riesser, a nineteenth-century Reform Jewish intellectual, once said that any Jew who preferred the nonexistent state and nation of Israel to the actual nation and state of Germany should be put under police protection, not because he was dangerous but because he was insane.[3] (Who looks to be the crazy one now?)

It was for similar reasons, based on similar hopes, that people like Magnes and Buber preferred a binational Jewish-Arab state in the time before the first Arab-Israeli war.[4] So this version of post-Zionism, at least, parallels the cultural, antipolitical Zionism of the prestate period. One may agree or disagree with it, think it practical or not, but it is clearly an intellectually respectable point of view. It descends into self-hatred only when it becomes obsessive: To disparage nationalism, it is not necessary for Jews to pick out only Jewish nationalism to despise. When they do so, one has to wonder if something more than philosophy is at work.

• • •

Some post-Zionism comes from the so-called New Historians—revisionists who have recast the politico-military history of the Yishuv (the Zionist presence in Palestine before 1948) and the state in maximally unflattering terms. To be sure, there was a mythology of Zionist purity built up in the early years of the state.[5] But most of these histories lean very far in the opposite direction. In recent times the worst offender has been Ilan Pappé, who has basically accused Zionism of ethnic cleansing and mass murder. Pappé, like his father before him, either was or still is a Communist, and seems to be a born contrarian. His scholarship has been called into question, but that has not stopped some Palestinians from quoting him approvingly. Daoud Kuttab, a Christian Palestinian from Jerusalem, has recently done so, and this is shameful.[6] Unlike the International Solidarity Movement, which is a front for Palestinian militant groups seeking the destruction of Israel, and which actively recruits Jews like Adam Shapiro to use as examples of selective representation, Kuttab is a genuine moderate.[7] To see him use Pappé as a bludgeon, when even reputable Palestinian scholars make no such outlandish claims, is sad. Pappé is being used by others in the anti-Semitic mode of selective representation, as in "If a Jew says it, I can say it." He is apparently happy to be of such use.

Avi Shlaim, who no longer lives in Israel, is another: in a book called *Collusion Across the Jordan*, he offered a skewed account of Zionist-Hashemite relations that cast Israeli behavior in the worst possible conspiratorial light. He is still at it, writing, for example, scathing attacks against Israel during the recent Gaza operation in the *Guardian*, one of which was in turn cited by the Turkish premier to justify his own criticism of Israel. This is a case of selective representation right out of central casting.[8] Daniel Barenboim serves a similar function as an anti-Israeli Jew when he sponsors anti-Israel petitions in the *New York Review of Books*. There are, alas, many examples. A historian of the 1948 war, Benny Morris, who was the most prominent of the New Historians and who in fact coined the term, has gradually changed his mind about the larger issues and considers himself now to be a Zionist. These historians as a group, however, have bolstered the post-Zionist cause by, in essence, replicating the admonition of Ahad Ha'am's "The Truth from Eretz Yisrael" and Herzl's reply to Nordau, and showing the consequences of ignoring these admonitions.

Support for post-Zionism has also come from archeologists, of all people. Some Israeli archeologists have been on a mission to debunk the Hebrew Bible. A good example is *The Bible Unearthed: Archeology's New Vision of Ancient Israel and the Origin of Its Sacred Texts*, a 2002 book by Tel-Aviv University professor Israel Finkelstein and Neil Asher Silberman, a Belgian scholar. In this book the authors argue that the Torah is a brilliant seventh- and eighth-century BCE construction, completed in the middle of the fifth century BCE, that aimed to unify otherwise disparate peoples in the country. There is no evidence of an exodus from Egypt, of a violent conquest of the land under Joshua, of a magnificent united kingdom under David and Solomon. There is evidence, in essence, that the Israelites were, in the main, Canaanites themselves, much of their religion taken from the general neighborhood to the north and east, particularly the ancient civilization at Ugarit. Schlomo Sand has argued further that there never was a Rome-era exile, and that the Palestinians who stayed put for the last eighteen centuries are to some extent the modern descendants of that era's Jews. The Jews of today, he says, are largely converts picked up through the centuries, add-ons, a polyglot mass of people with little "blood" in common. Sand thinks that by arguing this line he is undermining the Zionist narrative. Even if he is right in his historical scholarship (which is questionable) about Roman times, he is surely wrong about what it means. To repeat, Jews are not a race or an ethnicity so much as a people, a point that in no way undermines and in some ways strengthens the Jewish, and the Zionist, narrative.

Whether the scholarship represented and described in these and other books is motivated by scientific objectivity, or whether their authors have "found" more or less what they hoped to find for political reasons, is hard to say. But to the extent that what they say turns out to be true, or is widely believed to be true, it undermines faith in the Bible generally, and specifically undercuts religious justifications for Jewish chosenness—including the Zionist version. For those post-Zionists who argue on the basis of a postmodern antifoundationalism that the very idea of a Jewish "people" is an artificial construction, the polyglot origins of ancient Israel are a kind of gift from secular heaven.

This is not an entirely new idea either, as it happens. Starting as long ago as the 1930s and continuing well into the 1950s, some Israelis wanted to call themselves Canaanites. They wanted to distance themselves from the Diaspora and from Jewish history itself, preferring to see Israelis as a new, separate ethnicity, a new people. Some, like Yosef Rotosh, wrote poetry about it; had Baal worship still been popular in the general neighborhood, they probably would have been attracted to it, just as their ancestors—including some Judean kings like Ahaz and Menasseh—had been many centuries before. Though Canaanitism was never a movement with a large following in Israel, some aspects of post-Zionism harken back to it.

There is more. Another form of post-Zionism is best described as a kind of pro-green antidevelopmentalism. The idea is that since the Zionist pioneers did not really develop the land so much as despoil it—the draining of the Hula swamp is often cited as an example—one of the major achievements claimed by the movement is in fact a disaster. Post-Zionism in this sense means to reverse that "development" and return the land to its more natural and ecologically balanced state.

There is yet another source of post-Zionism that begs attention: the more modest view that while Zionism was a good thing for its time, it is now obsolete as much for its success as for any of its failures. For example, Avraham Burg, a former Knesset member and former head of the Jewish Agency, cites David Ben-Gurion himself as having said that Zionism is just a scaffolding that we will be able to take down once the house is built.[9] Bernard Avishai argues it, too, insisting exactly the reverse of the antinationalists: that all citizens of Israel should have Israeli nationality, but no official religious or other subcommunal identity, so that Israel can be a genuine egalitarian democracy. The only way for Israel to achieve this is to stop being a "Jewish" state but nevertheless to get everyone to speak Hebrew.[10] Good luck, Bernie.

The temporary functions of Zionism, namely the movement's role in building a viable Jewish society in Israel, provide the basis for a view argued by one of contemporary Israel's most original thinkers, the late Yeshayahu Leibowitz (1903–1994). Leibowitz was someone who could not exist, but did: an Orthodox Jew who was decidedly left-wing in terms of Israeli and other politics. There have been pro-peace Orthodox movements, one called Meimad, for example, in recent years. And there have been many figures who have combined the two in the past—remember Rabbi Ashlag, for example. But Leibowitz went beyond them all.

First of all, because of his Orthodoxy and Orthodox sensibility about history, Leibowitz never accepted the proposition that if the

State of Israel were to be destroyed, Judaism would be destroyed with it. He was religious, and in a practical sense he was a Zionist, but he was not a "religious Zionist" in the protomessianic mold of Rav Kook. Leibowitz always opposed the religious parties in Israel, referring to them as mere cogs in the state machinery and accusing them of damaging Judaism in the process. And most important for our purposes, he always turned aside questions about Zionism as being the wrong questions. "Zionism," he once said,

> was the tool that created a political matrix for the Jewish people. But a political matrix is no guarantee for the future. Zionism really fulfilled its mandate when it achieved the realization of the Jewish state; it doesn't have to be the watchdog of the Jewish people. . . . The Jews have been around before Zionism and Herzl. And only authentic Jewish content will guarantee its survival. . . . Our problem isn't Israel. It's the Jewish people. . . . [T]he crisis that began two centuries ago runs so deep that I am far from certain regarding the future of the Jewish people. What is the collective content of Jewish life? Because the existence of the people depends on that content. Do you know what it is? Because I don't. . . . No political content can fill a spiritual vacuum.[11]

Leibowitz's contention that Zionism's mandate ended when the state came into existence translates into the view that Zionism was a historical necessity but should never have become what amounts to an object of idol worship. He saw Zionism's success merely as an opportunity to address the real problems of the Jewish people, above all their postmodern conceptual disunity, not as the solution to those problems. If post-Zionism has a serious variant, this is it.

What are we to make of post-Zionism, then? First of all, it is not a great threat to Israel. Israelis will fight if they have to for their right to live, and live as Jews, in the Land of Israel. Their own sense of identity and pride remains strong. Israel as a society is a going concern, and a formidable one despite being cobbled together from so many disparate sources in a fairly short time. What is remarkable about Israeli society is not that there are tensions between religious and secular Jews, between Ashkenazi and Sephardi Jews, or even between Israeli Jews and Israeli Arabs; what is remarkable is that the tensions and difficulties are not much worse. Indeed, what the success of Israeli society shows is that there *is* a Jewish people after all—there is enough of a common sense of how to see the world, enough of a transgenerational memory, enough of a religious civilization, to persuade people that they belong together in a place where they can make a life for themselves and a future for their children. The proof of the concept is its existence. After all these years since 135 CE, that is extraordinary enough without having to resort to exaggerations.

That is why when Avraham Burg, for example, says that he feels the Jewish and the Israeli parts of him detracting from the human part of him, he has it exactly wrong. Burg and most other post-Zionists think that Jewish particularism of any sort—religious or not—is necessarily at cross-purposes with their broader, universalist sense of humanity. If that is what they think, then they put far too much stock in the securities of cosmopolitan life and they misunderstand the formula of Jewish civilization itself. But, as I have said, this is not important. Most Israelis are sensible enough to pay no attention to effete intellectuals, just as they are sensible enough not to take anything that their politicians tell them at face value.

As for what post-Zionism means in practical terms, let us look to history for help with an answer. As we have seen, in every generation and in almost every place Jews have lived, a certain number have always dropped away—as is happening in America today with alacrity. When this happened in Diaspora, apostate Jews could ultimately blend in with the larger population, easily or with more difficulty, depending on specific circumstances. When Jews in Israel peel off from the fold, from the consensus, from the mainstream community, they become the equivalent of the Haggadah's "wicked son" in that, though contrarian by disposition, they are still there, right at the table. The essence of the post-Zionist impulse is to put an end to chosenness. They want not to be special, and in not being special, they want not to be entitled to their own state, for only on the basis of the most improbable sequence of historical events can the present State of Israel even be imagined.

Many post-Zionists will leave Israel, as many native-born and other Israelis have left over the years. Some people simply do not wish to endure the hardships and pressures of life in a tight space, and it was always foolish to think that the Jewish instinct to keep on the move would entirely disappear in one fell swoop in 1948. I don't judge them. If Avraham Burg thinks the climes of the European Union a paradise on earth—"very Jewish," he says— then he can go live there, and few Israelis, I am fairly certain, will miss him.

I do think that, in our political age, when the passions of religion have in so many respects found their way into politics, it is fair to see at least some expressions of post-Zionism as a kind Jewish apostasy. But so what? There have always been Jewish apostates, just as there have always been converts into the fold. This some-out, some-in filtering process is still going on, now both in the Diaspora and in the Land of Israel itself. Perhaps this is something new under the sun, the words of Ecclesiastes notwithstanding. But, remembering Jason, Menelaus, and their associates, somehow I doubt it.

EPILOGUE

Now What?

An exaggeration is a truth that has lost its temper.
—KAHLIL GIBRAN

As the world moves, perhaps, toward a universal society for the first time, we do not know how the Jewish mission, whether self-ascribed or assigned by God, will fare. We do not know how the Abrahamic world will shape and be shaped by other global visions. Not that it isn't irresistible to think about it.

Max Dimont, a relatively benign Jewcentric soul despite his best efforts to resist, turned into something of a mystic toward the end of his 1962 book *Jews, God, and History*. Using the threefold drama of the kabbalistic system, which he combined with Hegelian dialectics, he speculated that the first two millennia of Jewish history, the period before the Second Exile, were devoted to the annealing of the Jewish people and their mission—corresponding to *tzimtzum* (self-concentration) and thesis. For the second two millennia, those people and that mission were pushed out into the world at large as a particularist vessel carrying a universalist message—corresponding to *shvirat ha-keilim* (the breaking of the vessels) and antithesis. With the reestablishment of the State of Israel, Dimont saw the beginning of another two-millennium period—corresponding to *tikkun* (restoration) and synthesis—and another two millennia of Jewish history "to fulfill an as yet unrevealed role."[1] Perhaps that role is to lay out the universal principles of a world civilization. Perhaps, in other words, the Jews will finally become what they always imagined they would be: a truly *global* kingdom of priests, a light unto the nations upon which the sun, so to speak, never sets.

Perhaps we learn from history, too, that it is, paradoxically, the enemies of the Jews who end up saving the Jews. When the Kingdom of Judah fell, it was Babylon that, in its own way, helped Jews and Judaism-in-the-making survive, for it prepared the people for the tribulations of Roman rule. When the Hasmoneans fell, it was Greek ideas that helped Jews and Judaism survive, through the logical system of the Talmud. And perhaps the anti- and post-Zionists will be proved right after all: that to place all the bets of the Jewish future on one small plot of Middle Eastern soil, no matter how fabled and special, is to risk being somewhere at the cost of being nowhere. Perhaps it signifies that the Jewish world mission is over and that Israel, like all fixed territorial political entities, will fade into the ether of history. But then, perhaps, as before, the enemies of the Jews will help save them for the next phase of their mission, whatever that turns out to be.

Alas, we don't know. That in itself, of course, is a quintessential Jewish thought: the past is beyond our grasp, the future we cannot know, so we have only now, only the present, in which to act purposefully. But since we know that our nows accumulate into our future, we can't help but think about it, any more than we should ignore the past for the lessons it bears.

Withal, one thing is for sure: as long as Jews are still around, someone will exaggerate their role in whatever transpires. Some will praise, some will blame, many will distort. Jews fit so poorly with standard historical expectations that exaggeration is to be expected. But it is not to be welcomed; as the Talmud says, "Whosoever adds to the truth subtracts from it."

It's all too bad, of course. Everyone, Jews and non-Jews alike, could profit from a little more inattention to the wrong things. Non-Jews should pay less attention to the Jews, and the Jews should pay more attention to themselves—meaning to the state of their spiritual and communal life. Too many Jews spend way too much time worrying about and exaggerating the implications of what others think of them. By exaggerating what others think, they ascribe to it and thus create for it far more influence than would otherwise be the case. If Jews would be a little less Jewcentric themselves, especially in public, there is just a chance, if only a small one, that non-Jews will become less Jewcentric, too.

Nonetheless, for all the damage that the cumulative discourse of Jewcentricity has done over the years, we might as well face the fact that there is a strict limit to how much Jews can do about how they are seen and understood. Jews can't change human nature, even their own, and exaggeration is as much a part of that nature as the sun and the snow, as a smile and a smirk. Jews can, however, teach their children well, something they have a lot of practice doing over the centuries. They can teach them, as the siddur says, to "guard our tongues from evil and our lips from speaking guile." They can teach them, as the Yom Kippur confessional has it, to avoid foolish speech and haughty airs. Children can be taught to understand, and to remember, that for every Jewcentric boast uttered, an equal and opposite anti-Jewish calumny will probably rise to meet it. Jews can choose to remember that. They are, anyway, free to do so.

Notes

1. Chosen

1. This idea isn't new; many meditations on the dynamics set in motion by the idea of Jews as the Chosen People exist. For a recent example see Avi Beker, *The Chosen: The History of an Idea and the Anatomy of an Obsession* (Palgrave Macmillan, 2008).
2. This, too, is a deeply rooted human impulse; see Mary Douglass, *Purity and Danger* (Praeger, 1966).
3. A. B. Yehoshua interviewed in *Haaretz*, March 19, 2004, quoted in Beker, *The Chosen*, 178 (emphasis added). Yehoshua detailed his argument in a 2005 essay in the Hebrew magazine *Alpayim*. This has been translated into English and appears in *Azure* 32 (Spring 5768/2008), 48–79.
4. *North American Review*, April 1895.
5. Luckily, Anthony Smith has done some of this for us in *Chosen Peoples* (Oxford, 2003). See also the interesting, possibly Jewcentric, claim that the Jews invented the first more or less modern concept of nationalism: Avi Erlich, *Ancient Zionism* (Free Press, 1995).
6. Jonathan Sacks, *To Heal a Fractured World* (Continuum, 2005), chap. 1.
7. Note Charles Tilly, *Credit and Blame* (Princeton University Press, 2008).
8. The Ten Tribes have reappeared in the mythologies of other believers, even as American Indian tribes. Chances are good that with the advance of genomics we will learn one day, perhaps soon, who the present-day descendants of the Lost Tribes really are. Pashtuns, Kurds, Kashmiris—who knows?
9. In the surviving Southern Kingdom were also descendants of Shimon and a few from Benjamin, and of course there were Levites and, among the Levites, Kohanim. No matter; over time all eventually became known as Jews, after the majority tribe.
10. Tel Aviv University history professor Schlomo Sands claims there was no exile of Jews from their land in Roman times (*Comment le peuple juif fut inventé* [Bayard, 2008]). We will return to Sands's contentions and what they do and don't mean in chapter 14.
11. See Shaye J. D. Cohen, *The Beginnings of Jewishness* (University of California Press, 1999), 303–304.
12. Why this happened when and as it did, and with what implications, is fascinating, but well beyond the scope of this discussion. The long-distance system of communication the Talmudists developed, however, becomes vitally important later on for reasons having to do with economics, as discussed in chapter 4.

13. The last line of the prayer quoted here was removed from Ashkenazi prayer books after the Aleynu was introduced into the daily prayer service in the fourteenth century because Christian authorities, alerted by Jewish apostates, interpreted it as a deliberate insult to Christianity by those touting their own chosenness. Since the prayer's origins predate Christianity, and since the supposedly offending words are quotes from Isaiah, this was clearly not the case by intent, but out the sentence came anyway. Muslim authorities agreed that it was an insult to Christianity for having materialized the concept of God, but, feeling the same way, they did not mind Jews saying it in majority-Islamic lands, so in Sephardi prayer books today the sentence is still found.

14. Jonathan Sacks, *Hagaddah* (Continuum, 2003), 14.

15. Jacob Neusner, *Neusner on Judaism* (Ashgate, 2005), 426.

16. The Jewish approach to history is a complex matter beyond the scope of this essay. Suffice it to say that although Jews have maintained an exquisite and long sense of history, they have not by and large been historians and certainly not historiographers. See Yosef Haim Hayerushalmi, *Zakhor: Jewish History and Jewish Memory* (University of Washington Press, 1983).

2. On Philo-Semitism

1. Max Dimont, *Jews, God, and History* (New American Library, 1962), 113.

2. Arnold Toynbee, *A Study of History*, vol. 4 (Oxford University Press, 1961), 262.

3. The quote comes from the *Sifre*, Numbers, section 69. The *Sifre* is a pre-Talmudic collection of midrashic writings on Numbers and Deuteronomy.

4. Dimont, *Jews, God, and History*, 248.

5. Lloyd George, quoted in Martin Gilbert, *Jewish History Atlas* (Macmillan, revised 1976), epigraph.

6. Salo Baron, *A Social and Religious History of the Jews*, vol. 1, 2nd ed. (Columbia University Press, 2001), 3, quoted in Avi Beker, *The Chosen: The History of an Idea and the Anatomy of an Obsession* (Palgrave Macmillan, 2008), 178.

7. For a map summarizing the phenomenon, see Martin Gilbert, *Jewish History Atlas*, rev. ed. (Macmillan, 1976), 65.

8. Perhaps this was the origin of a very Jewcentric group called the "Anglo-Israelites," British and some Danish Christians who believed that the Anglo-Saxon tribes were descended from one or more of the Ten Lost Tribes of Israel. Such authors as Edward Hine and William Carpenter propounded such views to the book-reading public in the 1870s. Around 1900, the Anglo-Israelites claimed some two million adherents—and that Queen Victoria was a direct descendant of King David!

9. Perhaps Disraeli had been influenced at a young age by Spinoza, whom he read well and who, in his *Tractatus Theologico-Politicus* (1670), had mentioned the idea that the Jews might one day take charge of the their own fate and reestablish the Jewish state—the earliest nonreligious, proto-nationalist Zionist expression by a Jew that I have found.

10. The phrase appears in Keith's 1843 book, *The Land of Israel According to the Covenant with Abraham, with Isaac, and with Jacob*. Keith, a Church of Scotland clergyman, was part of a phalanx of religious writers who influenced Darby at Trinity College.

11. I tracked this in "On the Origin, Meaning, Use and Abuse of a Phrase," *Middle Eastern Studies* (October 1991); to her credit, seventeen years later Diana Muir tracked the famous phase back to Keith, in "A Land without a People for a People without a Land," *Middle Eastern Quarterly* (Spring 2008), 55–62.

12. Scofield, *Scofield Bible Correspondence Course* (Moody Bible Institute, 1907), 45–46, quoted in John Scott, "Christian Zionism: Dispensationalism and the Roots of Sectarian Theology" (Information Clearing House, no date), 3.

13. See Danforth's *Faith and Politics* (Viking, 2006), and "A Conversation with Senator John Danforth," *American Interest* (Autumn 2006), 18–24.

3. Anti-Semitism, Properly Understood

1. See the study by Nicholas A. Christakis and James H. Fowler in the *New England Journal of Medicine* 357:4 (July 26, 2007), 370–379, and a report on follow-up research by Rob Stein, "Social Networks' Sway May Be Underestimated," *New York Times*, May 26, 2008.

2. For a concise discussion, see Joseph Joffe, "Dissecting Anti-isms," *American Interest* (Summer 2006), 164–170.

3. Edouard Drumont, quoted in Robert S. Wistrich, "The Old-New Anti-Semitism," *National Interest* (Summer 2003), 61.

4. Described in Sandra Blakeslee, "What Other People Say May Change What You See," *New York Times*, June 28, 2005.

5. Hailan Hu, Eleonore Real, Kogo Takamiya, Myoung-Goo Kang, Joseph Ledoux, Richard L. Huganir, and Roberto Malinow, "Emotion Enhances Learning via Norepinephrine Regulation of AMPA-Receptor Trafficking," *Cell*, October 5, 2007.

6. There were some exceptions. See Elliott Horowitz, *Reckless Rites: Purim and the Legacy of Jewish Violence* (Princeton University Press, 2006).

7. This is a main theme of Ruth Wisse's *Jews and Power* (Schocken, 2007).

8. The iconic figure of six million Jews comes, ironically enough, from Adolf Eichmann. Early estimates, by Raul Hilberg for example, were around 5.1 million, while others were as high as 5.75 million and as low as 4.2 million. For the latter, see Howard Morely Sacher, *The Course of Modern Jewish History* (Delta, 1958), 457.

9. A meticulous history of court Jews, written originally in German in the 1940s, is Selma Stern, *The Court Jew* (Jewish Publication Society of America, 1950).

10. This argument is advanced in Dennis Prager and Joseph Telushkin, *Why the Jews? The Reason for Antisemitism* (Harper Torchbook, 2003). Their assertion that all anti-Semitism comes down to hatred of ethnical monotheism seems fairly obviously wrong in the face of religiously inspired Christian, and especially Muslim, anti-Semitism.

11. This argument follows, among others, Bernard Lewis, "Anti-Semitism's New Rationale," *American Scholar* (Winter 2006) 25–36; and Walter Laqueur, *The Changing Face of Anti-Semitism: From Ancient Times to the Present Day* (Oxford University Press, 2006). For a slightly different expression of the same idea, see Bernard-Henri Lévy, "The Task of the Jews," *American Interest* (Autumn 2008), 144–149.

12. Michael Scheuer, *Marching toward Hell* (Free Press, 2008), 51, 56.

13. The closest any Jewish government in Israel came to being a theocracy was in the five-hundred-year period of Persian and Greek overlordship, when a high priest was the titular head of the Jewish community. This was because a temporal Jewish leader would have symbolically contradicted Persian and then Greek imperial sovereignty, so it was not allowed. In fact, the Sanhedrin and a variety of popular assemblies kept government under secular control.

14. Dr. William Pierce, "How It Fits Together," ADV Broadcast, December 12, 1998, at library.flawlesslogic.com/media.htm.

15. Ibid.

16. For the science and the data, see Ellen Levy-Coffman, "A Mosaic of People: The Jewish Story and a Reassessment of the DNA Evidence," *Journal of Genetic Genealogy* 1, no. 1 (Spring 2005), 1–16.
17. We will return to this topic in chapter 8, in the context of analyzing the sources of Jewish intelligence.
18. Nicholas Wade, *Before the Dawn: Recovering the Lost History of Our Ancestors* (Penguin, 2006), 147.

4. Jewcentricity Globalized

1. See Philip Jenkins, *The Next Christendom: The Coming of Global Christianity* (Oxford University Press, 2002).
2. See David G. Goodman and Masanori Miyazawa, *Jews in the Japanese Mind* (Basic Books, 2004).
3. See Ian Buruma, "The Jewish Conspiracy in Asia," Project Syndicate, 2009.
4. Jason Lim, "Am I a Korean Racist?" *Korea Times*, December 24, 2007.
5. Quoted in Choe Sang-hun, "Anti-Semitic Comic Book in Korea Stirs Anger in the U.S.," *International Herald Tribune*, February 25, 2007.
6. Buruma, op. cit.
7. King Abdullah's remarks may be found on the Saudi Press Agency Web site at www.spa.gov.sa/english, October 26, 2008.
8. Before Ms. Nunu's appointment, most people did not know that there *were* any Bahraini Jews. Bahrain's Jewish community was never large—at its maximum in the 1940s it numbered about five hundred, most of its members having come for business reasons from Iraq or India. Now it reportedly numbers thirty-seven.
9. Philip Zelikow, "The Transformation of National Security: Five Redefinitions," *National Interest* (Spring 2003), 18.
10. Quoted in *The Economist*, January 31-February 6, 2009.
11. See Shlomo Shamir, "Top UN Official: Israel's Policies Are Like Apartheid of Bygone Era," *Ha`aretz*, November 24, 2008.
12. Zelikow, op. cit.
13. See Bernard Lewis, *The Muslim Discovery of Europe* (Princeton University Press, 1982).
14. The original book, *Die Juden und das Wirtschaftsleben*, was published in Leipzig by Duncker in 1911. A translation called *The Jews and Modern Capitalism*, with an excellent introduction by Samuel Z. Klausner, was published by the Free Press in 1951.
15. Max Dimont, *Jews, God, and History* (New American Library, 1962), 260.
16. A book of historical fiction by David Liss, *The Coffee Trader* (Random House, 2003), brilliantly recreates the flavor of the times.
17. The books, still classics in their field, are de la Vega, *Confusión de confusiones* (1688) and Pinto, *Traité de la Circulation et du Crédit* (1771).
18. Well recounted in Amy Chua, *Day of Empire* (Doubleday, 2008), 195.
19. Ayaan Hirsi Ali, "Why They Deny the Holocaust," *Los Angeles Times*, December 16, 2006.
20. Quoted in Judea Pearl, "The Daniel Pearl Standard," *Wall Street Journal*, January 30, 2008.
21. Mahathir's anti-Semitism exploded in 1997 during the Asian financial crisis, but it did have a pretext: George Soros's currency manipulations did, in fact, help cause the crisis. More on the method to Mahathir's madness in chapter 13; more on Soros in chapter 10.
22. See Mustafa Akyol, "The Latest Jewish Conspiracy: 'Moderate Islam' & the AKP!" *Turkish Daily News*, May 5, 2007.

5. Jewcentricity Central

1. See Michael Oren, *Power, Faith, and Fantasy: America in the Middle East* (Norton, 2007); the essay by Walter Russell Mead, "The New Israel and the Old," *Foreign Affairs* (July/August 2008), 28–46; and the sources listed below.
2. Moshe Davis, *America and the Holy Land: With Eyes toward Zion IV* (Praeger, 1995), 16–17.
3. John Adams and Charles Francis Adams, *The Works of John Adams, Second President of the United States: With a Life of the Author, Notes and Illustrations* (Little, Brown, 1854), 609.
4. "Hearth culture" refers to David Hackett Fischer's phrase in *Albion's Seed: Four British Folkways in America* (Oxford University Press, 1989).
5. Thomas Cahill, *The Gifts of the Jews: How a Tribe of Desert Nomads Changed the Way Everyone Thinks and Feels* (Anchor Books, 1998), 239–241; italics in the original.
6. President Lincoln countermanded the order, and Grant, although he never publicly apologized, later came to regret what he called "that obnoxious order." See John Simon, "That Obnoxious Order," *Civil War Times Illustrated* 23, no. 6 (1984): 12–17.
7. Jay Gould and James Fisk caused Black Friday, September 24, 1869, when they tried to corner the gold market.
8. Richard Holbrooke, "Washington's Battle Over Israel's Birth," *Washington Post*, May 7, 2008.
9. For details, see my article "Here's to You, Harry," *American Interest* (Vacation 2008), 130–131.
10. Quoted in Oren, *Power, Faith, and Fantasy*, 523.
11. Quoted in Bob Michael, "Mark Twain and the Jews," 1993, at www.twainweb.net/filelist/jews.html.
12. Charles Neider, ed., *The Complete Essays of Mark Twain* (Garden City, 1963).
13. *John L. Stoddard's Lectures: Illuminated and Embellished with Views of the World's Most Famous Places and People, Being the Identical Discourses Delivered During the Past Eighteen Years under the title of the Stoddard Lectures*, Vol. II (Balch Brothers, 1897).
14. Cited in Oren, *Power, Faith, and Fantasy*, 221.
15. See Tim Townsend, "New Jews, New Hope," *Washington Post*, February 2, 2008.
16. See Angela Valdez, "The Real Jews," *Washington City Paper*, March 19, 2008. For a fascinating account of the black Hebrew movement, see Zev Chafetz, "Obama's Rabbi," *New York Times Magazine*, April 5, 2009.
17. See Steve Lipman, "Ordained by the Shoah," *Jewish Week*, November 4, 2008.
18. For details, see Charles Lane, "The Double Man," *New Republic*, July 28, 1997.
19. Thomas Frank, "The GOP Loves the Heartland to Death," *Wall Street Journal*, September 10, 2008.

6. The Two Religions of American Jews

1. A translation may be found in Jonathan Decter, *Iberian Jewish Literature: Between al-Andalus and Christian Europe* (Indiana University Press, 2007).
2. A translation may be found in Franz Kobler, ed., *A Treasury of Jewish Letters* (Jewish Publication Society, 1953).
3. I thank Jonathan Decter of Brandeis University and Shulamit Elizur of Hebrew University for helping me locate these poems and letters.
4. See Joseph Epstein, "'Uncle Bernie' and the Jews," *Newsweek*, January 19, 2009.
5. Let's be specific about what is meant here by mainstream: The 1.7 percent of the U.S. population that identifies itself as Jewish breaks down as follows: 0.7 percent Reform,

0.5 percent Conservative, 0.3 percent unaffiliated, and less than 0.3 percent Orthodox. Reform Judaism essentially repudiates the ben-Zakkai system that defines rabbinic Judaism. The Conservative movement affirms most of the system in theory, but its members in practice do not act in accordance with much or most of it. That means that at least three-quarters of the Jews in the United States—the mainstream—are non-halachic Jews, and that is a generous estimate.

6. *Ethics of the Fathers*, I:10.
7. The rather antiseptically patriotic times of the Cold War, which coincided with rising Jewish social and intellectual mobility in the United States, proved a great stimulus for arguments of this kind. A somewhat later effort, better than the rest, is Abraham I. Katsch, *The Biblical Heritage of American Democracy* (KTAV, 1977). See also Rabbi Ken Spiro, *WorldPerfect: The Jewish Impact on Civilization* (Simcha Press, 2002), a very Jewcentric book.
8. See Andrew M. Greeley, "Hanukkah, Christmas—In the Same Light," *New York Times*, December 11, 1990.
9. On this theme, Max Dimont, who is usually careful not to exaggerate, is himself very Jewcentric; see *Jews, God, and History* (New American Library, 1962), 48.
10. Thomas Cahill, *The Gifts of the Jews: How a Tribe of Desert Nomads Changed the Way Everyone Thinks and Feels* (Anchor Books, 1998), 249.
11. The answers are discussed in my essay "The Two Religions of American Jews: A Provocation for the Sake of Heaven," *Conservative Judaism* 48, no. 2 (Winter 1996).
12. Some American Jews have gone even further, from acknowledging assimilation to celebrating it. See Edward Rothstein, "Museum's Vision: West Coast Paradise," *New York Times*, June 9, 2008.
13. "Survey of Voters: Who They Were," *New York Times*, November 9, 2006.
14. David Frum and Richard Perle, *An End to Evil: How to Win the War on Terror* (Random House, 2003), 239.
15. David Gelernter, *Americanism: The Fourth Great Western Religion* (Doubleday, 2007), 156.
16. Irving Howe, quoted in Morris Dickstein, "A World Away, a Generation Later," *New York Times Book Review*, April 6, 1997, 35.
17. Milton Himmelfarb, "Secular Society? A Jewish Perspective," *Daedalus* (Winter 1967), 220–235.

7. Adjewlation: Jews in American Celebrity Culture

1. Carol Leifer, quoted in Frank Rich, "TV's New Jew," *New York Times*, November 23, 1996.
2. For details, see Lawrence Maslon, "The Wizards of Oz," *American Interest* (Vacation 2007).
3. David Kirby, "Celebrities R Us," *American Interest* (Spring 2006), 88.
4. Pierre Paul Leroy-Beaulieu, *Israel Among the Nations* (1895), 169.
5. See my conversation with Dr. Putnam in "Bowling with Robert Putnam," *American Interest* (Winter 2008).
6. See Rod Dreher, *Crunchy Cons* (Crown Forum, 2006).
7. Walter Kirn, "Prisoner of Hollywood," *New York Times Book Review*, February 25, 2007, 9.
8. David Mamet, *Bambi vs. Godzilla: On the Nature, Purpose, and Practice of the Movie Business* (Pantheon, 2007).
9. Barbra Streisand attended a Jewish day school, a yeshiva, in Flatbush as a child, and Kirk Douglas took to taking Talmud lessons in old age after his health began to fail, but these are exceptions to the rule.

10. See Natalie Clark, "Adopt a Baby? No, Madonna wants to take over a nation," *Daily Mail*, April 22, 2007.
11. As reported by the Associated Press on September 16, 2007.
12. See Daphne Merkin, "In Search of the Skeptical, Hopeful, Mystical Jew That Could Be Me," *New York Times Magazine*, April 13, 2008.
13. Ibid., 53.
14. See the confessional of a recovering cultist in Sharon Van Geuns, "Is Madonna's Kabbalah a Cult?" *Star*, October 18, 2004.
15. Quoted in Olivia Barker, "Madonna Has Faith on a String," *USA Today*, May 25, 2004.

8. Meet the JACs

1. Yitzchok Levine, "Glimpses into American Jewish History: Part 26—The Jews of Nevis and Alexander Hamilton," *Jewish Press*, May 2, 2007.
2. Nicholas Wade, "Study Raises Possibility of Jewish Tie for Jefferson," *New York Times*, February 28, 2007.
3. See Adam Kirsch, *Benjamin Disraeli* (Nextbook/Schocken, 2009).
4. As did several other men I remember from my youth who worked in the Garfinkle family shoe-finding business near Seventh and I Streets, N.W., in Washington. When Powell first demonstrated his Yiddish vocabulary to me, when I worked as his speechwriter at the State Department, I think he expected me to be surprised. I was amused, sure, but having read his autobiography, *An American Life*, I wasn't surprised. When I told him why, he wasn't surprised either.
5. Thomas Brothers, ed., *Louis Armstrong, in His Own Words* (Oxford University Press, 1999).
6. Nate Bloom, "Jewz in the Newz," *Jewish World Review*, May 17, 2004, referencing *Modern Maturity*, March 2004.
7. See here James R. Flynn, *What Is Intelligence?* (Cambridge University Press, 2007).
8. Discussed in Nicholas Wade, *Before the Dawn: Recovering the Lost History of Our Ancestors* (Penguin, 2006), 196.
9. Summarized sympathetically and entertainingly by Mark Edmundson, "Defender of the Faith?" *New York Times Magazine*, September 7, 2007, 15–19.

9. Professional Jews

1. See Sue Fishkoff, "Survey Finds One in Five Americans Holds 'Strongly Antisemitic Opinions,'" *Jewish Exponent*, November 17, 1992, 1.
2. ADL Statement, July 11, 2003.
3. Abraham H. Foxman, "Harry Truman, My Flawed Hero," *Forward*, July 18, 2003.
4. Harry S. Truman, *Truman Memoirs*, vol. 2 (Doubleday, 1955), 158.
5. Quoted in Margaret Truman, *Harry S. Truman* (William Morrow, 1973), 420.
6. The Truman diary excerpt for July 21, 1947, with photos of the actual handwritten pages, can be found at www.trumanlibrary.org/diary/page21.htm.
7. Charles Krauthammer, "Marge Schott: Who Cares?" *Washington Post*, May 10, 1996.
8. Jacob Neusner, "A Fading Memory," *Jerusalem Post*, May 2, 1993.
9. The best example is perhaps Hannah Arendt. See Ron H. Feldman, ed., *The Jew as Pariah* (Grove Press, 1978). Philip Rieff called these people "Jews of Culture." See his *Sacred Order/Social Order, Volume 3: The Jew of Culture: Freud, Moses, and Modernity* (University of Virginia Press, 2008).
10. Hirsh Goodman, "The Real Threat," *Jerusalem Report*, September 23, 1993, 64.
11. Aqiva Eldar, "Jewish Chutzpah," *Haaretz*, March 21, 1994.

12. For a report on the UJA/Israel donations drop-off, see Karen W. Arenson, "Donations to a Jewish Philanthropy Ebbs," *New York Times*, December 27, 1995.
13. Charles Krauthammer, "The Holocaust Scandal," *Washington Post*, December 4, 1998.
14. Neusner, "A Fading Memory."
15. Alan M. Dershowitz, *The Vanishing American Jew* (Little, Brown, 1997).
16. Marshall Breger, "The Anti-anti-Semitic Thought Police," *Moment* (December 1996), 24.
17. See Irving Kristol, "Why Religion Is Good for the Jews," *Commentary* (August 1994), 20.
18. Quoted in J. J. Goldberg, *Jewish Power* (Basic Books, 1997) 16–17. For Goldman's own illuminating account, see his book *The Jewish Paradox* (Grosset & Dunlap, 1978).
19. Foxman, quoted in Goldberg, 17.

10. Self-Hating Jews

1. To my knowledge, there is no English-language biography of Reuchlin, which is a shame. Reuchlin was a diplomat, judge, and scholar who mastered Hebrew and became fascinated with Judaism. On a trip to Rome, Reuchlin met Giovanni Pico della Mirandola, author of the essay that launched the Renaissance, the *Oration on the Dignity of Man*. Pico interested Reuchlin in kabbalah, which he had learned about from the aforementioned Rabbi Delmedigo. Reuchlin pursued Hebrew language study with Rabbi Obadiah of Sforno, under whom Reuchlin also studied Talmud and kabbalah. Reuchlin was the first to teach Hebrew in a European university and the first non-Jew ever to attempt the writing of a Hebrew grammar.
2. David Mamet, *The Wicked Son: Anti-Semitism, Self-Hatred, and the Jews* (Schocken, 2006).
3. Ibid., 38.
4. See Sander L. Gilman, *Jewish Self-Hatred* (Johns Hopkins University Press, 1986).
5. See Meg Barnette and Brad Lander, "To our son, Marke Alexander Barnette, on the occasion of his naming," in *Wrestling with Zion*, ed. Tony Kushner and Aliza Salomon (Grove, 2003), 5.
6. For an obscure but revealing example, see Bertell Ollman, "Letter of Resignation from the Jewish People," *Tikkun* (January–February 2005).
7. See Richard Falk, "Slouching Toward a Palestinian Holocaust," *Palestine Chronicle*, July 7, 2007.
8. Norman Finkelstein, *The Holocaust Industry: Reflections on the Exploitation of Jewish Suffering*, 2nd ed. (Verso, 2003).
9. A longer list, complete with citations, is available in Emanuele Ottolenghi, "Anti-Semites, Anti-Zionists, and European Culture," *Aspenia* no. 37–38 (2007), 142–145.
10. Ottolenghi, "Anti-Semites, Anti-Zionists," 144.
11. Erich Kähler, *The Jews among the Nations* (Transaction, 1989), xi.
12. Steiner knows it, too; see his illuminating essay "Some Meta-Rabbis," in *Next Year in Jerusalem*, ed. Douglas Villiers (Viking Press, 1976).
13. Melanie Phillips, in *Daily Mail*, March 7, 2002.
14. See Martin Peretz, "Capitalist Tools," *New Republic*, November 24, 1997. Soros has defended himself and, in the process, said things publicly about his concern for Israel and for Jews that he had never before expressed. See "On Israel, America & AIPAC," *New York Review of Books*, April 12, 2007. Peretz has also attacked Steiner; see "Red Dusk: The Rosenberg Bombshell," *New Republic*, October 8, 2008.

11. The Anti-Israel Lobby

1. Abraham H. Foxman, *The Deadliest Lies: The Israel Lobby and the Myth of Jewish Control* (Palgrave Macmillan, 2008).

2. Robert Strausz-Hupé, "The Balance of Tomorrow," *Orbis* 1, no. 1 (Fall 1957), 22.

3. John Foster Dulles, quoted in George Ball and Douglas B. Ball, *The Passionate Attachment: America's Involvement with Israel 1947 to the Present* (Norton, 1992), 47.

4. In 2002, the respected British magazine *Prospect* ran a cover essay by an American writer, Michael Lind, called "The Israel Lobby and American Power." I was asked to reply to it, which I did. See *Prospects'* April, September, October, and November 2002 issues for the full debate.

5. Michael Gerson, "Seeds of Anti-Semitism," *Washington Post*, September 21, 2007.

6. Harvey Sicherman, "The Israel Lobby and U.S. Foreign Policy: A Working Paper that Does Not Work," Foreign Policy Research Institute E-Note, March 28, 2006.

7. Quoted in Moshe Davis, *America and the Holy Land* (Greenwood, 1995), 31.

8. This remark, which Secretary Baker never denied making, has been cited at least a thousand times, but never the original, of course, since it was a private remark later leaked. For one source, as good as any other under the circumstances, see Craig Horowitz, "The Zion Game," *New York Times Magazine*, October 30, 2000.

9. See Itamar Rabinovich, "Testing the 'Israel Lobby' Thesis," *American Interest* (Spring 2008), 139.

12. The (Non)-Centrality of the Arab-Israeli Conflict

1. Interesting arguments to this effect have been made by Philip E. Auerswald, "Does the Middle East Matter?" *American Interest* (Summer 2007), and Edward Luttwak, "The Middle of Nowhere," *Prospect* (May 2007). An opposing view has been advanced by Niall Ferguson in the June 17, 2007, *Telegraph*, and Josef Joffe in the Aug. 27, 2007, *Wall Street Journal*.

2. See my "Comte's Caveat: How We Misunderstand Terrorism," *Orbis* (Summer 2008).

3. Jimmy Carter and Zbigniew Brzezinski, quoted in Martin Kramer, "The Myth of Linkage," Middle East Strategy at Harvard, June 12, 2008.

4. Leslie Gelb, "Dual Loyalties," *New York Times Book Review*, September 23, 2007.

5. Saud al-Faisal quoted in *Arab News*, September 30, 2007, 1.

6. Romano Prodi, interviewed by Jeff Israely in *Time*, May 1, 2006.

7. For a good summary, see Philip Stevens, "This time, will Blair really be heard?" *Financial Times*, November 14, 2006.

8. As an example, see Blair quoted in Kevin Sullivan and Mary Jordan, "Blair Sees Chance for Progress on Middle East Conflict," *Washington Post*, November 17, 2006.

9. Daniel Kurtzer quoted in Ethan Bronner, "Israel Is Not Linked to Iraq, Except That It Is," *New York Times*, December 10, 2006, Week in Review, 5.

10. James A. Baker III and Lee H. Hamilton, cochairs, *The Iraq Study Group Report: The Way Forward—A New Approach* (Vintage, 2006), xv.

11. Rob Satloff, "Forget the Domino Theories," *Washington Post*, December 19, 2006.

12. See Dennis Ross, "Internal Affairs," *New Republic*, December 18, 2006.

13. See the discussion and the statistics in Walter Russell Mead, "God's Country?" *Foreign Affairs* (September/October 2006).

14. See Michael Scott Doran, "Palestine, Iraq, and American Strategy," *Foreign Affairs* (January/February 2003).

15. See Paul Haven, "Survey: European Anti-Semitism Strong," *Miami Herald*, February 10, 2009.

13. Muslim Jewcentricity

1. Michael Slackman, "9/11 Rumors That Become Conventional Wisdom," *New York Times*, September 8, 2008.

2. See Andrew Bostom, *The Legacy of Islamic Anti-Semitism: From Sacred Texts to Solemn History* (Prometheus, 2008), for an informed if perhaps exaggerated account.

3. As the great scholar of Islam W. Montgomery Watt noted: "One of the most remarkable features of the relationship between Muslims and Christians is that neither Mohammed nor any of his Companions seems to have been aware of some of the fundamental Christian doctrines." Watt, *Muhammad at Medina* (Oxford University Press, 1956), 320.

4. See Matthias Kuentzel, *Jihad and Jew-Hatred: Islamism, Nazism and the Roots of 9/11* (Telos, 2007).

5. Quoted in Avi Beker, *The Chosen: The History of an Idea and the Anatomy of an Obsession* (Palgrave Macmillan, 2008), 7–8.

6. Good periodic surveys of anti-Semitism in the Arab and Iranian press can be found in the publications of the Middle East Media Research Institute (MEMRI).

7. See note 4101, p. 1357, of the Quran published by the Presidency of Islamic Researchers, IFTA, Call and Guidance, King Fahd Holy Quran Printing Complex, Riyadh, Saudi Arabia (no date).

8. This is called *tahrif*, or "corruption," in Arabic. For an excellent discussion, see W. Montgomery Watt, *Islamic Political Thought* (Edinburgh at the University Press, 1968), chap. 6.

9. See here, among other sources, Jean-Pierre Filiu, *L'Apocalypse dans l'Islam* (Fayard, 2006).

10. Marcus Nathan Adler, ed. and trans., *The Itinerary of Benjamin of Tudela* (Oxford University Press, 1907), 39–40.

11. See Jeremy Black, *Maps and Politics* (University of Chicago Press, 1997).

12. It will not do to exaggerate this, however, as so many are wont to do. The most significant expansions of Islam, whether in Africa or in Moghul India, did *not* come at the expense of Christians. Moreover, one should not assume Christian military superiority throughout; there are many cases where Muslim armies defeated Christian ones.

13. The verses are 2:65, 5:60, and 7:166.

14. Abraham Cooper and Harold Brackman, "Mumbai's Aftermath: Euphemisms, Apologetics and Double Standards Becloud the War on Terrorism," *National Post* (Toronto), December 2, 2008.

14. Post-Zionism

1. For samplings of post-Zionist writings in English, see Akiva Orr, *Israel: Politics, Myths and Identity Crises* (Pluto Press, 1994), and Boas Evron, *Jewish State of Israeli Nation?* (Indiana University Press, 1995).

2. Conor Cruise O'Brien, *The Siege* (Weidenfeld and Nicolson, 1986), 18.

3. Walter Laqueur, *A History of Zionism* (Holt, Rinehart and Winston, 1972), 8.

4. For Magnes's writings, see Arthur A. Goren, ed., *Dissenter in Zion: From the Writings of Judah L. Magnes* (Harvard University Press, 1982). For Buber's views on this subject, see Paul R. Mendes-Flohr, *A Land of Two Peoples: Martin Buber on Jews and Arabs* (Oxford University Press, 1983).

5. I have analyzed this in my essay "History and Peace: Revisiting Zionist Mythology," *Israel Affairs* (Autumn 1998).

6. Daoud Kuttab, "Priority Statehood," *Washington Post*, May 12, 2008.

7. I even published him myself: See Kuttab, "A Civilized Way to Fight Terror," in *A Practical Guide to Winning the War on Terrorism*, ed. Adam Garfinkle (Hoover Institution, 2004).

8. Avi Shlaim, "How Israel Brought Gaza to the Brink of Humanitarian Catastrophe," *Guardian*, January 7, 2009.

9. See "Leaving the Zionist Ghetto: A Conversation with Avraham Burg by Ari Sharvit," *Haaretz*, June 13, 2007.

10. See Bernard Avishai, *The Hebrew Republic: How Secular Democracy and Global Enterprise Will Bring Israel Peace at Last* (Harcourt, 2008).

11. Egon Friedler, "Letting Leibovitz Speak for Himself," World Zionist Organization Archive, October 11, 2000.

Epilogue. Now What?

1. Max Dimont, *Jews, God, and History* (New American Library, 1962), 420.

Index

Abraham, 11–13, 15, 18, 41, 247
Adams, John, 46, 94, 119
"adjewlations," 148
advocacy organizations, 164–165
  anti-Israel lobby and, 218
  anti-Semitism and, 171–177
  power of, 179–182
  as "professional" Jews, 165–167
  purpose of, 167–171
  secular Jewish culture and,
    178–179
African Americans, 96, 105,
    154–157, 188
Ahmadinejad, Mahmoud, 79, 251, 257
Albright, Madeleine, 106–107, 201
Alexander the Great, 21, 185
Ali, Muhammad, 45
Allen, Etty, 106, 201
Allen, George, 105–106, 201
Allen, Woody, 188–189
Altneuland (Herzl), 266
America-Israel Public Affairs
    Committee (AIPAC), 174,
    179–181, 214, 216
American Conservative, 208
American Educational Trust, 208
Americanism, 115–127
American Jewry, 110–113
  cultural influence of Jews and,
    132–137

Holocaust identification by,
    115–116, 125–126
  incompatibility of Judaism and
    Americanism, 116–118
  "Jewish Americans"/"American
    Jews," defined, 113–116
  modernity and, 120–123, 126–127
  neoconservatives and, 123–125
  social values and, 118–120
  See also secular Jewish culture
"American Jews," defined, 113–116
American Nazi Party, 66–67
American philo-Semitism, 93
  conversion and, 105–107
  dispensationalism and, 40, 98,
    108–109
  founding of America and, 93–98
  media and, 107–108
  Palin and, 108–109
  Stoddard and, 101–104
  "The Jewish Cemetery at
    Newport" (Longfellow), 98–99
  Twain and, 99–101
American Revolution, 82, 148
Annapolis Summit (2007), 229
ANSWER (Act Now to Stop War
    and End Racism), 208
anti-Christ, 50
Anti-Defamation League (ADL),
    167, 168–169, 176, 178, 237

intermarriage, 22, 114–115, 177,
178–179
Internet, 136, 138
celebrity culture and, 145
e-mails circulated on, 148, 153,
154, 157, 177
globalization and, 72, 86
Muslim anti-Semitism and, 245
See also celebrity culture
(American)
intifada, 257
IQ (intelligence quotient), 158–162
Iran
Iran-Iraq War (1980–1988), 224
Iraq Study Group Report and,
230
Muslim anti-Semitism and,
257–258
Palin on, 109
shah of Iran, 223
U.S. relations with, 226, 232
weapons of, 239, 258
Iraq, 12
Baathist regime, 213, 254
Gulf War, 215, 224
Iran-Iraq War (1980–1988), 224
Iraq War, 206–207, 212–213,
222–225, 230–231
Saddam Hussein, 213
Iraq Study Group Report (2006),
230–231
Irgun, 96
Isaac, 15, 247–249
Isaiah, 19, 120
Ishmael, 12, 247
Islam
Dar al-Islam, 71, 243–244
European immigration and, 236
evangelism and, 249–251, 257
Jewish American chauvinism and,
157
Muslim anti-Semitism and,
251–259
radical Islam, 222–225, 238-239

Salafi Muslims, 139
Shi'a, 251, 257
Sunni, 249–251, 255
See also Muslim anti-Semitism
Islamic Jihad, 238–239, 222-225
Israel (ancient), 16, 19
Israel (modern State of Israel)
American Jewish identification
with, 173–177
anti-Semitism and Zionism, 63–67
Egyptian-Israeli peace treaty of
1979, 234
evangelism and, 50, 209, 233
Gaza war (2009), 237, 238, 271
Hezbollah War (2006), 232
"Israel," English translation of,
269
Israeli bonds, 174–175
Jewish identification and Zionism,
69–70
land developed in, 273
Lebanon War (1982), 69
Madonna in, 142, 146
as "night shelter," 267
1973 War (Yom Kippur War),
69, 215
non-Jews of, 65
right of return and, 211
Six Day War of 1967, 173–174,
208, 255
See also anti-Israel lobby; Arab-
Israeli conflict; post-Zionism;
Zionism
Israelite Church of God in Jesus
Christ (ICGJC), 105
Israelites, 11, 247
"Israel Lobby, The" (Mearsheimer,
Walt), 194
Israel Lobby, The (Mearsheimer,
Walt), 206–218
Italy, 56, 229

Jabotinsky, Vladimir Zeev, 269
Jacob, 15